THE PRECINCT

™

A STEAMPUNK ADVENTURE

Nick Barrucci, CEO / Publisher
Juan Collado, President / COO

Joe Rybandt, Executive Editor
Matt Idelson, Senior Editor
Rachel Pinnelas, Associate Editor
Anthony Marques, Assistant Editor
Kevin Ketner, Editorial Assistant

Jason Ullmeyer, Art Director
Geoff Harkins, Senior Graphic Designer
Cathleen Heard, Graphic Designer
Alexis Persson, Production Artist

Chris Caniano, Digital Associate
Rachel Kilbury, Digital Assistant

Brandon Dante Primavera, V.P. of IT and Operations
Rich Young, Director of Business Development

Alan Payne, V.P. of Sales and Marketing
Keith Davidsen, Marketing Director
Pat O'Connell, Sales Manager

Online at **www.DYNAMITE.com**
On Facebook **/Dynamitecomics**
On Instagram **/Dynamitecomics**
On Tumblr **dynamitecomics.tumblr.com**
On Twitter **@dynamitecomics**
On YouTube **/Dynamitecomics**

First Printing

ISBN-13: 978-1-5241-0060-5

10 9 8 7 6 5 4 3 2 1

Writer
FRANK J. BARBIERE

Artist
CRIZAM CRISTHIAN ZAMORA

Colors
DINEI RIBEIRO

Letters
TROY PETERI (Issue #1)
A LARGER WORLD STUDIOS (Issues #2-5)

Collection cover art
JOE BENITEZ art SABINE RICH

Collection Design
GEOFF HARKINS

This volume collects issues 1-5 of
"The Precinct"
from Dynamite Entertainment.

Greetings, fair traveler, and welcome to The Big City, a sprawling metropolis fueled by steam and adventure! By the light of day, enjoy our bustling streets, metalwork marvels, and the splendors of airship transportation. By night, however...

Let's just say that, in the shadows of our cast-iron kingdom, danger is afoot. Use caution... and know that the protective services of The Precinct are available, should you require them.

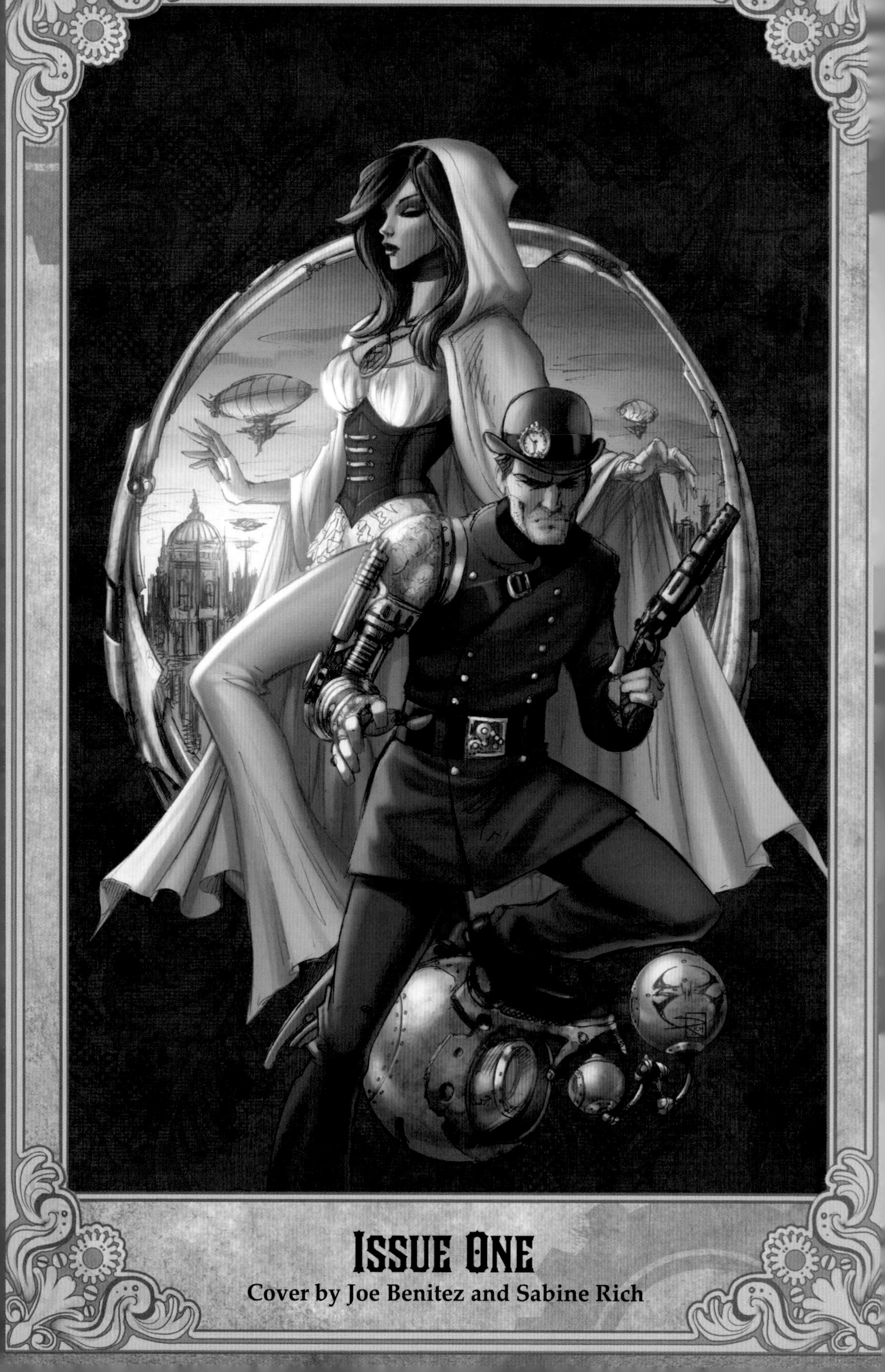

Issue One

Cover by Joe Benitez and Sabine Rich

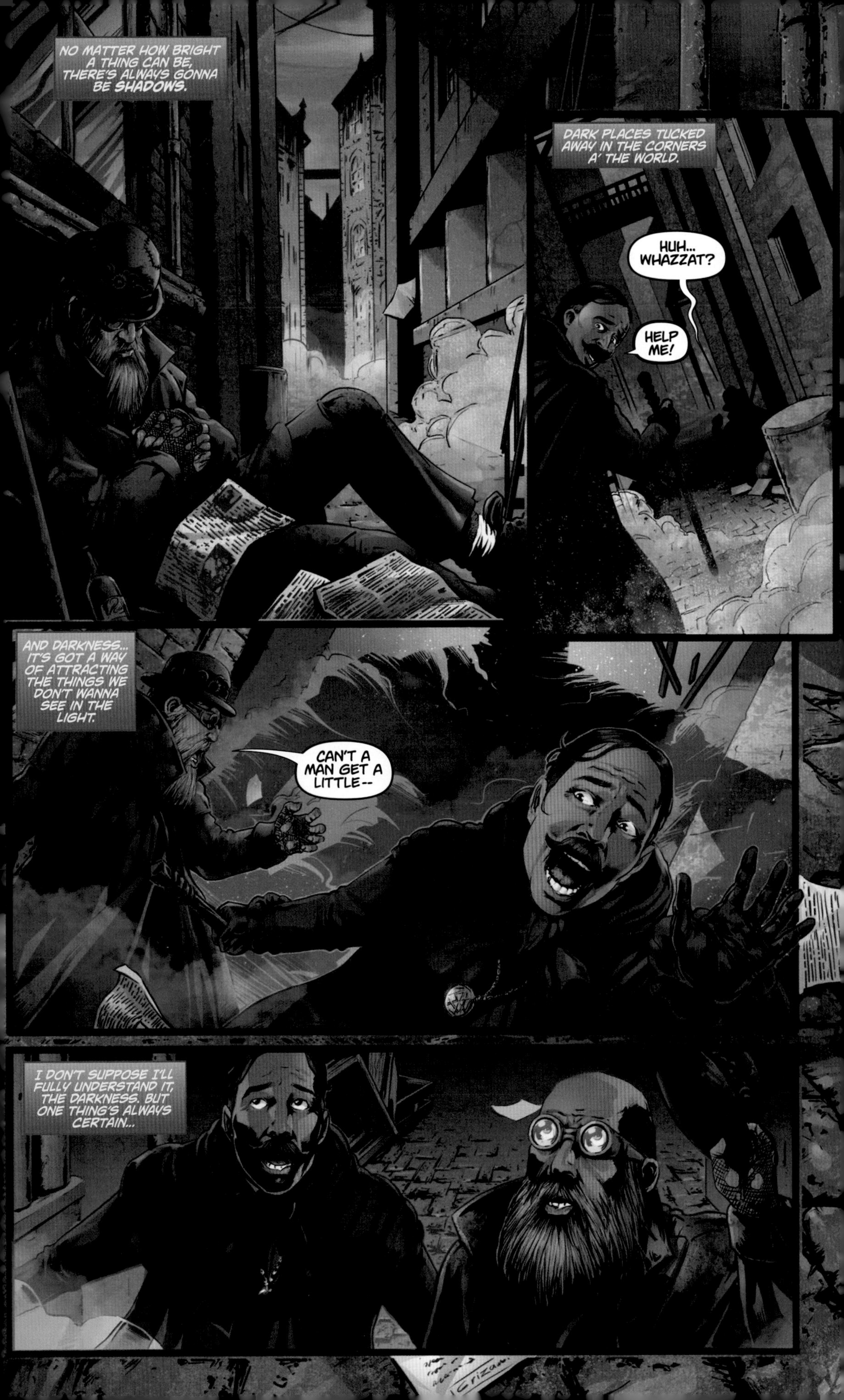
NO MATTER HOW BRIGHT A THING CAN BE, THERE'S ALWAYS GONNA BE SHADOWS.
DARK PLACES TUCKED AWAY IN THE CORNERS A' THE WORLD.
HUH... WHAZZAT?
HELP ME!
AND DARKNESS... IT'S GOT A WAY OF ATTRACTING THE THINGS WE DON'T WANNA SEE IN THE LIGHT.
CAN'T A MAN GET A LITTLE--
I DON'T SUPPOSE I'LL FULLY UNDERSTAND IT, THE DARKNESS. BUT ONE THING'S ALWAYS CERTAIN...

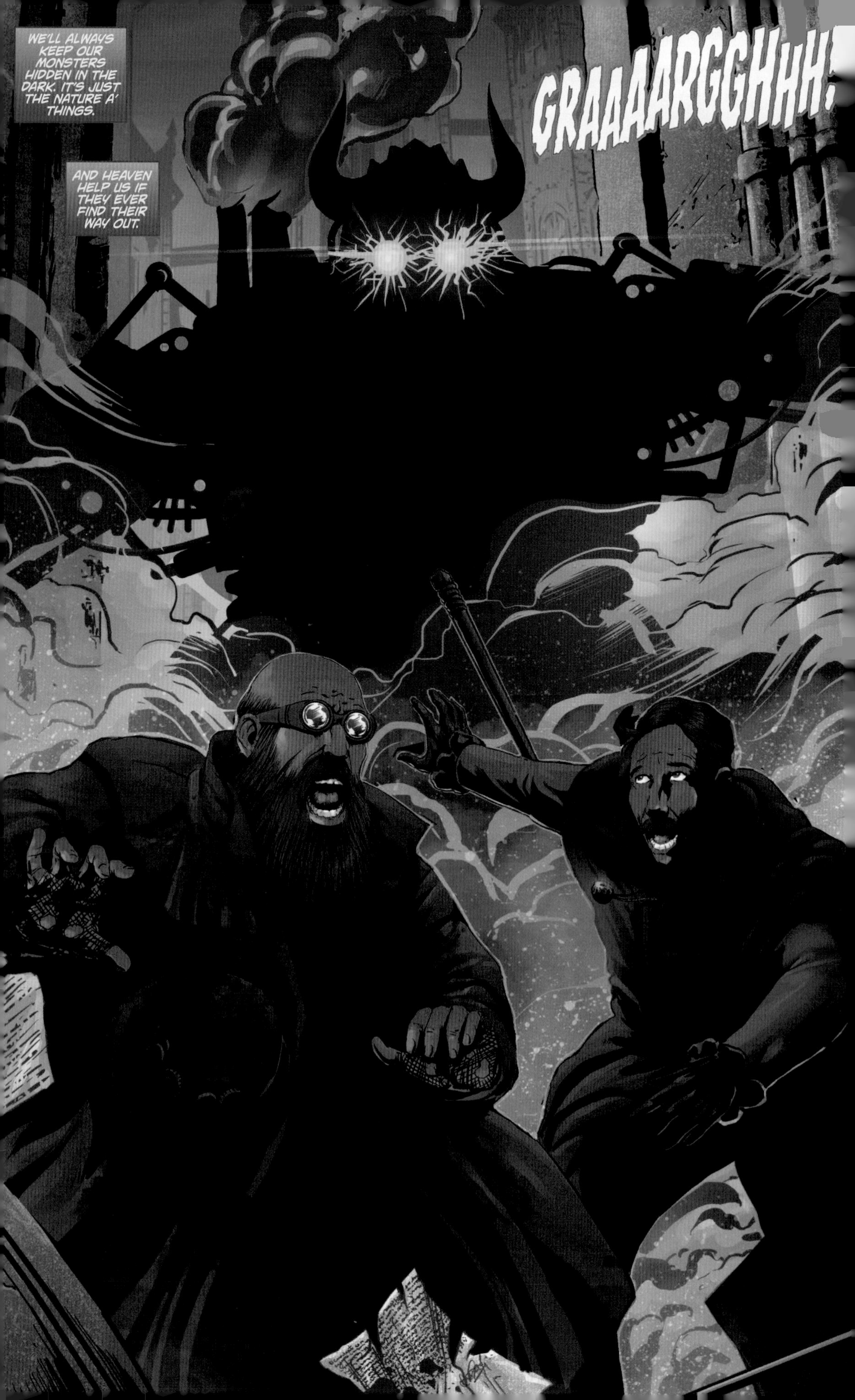

WE'LL ALWAYS KEEP OUR MONSTERS HIDDEN IN THE DARK. IT'S JUST THE NATURE A' THINGS.
AND HEAVEN HELP US IF THEY EVER FIND THEIR WAY OUT.
GRAAAARGGHHH!

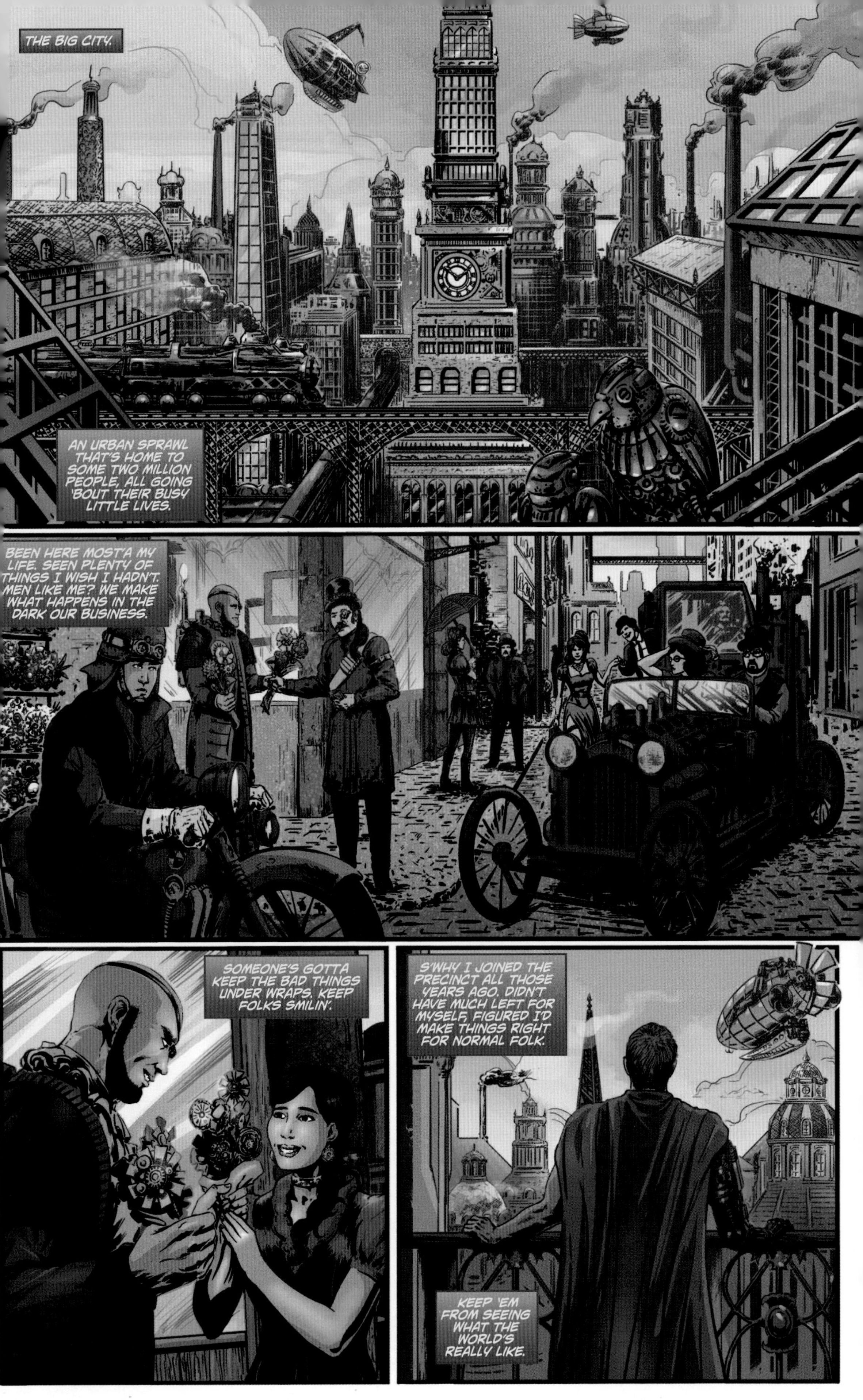
THE BIG CITY.
AN URBAN SPRAWL THAT'S HOME TO SOME TWO MILLION PEOPLE, ALL GOING 'BOUT THEIR BUSY LITTLE LIVES.
BEEN HERE MOST'A MY LIFE. SEEN PLENTY OF THINGS I WISH I HADN'T. MEN LIKE ME? WE MAKE WHAT HAPPENS IN THE DARK OUR BUSINESS.
SOMEONE'S GOTTA KEEP THE BAD THINGS UNDER WRAPS. KEEP FOLKS SMILIN'.
S'WHY I JOINED THE PRECINCT ALL THOSE YEARS AGO. DIDN'T HAVE MUCH LEFT FOR MYSELF, FIGURED I'D MAKE THINGS RIGHT FOR NORMAL FOLK.
KEEP 'EM FROM SEEING WHAT THE WORLD'S REALLY LIKE.

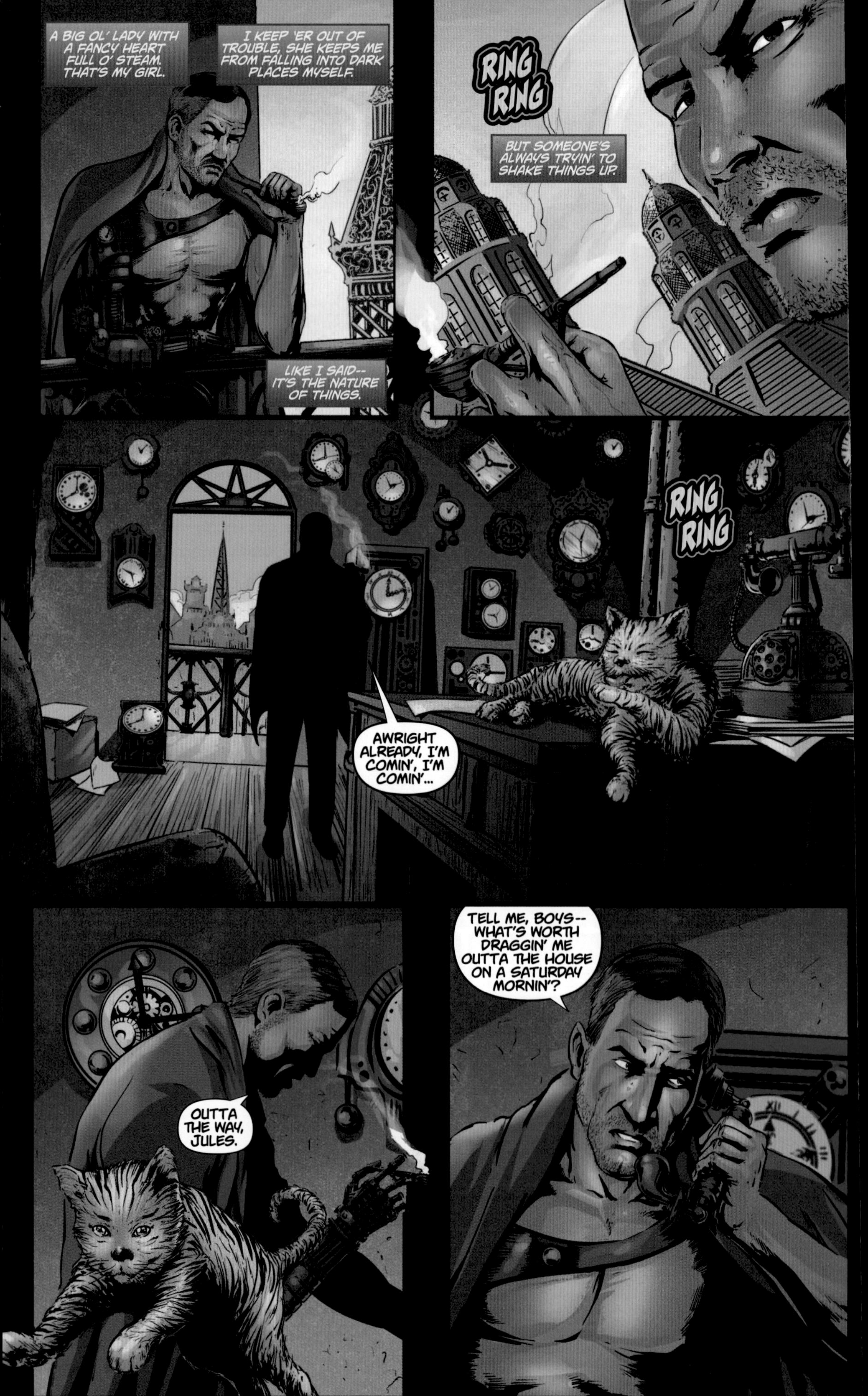
A BIG OL' LADY WITH A FANCY HEART FULL O' STEAM. THAT'S MY GIRL.
I KEEP 'ER OUT OF TROUBLE, SHE KEEPS ME FROM FALLING INTO DARK PLACES MYSELF.
LIKE I SAID-- IT'S THE NATURE OF THINGS.
RING RING
BUT SOMEONE'S ALWAYS TRYIN' TO SHAKE THINGS UP.
RING RING
AWRIGHT ALREADY, I'M COMIN', I'M COMIN'...
OUTTA THE WAY, JULES.
TELL ME, BOYS-- WHAT'S WORTH DRAGGIN' ME OUTTA THE HOUSE ON A SATURDAY MORNIN'?

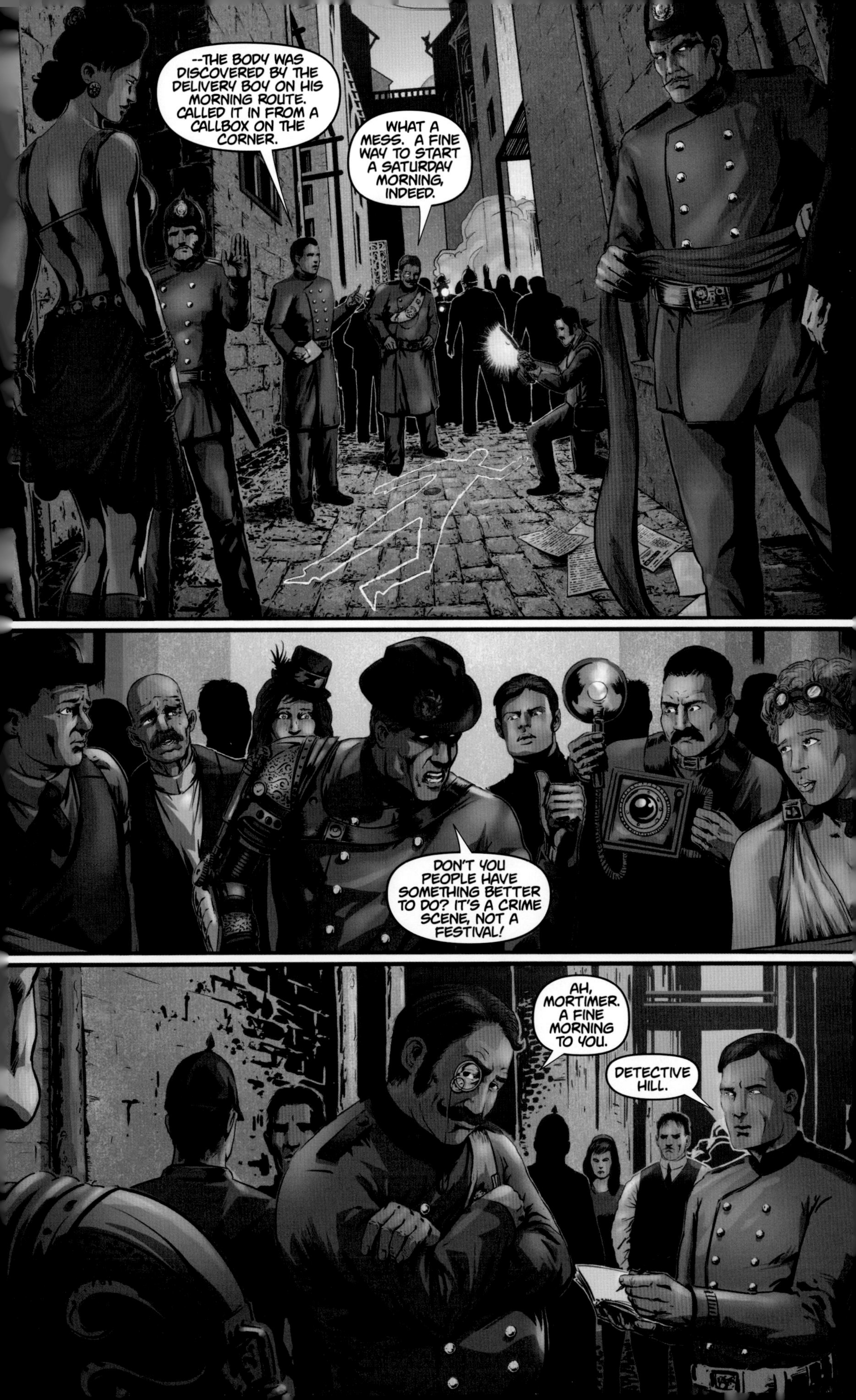
--THE BODY WAS DISCOVERED BY THE DELIVERY BOY ON HIS MORNING ROUTE. CALLED IT IN FROM A CALLBOX ON THE CORNER.
WHAT A MESS. A FINE WAY TO START A SATURDAY MORNING, INDEED.
DON'T YOU PEOPLE HAVE SOMETHING BETTER TO DO? IT'S A CRIME SCENE, NOT A FESTIVAL!
AH, MORTIMER. A FINE MORNING TO YOU.
DETECTIVE HILL.

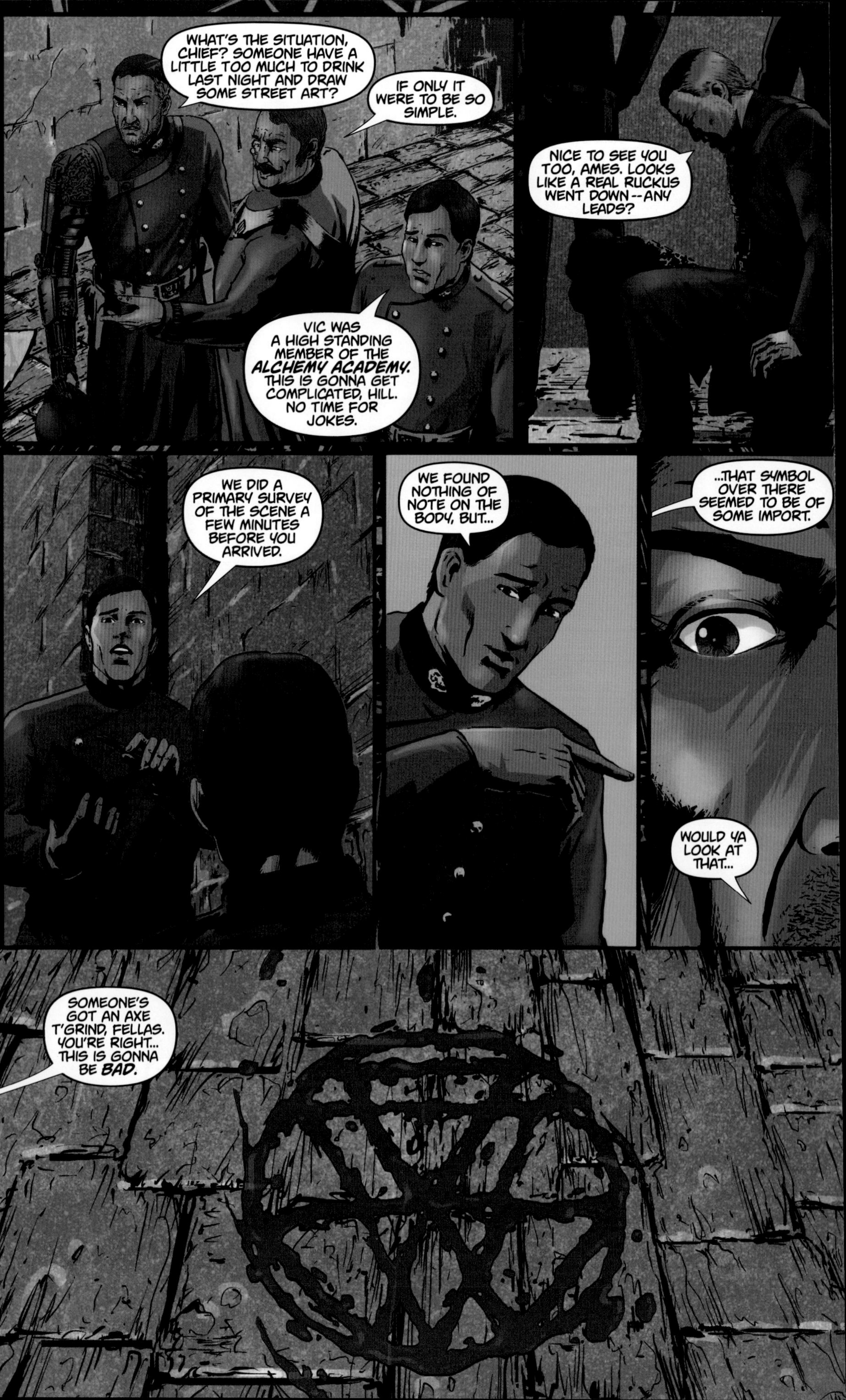
WHAT'S THE SITUATION, CHIEF? SOMEONE HAVE A LITTLE TOO MUCH TO DRINK LAST NIGHT AND DRAW SOME STREET ART?
IF ONLY IT WERE TO BE SO SIMPLE.
VIC WAS A HIGH STANDING MEMBER OF THE ALCHEMY ACADEMY. THIS IS GONNA GET COMPLICATED, HILL. NO TIME FOR JOKES.
NICE TO SEE YOU TOO, AMES. LOOKS LIKE A REAL RUCKUS WENT DOWN--ANY LEADS?
WE DID A PRIMARY SURVEY OF THE SCENE A FEW MINUTES BEFORE YOU ARRIVED.
WE FOUND NOTHING OF NOTE ON THE BODY, BUT...
...THAT SYMBOL OVER THERE SEEMED TO BE OF SOME IMPORT.
WOULD YA LOOK AT THAT...
SOMEONE'S GOT AN AXE T'GRIND, FELLAS. YOU'RE RIGHT... THIS IS GONNA BE BAD.

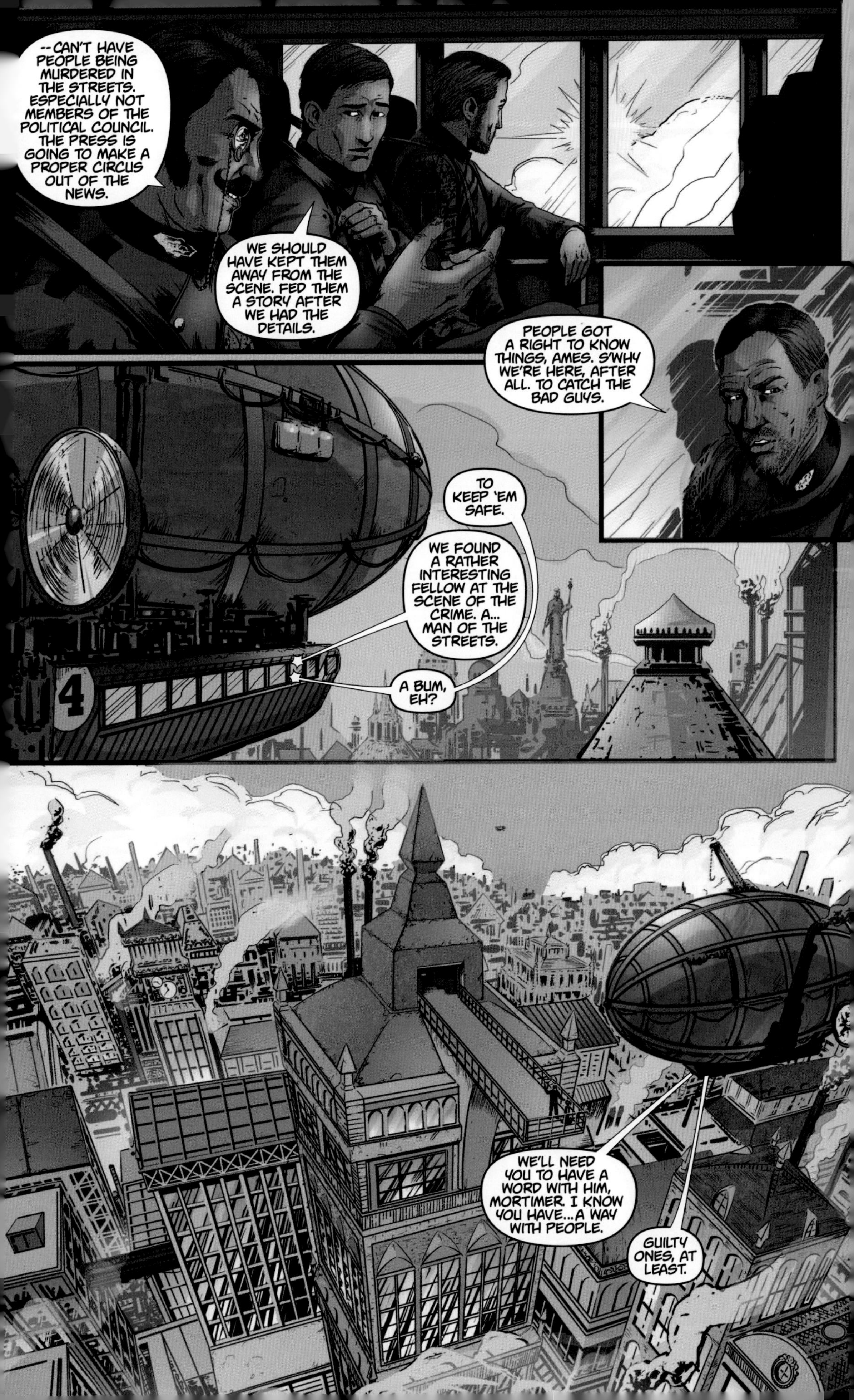
--CAN'T HAVE PEOPLE BEING MURDERED IN THE STREETS. ESPECIALLY NOT MEMBERS OF THE POLITICAL COUNCIL. THE PRESS IS GOING TO MAKE A PROPER CIRCUS OUT OF THE NEWS.
WE SHOULD HAVE KEPT THEM AWAY FROM THE SCENE. FED THEM A STORY AFTER WE HAD THE DETAILS.
PEOPLE GOT A RIGHT TO KNOW THINGS, AMES. S'WHY WE'RE HERE, AFTER ALL. TO CATCH THE BAD GUYS.
TO KEEP 'EM SAFE.
WE FOUND A RATHER INTERESTING FELLOW AT THE SCENE OF THE CRIME. A... MAN OF THE STREETS.
A BUM, EH?
4
WE'LL NEED YOU TO HAVE A WORD WITH HIM, MORTIMER. I KNOW YOU HAVE...A WAY WITH PEOPLE.
GUILTY ONES, AT LEAST.

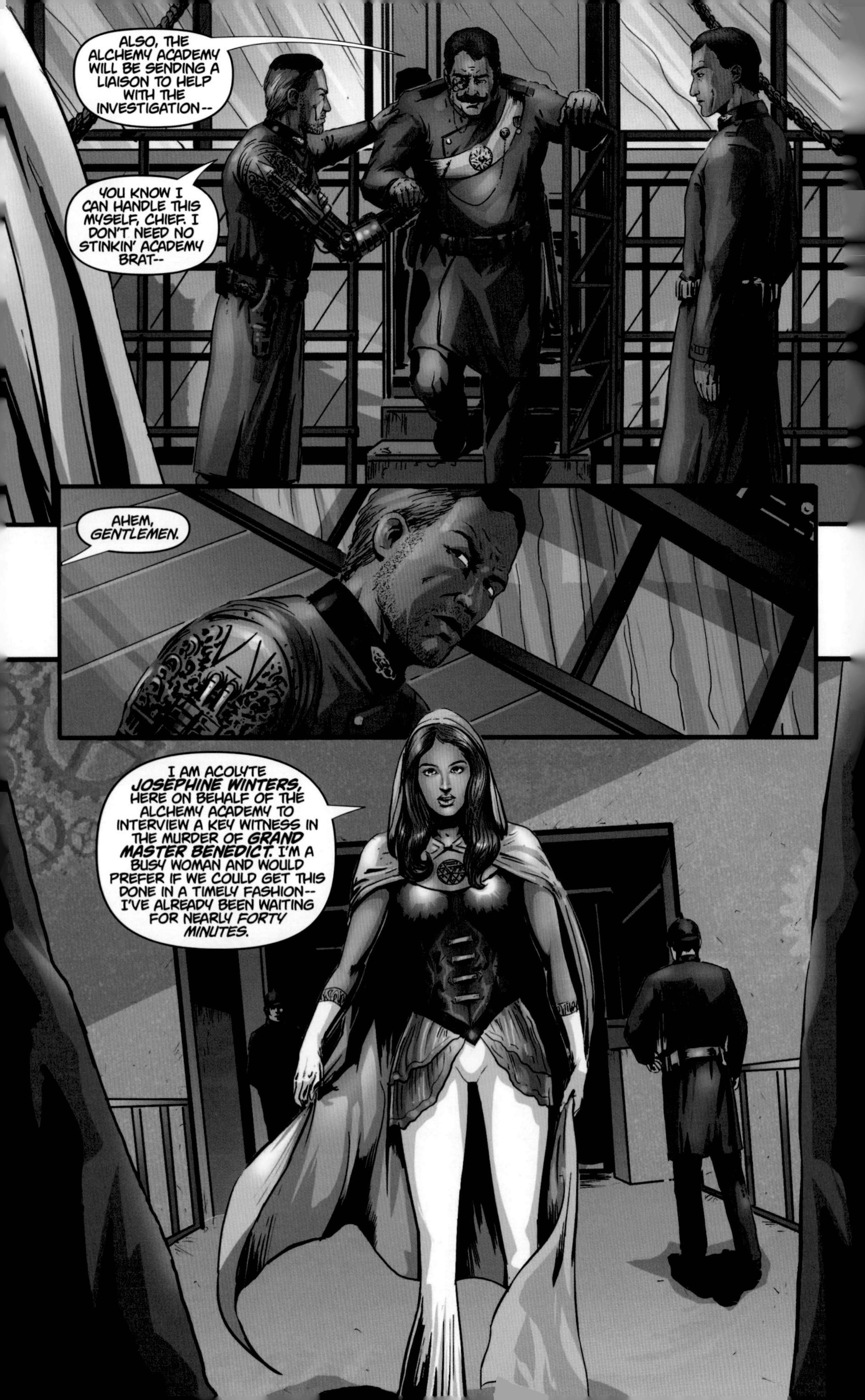
ALSO, THE ALCHEMY ACADEMY WILL BE SENDING A LIAISON TO HELP WITH THE INVESTIGATION--
YOU KNOW I CAN HANDLE THIS MYSELF, CHIEF. I DON'T NEED NO STINKIN' ACADEMY BRAT--
AHEM, GENTLEMEN.
I AM ACOLYTE *JOSEPHINE WINTERS*, HERE ON BEHALF OF THE ALCHEMY ACADEMY TO INTERVIEW A KEY WITNESS IN THE MURDER OF *GRAND MASTER BENEDICT*. I'M A BUSY WOMAN AND WOULD PREFER IF WE COULD GET THIS DONE IN A TIMELY FASHION-- I'VE ALREADY BEEN WAITING FOR NEARLY *FORTY* MINUTES.

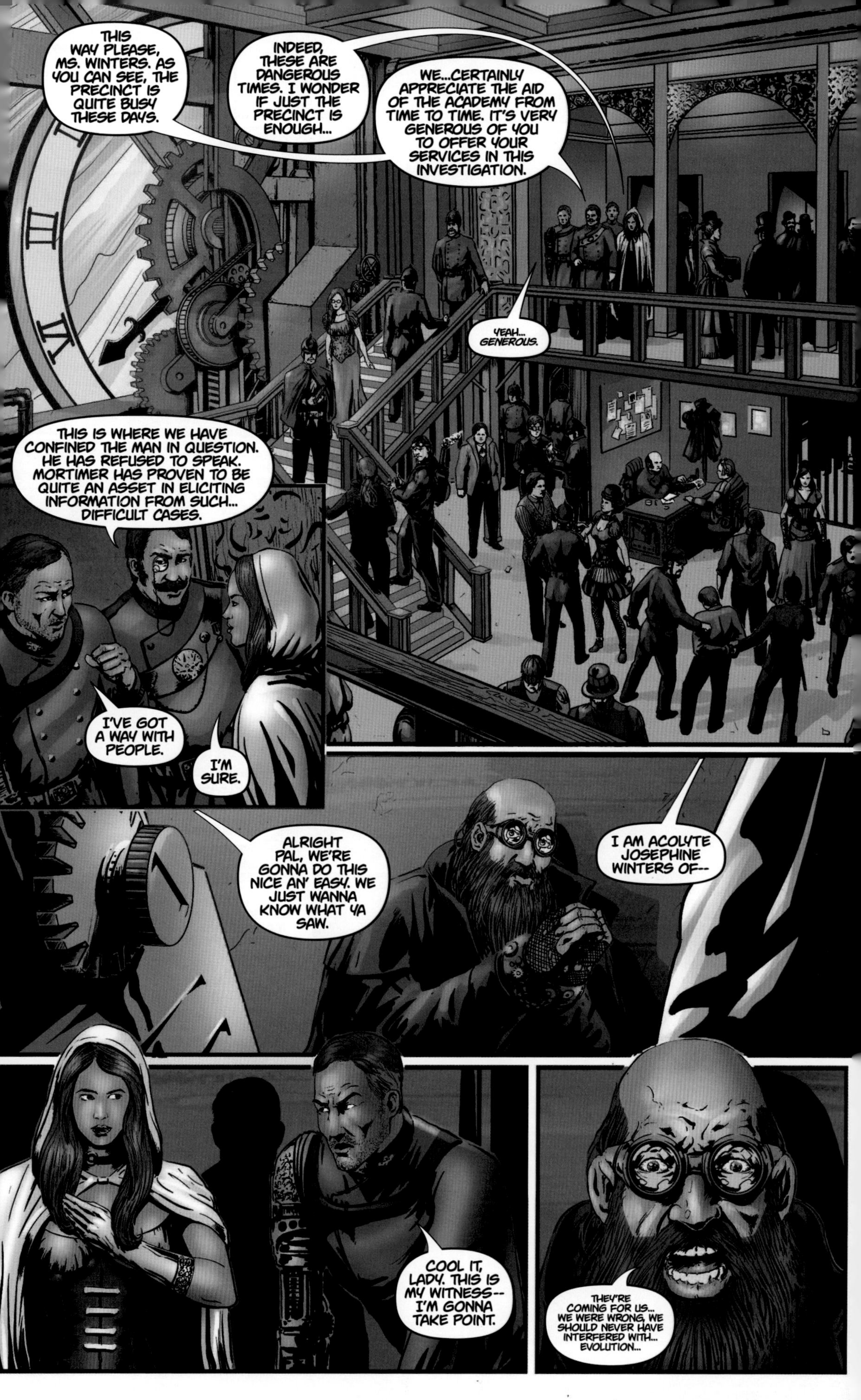
THIS WAY PLEASE, MS. WINTERS. AS YOU CAN SEE, THE PRECINCT IS QUITE BUSY THESE DAYS.
INDEED, THESE ARE DANGEROUS TIMES. I WONDER IF JUST THE PRECINCT IS ENOUGH...
WE...CERTAINLY APPRECIATE THE AID OF THE ACADEMY FROM TIME TO TIME. IT'S VERY GENEROUS OF YOU TO OFFER YOUR SERVICES IN THIS INVESTIGATION.
YEAH... GENEROUS.
THIS IS WHERE WE HAVE CONFINED THE MAN IN QUESTION. HE HAS REFUSED TO SPEAK. MORTIMER HAS PROVEN TO BE QUITE AN ASSET IN ELICITING INFORMATION FROM SUCH... DIFFICULT CASES.
I'VE GOT A WAY WITH PEOPLE.
I'M SURE.
ALRIGHT PAL, WE'RE GONNA DO THIS NICE AN' EASY. WE JUST WANNA KNOW WHAT YA SAW.
I AM ACOLYTE JOSEPHINE WINTERS OF--
COOL IT, LADY. THIS IS MY WITNESS-- I'M GONNA TAKE POINT.
THEY'RE COMING FOR US... WE WERE WRONG, WE SHOULD NEVER HAVE INTERFERED WITH... EVOLUTION...

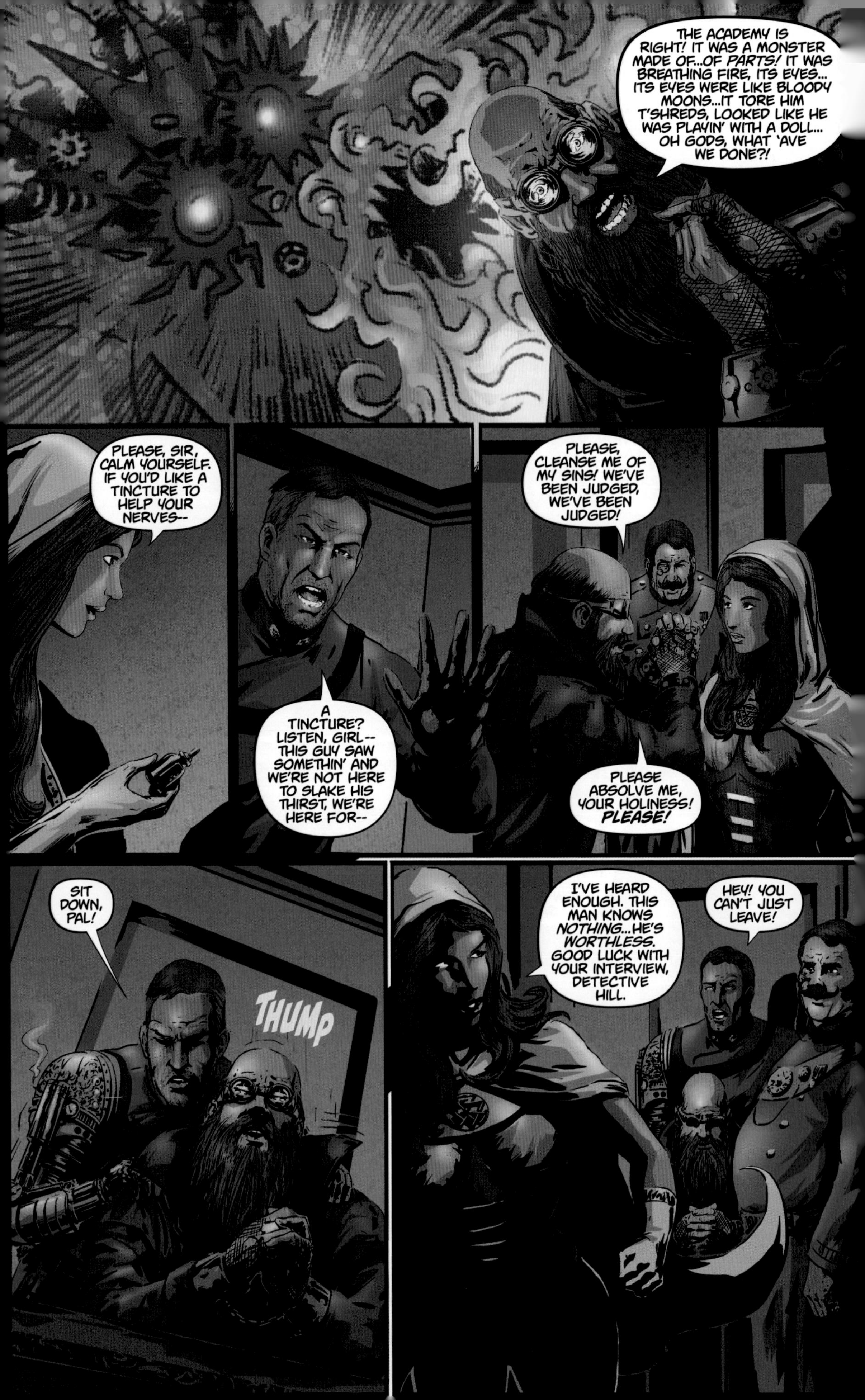
THE ACADEMY IS RIGHT! IT WAS A MONSTER MADE OF...OF *PARTS!* IT WAS BREATHING FIRE, ITS EYES... ITS EYES WERE LIKE BLOODY MOONS...IT TORE HIM T'SHREDS, LOOKED LIKE HE WAS PLAYIN' WITH A DOLL... OH GODS, WHAT 'AVE WE DONE?!
PLEASE, SIR, CALM YOURSELF. IF YOU'D LIKE A TINCTURE TO HELP YOUR NERVES--
A TINCTURE? LISTEN, GIRL-- THIS GUY SAW SOMETHIN' AND WE'RE NOT HERE TO SLAKE HIS THIRST, WE'RE HERE FOR--
PLEASE, CLEANSE ME OF MY SINS! WE'VE BEEN JUDGED, WE'VE BEEN JUDGED!
PLEASE ABSOLVE ME, YOUR HOLINESS! ***PLEASE!***
SIT DOWN, PAL!
THUMP
I'VE HEARD ENOUGH. THIS MAN KNOWS *NOTHING*...HE'S *WORTHLESS*. GOOD LUCK WITH YOUR INTERVIEW, DETECTIVE HILL.
HEY! YOU CAN'T JUST LEAVE!

THE HELL WAS THAT ALL ABOUT, LADY?

I DON'T HAVE TO EXPLAIN MYSELF TO YOU.

THE HELL YOU DON'T!

SOMETHIN' ABOUT YOU GOT HIM ALL RILED UP AND YOU JUST LEFT THE ROOM? WHAT'VE YOU GOT TO HIDE? YOU ACADEMY CREEPS ARE ALL THE SAME...

SOME FOLKS ARE JUST MORE COMFORTABLE DEALING WITH ACOLYTES. YOU? YOU'RE A BIT ROUGH AROUND THE EDGES. AND DON'T THINK I DIDN'T SEE THAT ARM...

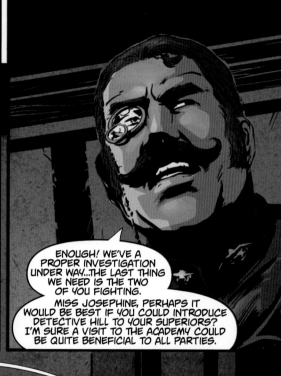

ENOUGH! WE'VE A PROPER INVESTIGATION UNDER WAY...THE LAST THING WE NEED IS THE TWO OF YOU FIGHTING.

MISS JOSEPHINE, PERHAPS IT WOULD BE BEST IF YOU COULD INTRODUCE DETECTIVE HILL TO YOUR SUPERIORS? I'M SURE A VISIT TO THE ACADEMY COULD BE QUITE BENEFICIAL TO ALL PARTIES.

IF YOU INSIST, SIR. IT'D BE...MY PLEASURE.

HRMPH.

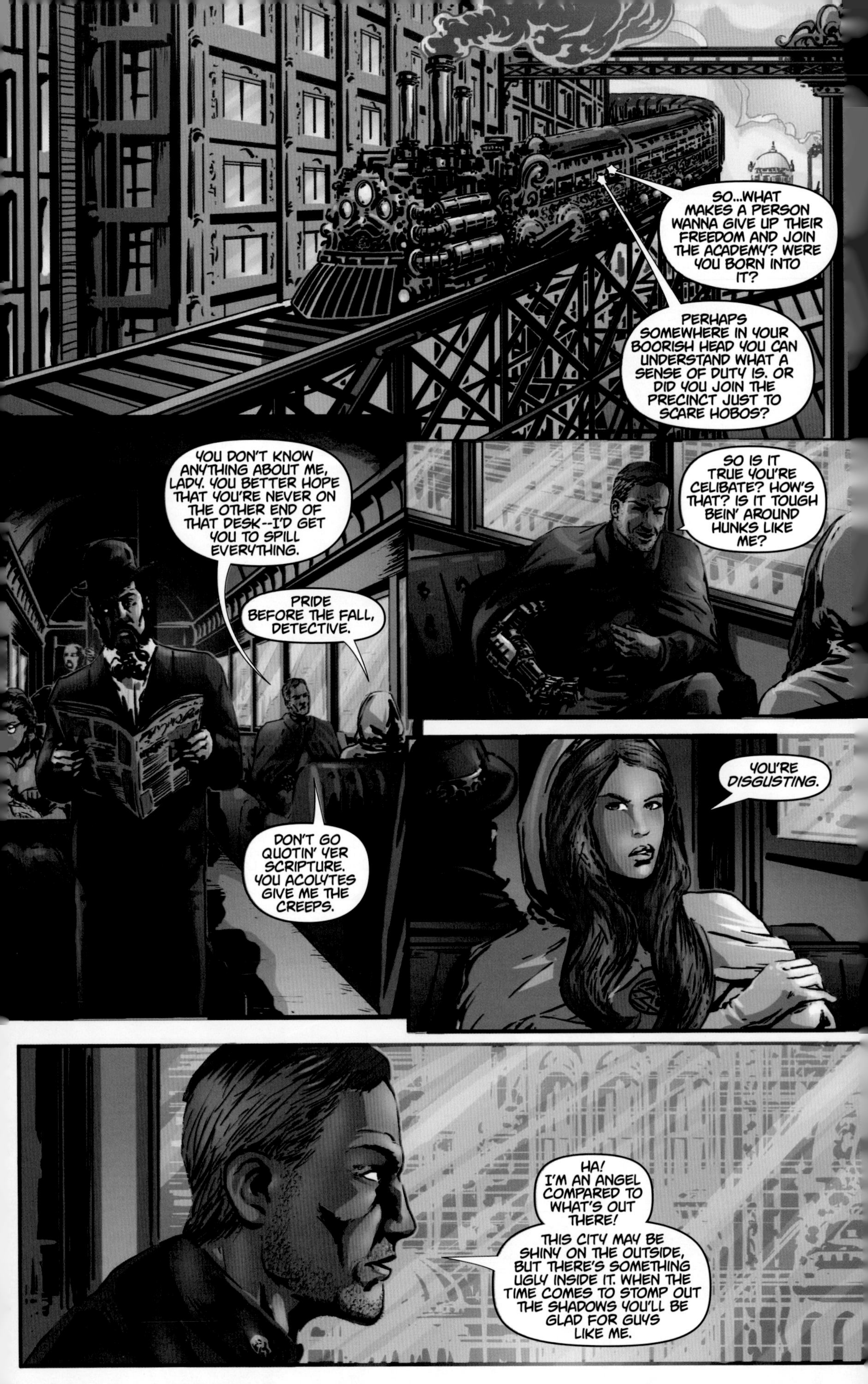
SO...WHAT MAKES A PERSON WANNA GIVE UP THEIR FREEDOM AND JOIN THE ACADEMY? WERE YOU BORN INTO IT?
PERHAPS SOMEWHERE IN YOUR BOORISH HEAD YOU CAN UNDERSTAND WHAT A SENSE OF DUTY IS. OR DID YOU JOIN THE PRECINCT JUST TO SCARE HOBOS?
YOU DON'T KNOW ANYTHING ABOUT ME, LADY. YOU BETTER HOPE THAT YOU'RE NEVER ON THE OTHER END OF THAT DESK--I'D GET YOU TO SPILL EVERYTHING.
PRIDE BEFORE THE FALL, DETECTIVE.
DON'T GO QUOTIN' YER SCRIPTURE. YOU ACOLYTES GIVE ME THE CREEPS.
SO IS IT TRUE YOU'RE CELIBATE? HOW'S THAT? IS IT TOUGH BEIN' AROUND HUNKS LIKE ME?
YOU'RE DISGUSTING.
HA! I'M AN ANGEL COMPARED TO WHAT'S OUT THERE!
THIS CITY MAY BE SHINY ON THE OUTSIDE, BUT THERE'S SOMETHING UGLY INSIDE IT. WHEN THE TIME COMES TO STOMP OUT THE SHADOWS YOU'LL BE GLAD FOR GUYS LIKE ME.

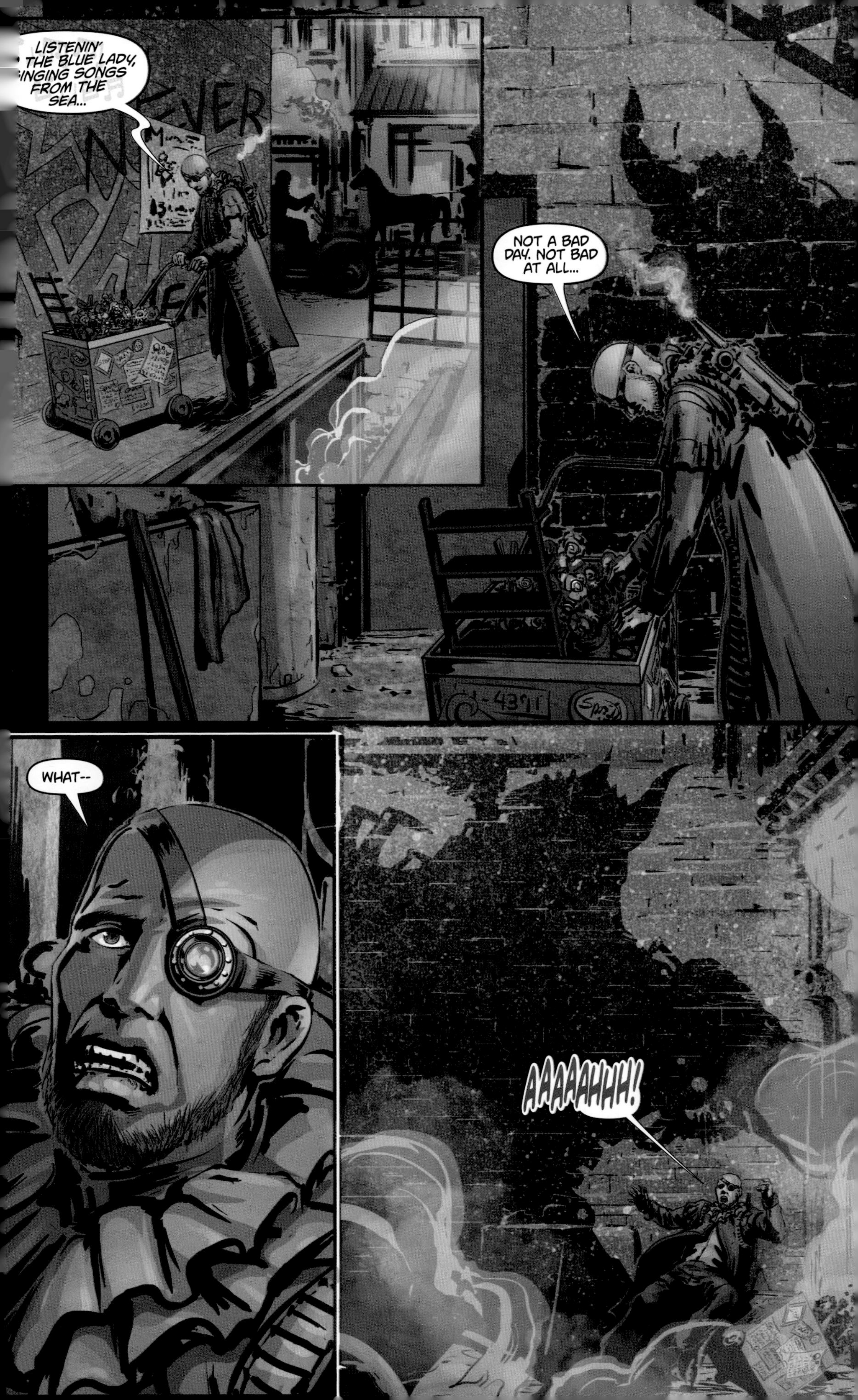
LISTENIN' TO THE BLUE LADY, SINGING SONGS FROM THE SEA...
NOT A BAD DAY. NOT BAD AT ALL...
WHAT--
AAAAAHHH!

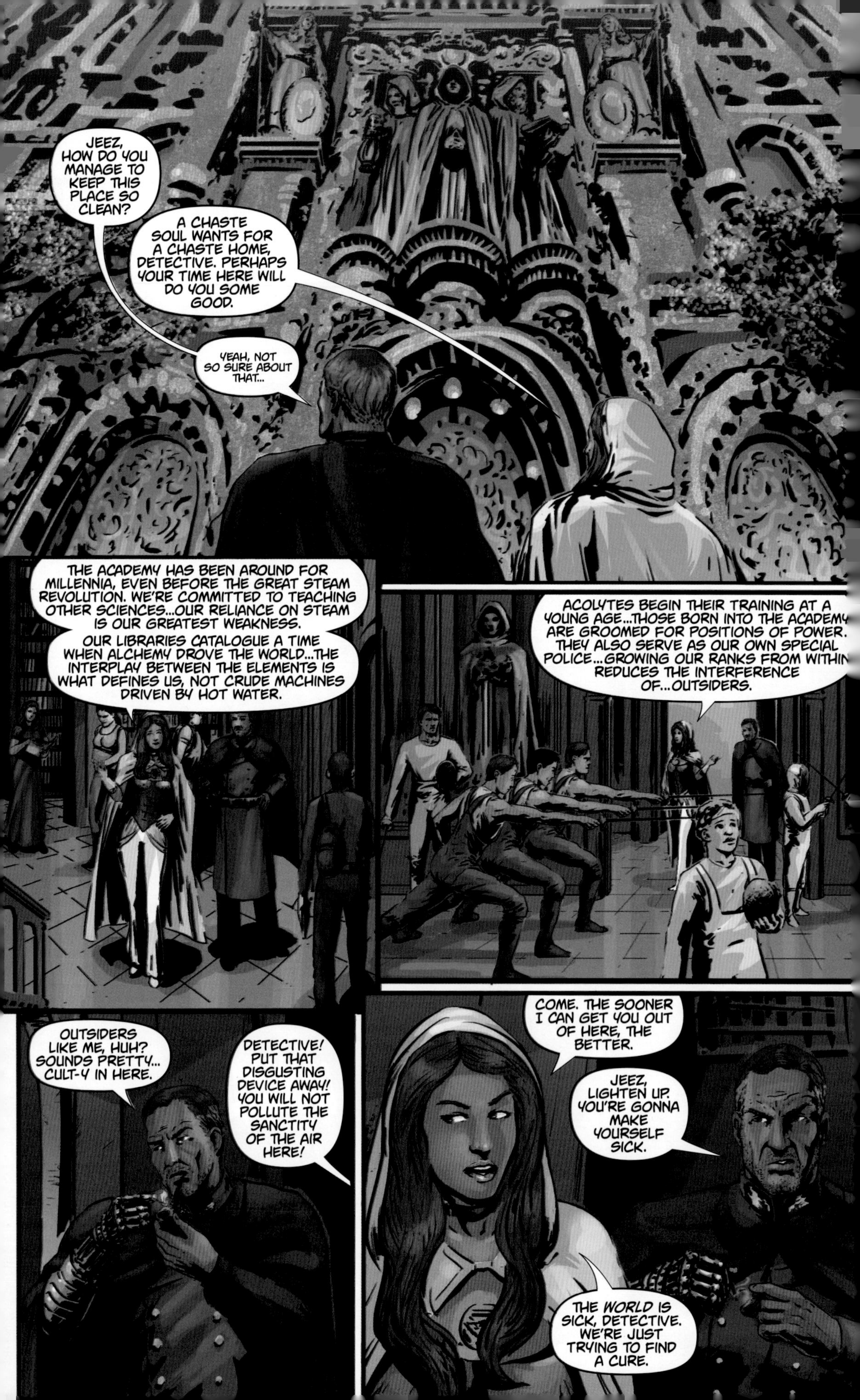
JEEZ, HOW DO YOU MANAGE TO KEEP THIS PLACE SO CLEAN?
A CHASTE SOUL WANTS FOR A CHASTE HOME, DETECTIVE. PERHAPS YOUR TIME HERE WILL DO YOU SOME GOOD.
YEAH, NOT SO SURE ABOUT THAT...
THE ACADEMY HAS BEEN AROUND FOR MILLENNIA, EVEN BEFORE THE GREAT STEAM REVOLUTION. WE'RE COMMITTED TO TEACHING OTHER SCIENCES...OUR RELIANCE ON STEAM IS OUR GREATEST WEAKNESS.
OUR LIBRARIES CATALOGUE A TIME WHEN ALCHEMY DROVE THE WORLD...THE INTERPLAY BETWEEN THE ELEMENTS IS WHAT DEFINES US, NOT CRUDE MACHINES DRIVEN BY HOT WATER.
ACOLYTES BEGIN THEIR TRAINING AT A YOUNG AGE...THOSE BORN INTO THE ACADEMY ARE GROOMED FOR POSITIONS OF POWER. THEY ALSO SERVE AS OUR OWN SPECIAL POLICE...GROWING OUR RANKS FROM WITHIN REDUCES THE INTERFERENCE OF...OUTSIDERS.
OUTSIDERS LIKE ME, HUH? SOUNDS PRETTY... CULT-Y IN HERE.
DETECTIVE! PUT THAT DISGUSTING DEVICE AWAY! YOU WILL NOT POLLUTE THE SANCTITY OF THE AIR HERE!
COME. THE SOONER I CAN GET YOU OUT OF HERE, THE BETTER.
JEEZ, LIGHTEN UP. YOU'RE GONNA MAKE YOURSELF SICK.
THE WORLD IS SICK, DETECTIVE. WE'RE JUST TRYING TO FIND A CURE.

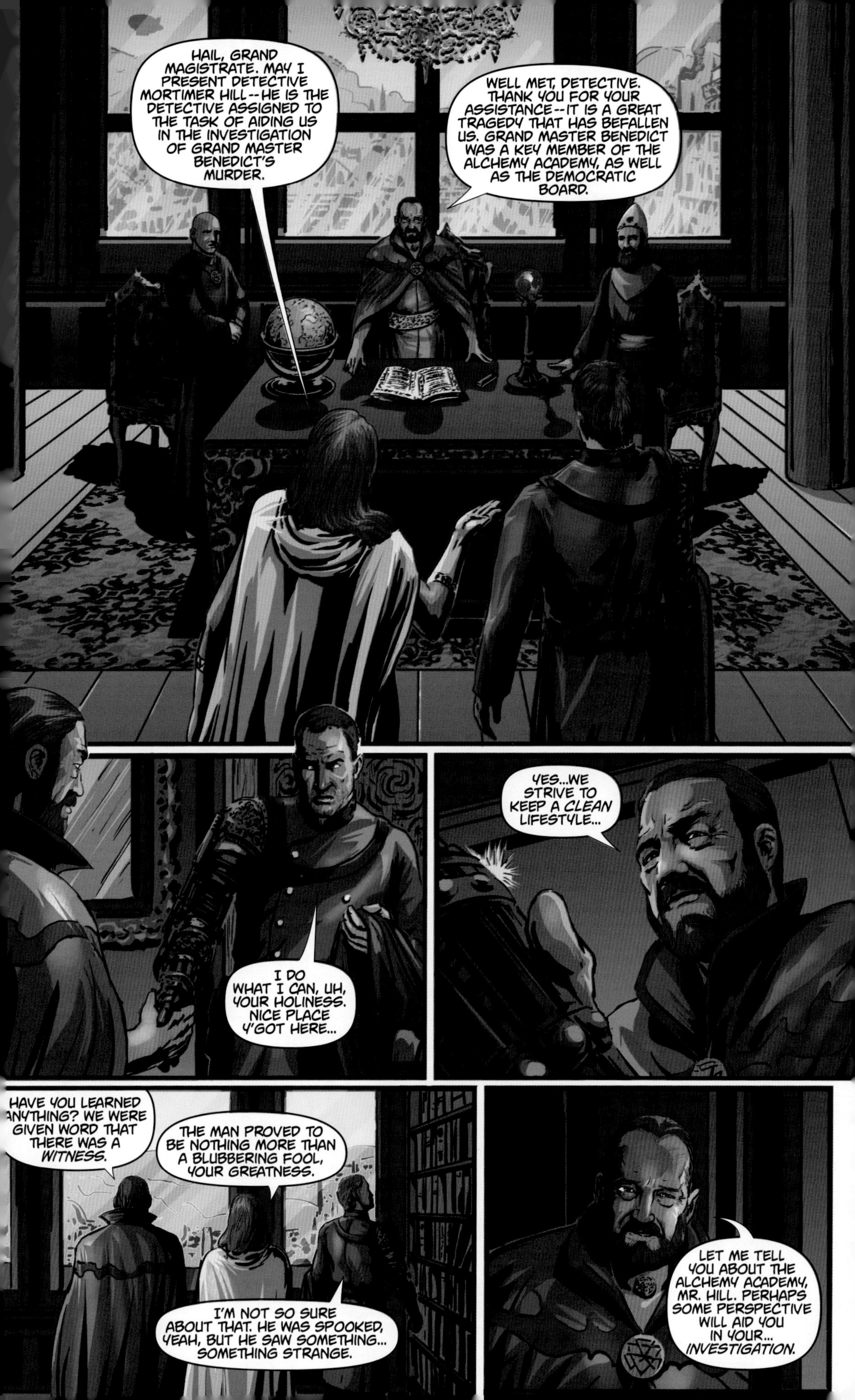
HAIL, GRAND MAGISTRATE. MAY I PRESENT DETECTIVE MORTIMER HILL--HE IS THE DETECTIVE ASSIGNED TO THE TASK OF AIDING US IN THE INVESTIGATION OF GRAND MASTER BENEDICT'S MURDER.
WELL MET, DETECTIVE. THANK YOU FOR YOUR ASSISTANCE--IT IS A GREAT TRAGEDY THAT HAS BEFALLEN US. GRAND MASTER BENEDICT WAS A KEY MEMBER OF THE ALCHEMY ACADEMY, AS WELL AS THE DEMOCRATIC BOARD.
I DO WHAT I CAN, UH, YOUR HOLINESS. NICE PLACE Y'GOT HERE...
YES...WE STRIVE TO KEEP A *CLEAN* LIFESTYLE...
HAVE YOU LEARNED ANYTHING? WE WERE GIVEN WORD THAT THERE WAS A *WITNESS*.
THE MAN PROVED TO BE NOTHING MORE THAN A BLUBBERING FOOL, YOUR GREATNESS.
I'M NOT SO SURE ABOUT THAT. HE WAS SPOOKED, YEAH, BUT HE SAW SOMETHING... SOMETHING STRANGE.
LET ME TELL YOU ABOUT THE ALCHEMY ACADEMY, MR. HILL. PERHAPS SOME PERSPECTIVE WILL AID YOU IN YOUR... *INVESTIGATION*.

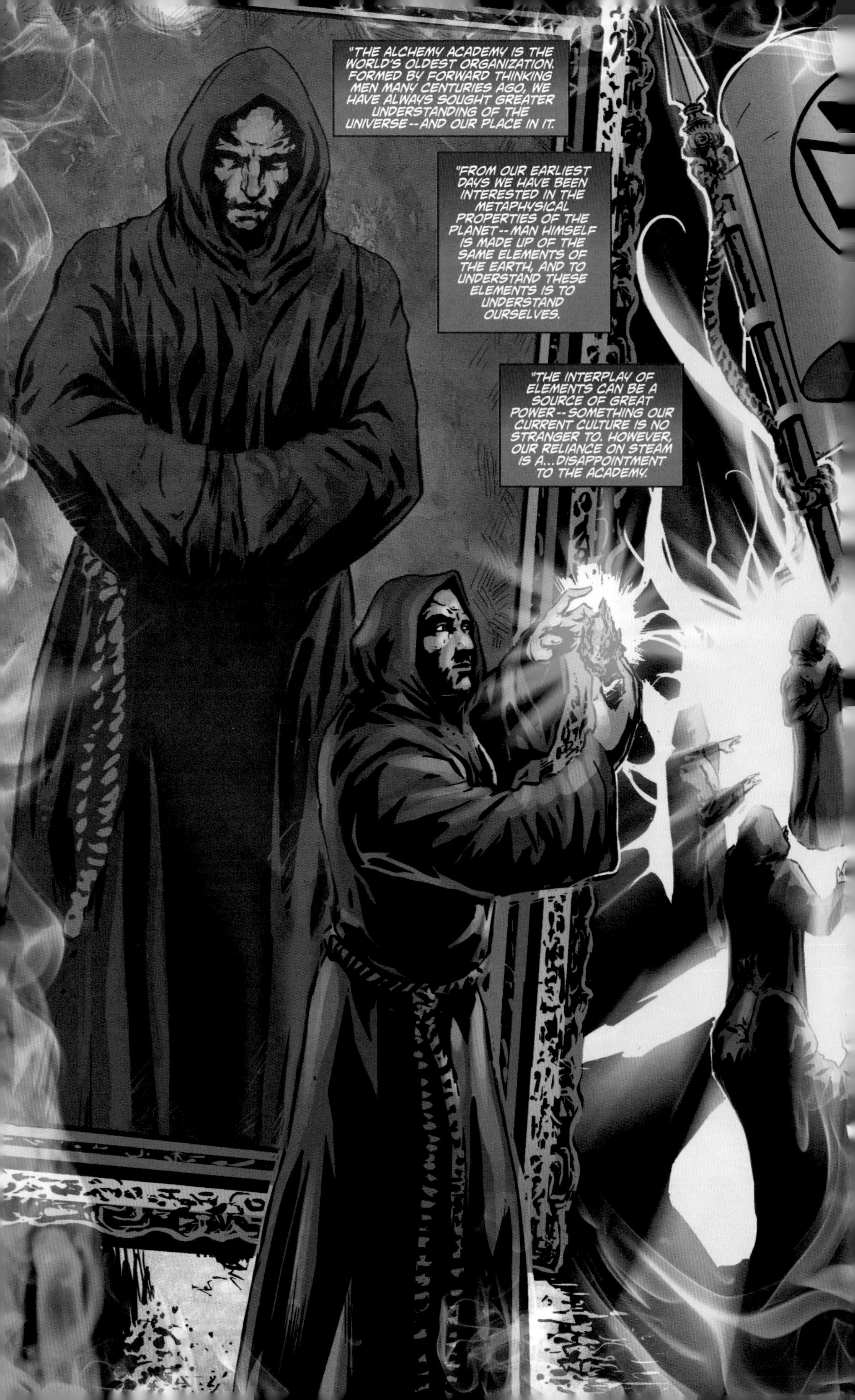
"THE ALCHEMY ACADEMY IS THE WORLD'S OLDEST ORGANIZATION. FORMED BY FORWARD THINKING MEN MANY CENTURIES AGO, WE HAVE ALWAYS SOUGHT GREATER UNDERSTANDING OF THE UNIVERSE--AND OUR PLACE IN IT.
"FROM OUR EARLIEST DAYS WE HAVE BEEN INTERESTED IN THE METAPHYSICAL PROPERTIES OF THE PLANET--MAN HIMSELF IS MADE UP OF THE SAME ELEMENTS OF THE EARTH, AND TO UNDERSTAND THESE ELEMENTS IS TO UNDERSTAND OURSELVES.
"THE INTERPLAY OF ELEMENTS CAN BE A SOURCE OF GREAT POWER--SOMETHING OUR CURRENT CULTURE IS NO STRANGER TO. HOWEVER, OUR RELIANCE ON STEAM IS A...DISAPPOINTMENT TO THE ACADEMY.

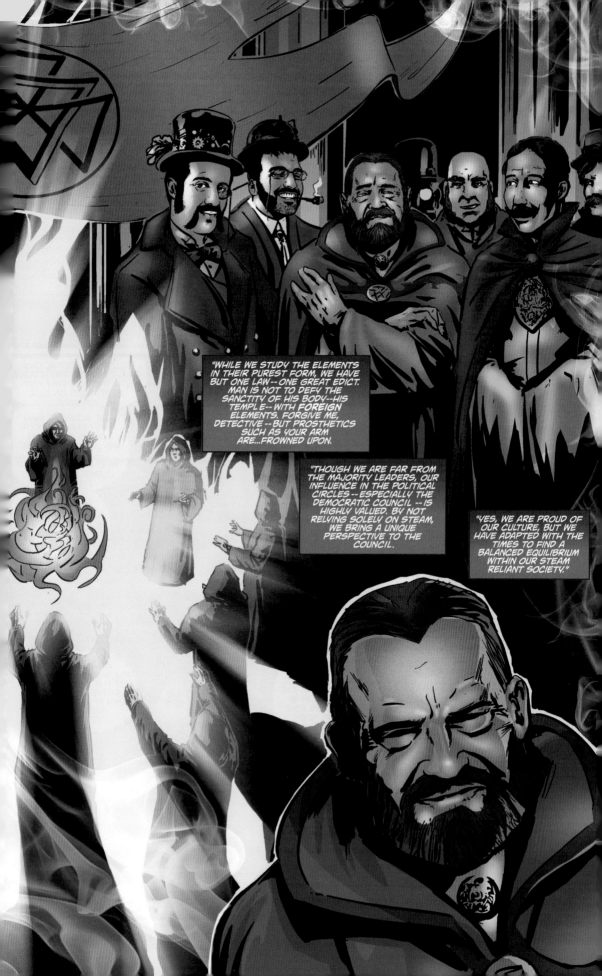

"WHILE WE STUDY THE ELEMENTS IN THEIR PUREST FORM, WE HAVE BUT ONE LAW--ONE GREAT EDICT. MAN IS NOT TO DEFY THE SANCTITY OF HIS BODY--HIS TEMPLE-- WITH FOREIGN ELEMENTS. FORGIVE ME, DETECTIVE -- BUT PROSTHETICS SUCH AS YOUR ARM ARE...FROWNED UPON.

"THOUGH WE ARE FAR FROM THE MAJORITY LEADERS, OUR INFLUENCE IN THE POLITICAL CIRCLES -- ESPECIALLY THE DEMOCRATIC COUNCIL -- IS HIGHLY VALUED. BY NOT RELYING SOLELY ON STEAM, WE BRING A UNIQUE PERSPECTIVE TO THE COUNCIL.

"YES, WE ARE PROUD OF OUR CULTURE, BUT WE HAVE ADAPTED WITH THE TIMES TO FIND A BALANCED EQUILIBRIUM WITHIN OUR STEAM RELIANT SOCIETY."

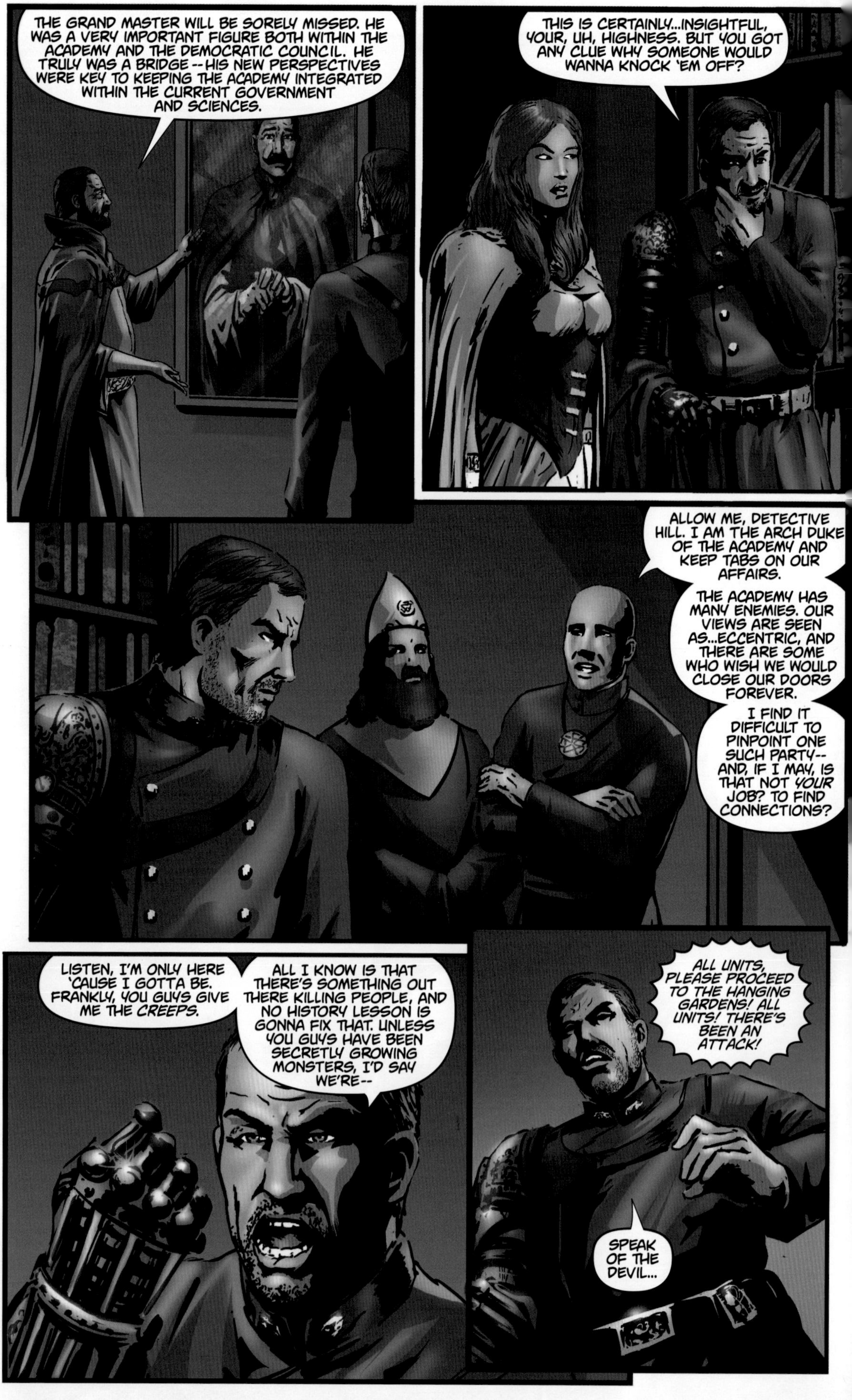
THE GRAND MASTER WILL BE SORELY MISSED. HE WAS A VERY IMPORTANT FIGURE BOTH WITHIN THE ACADEMY AND THE DEMOCRATIC COUNCIL. HE TRULY WAS A BRIDGE --HIS NEW PERSPECTIVES WERE KEY TO KEEPING THE ACADEMY INTEGRATED WITHIN THE CURRENT GOVERNMENT AND SCIENCES.
THIS IS CERTAINLY...INSIGHTFUL, YOUR, UH, HIGHNESS. BUT YOU GOT ANY CLUE WHY SOMEONE WOULD WANNA KNOCK 'EM OFF?
ALLOW ME, DETECTIVE HILL. I AM THE ARCH DUKE OF THE ACADEMY AND KEEP TABS ON OUR AFFAIRS.
THE ACADEMY HAS MANY ENEMIES. OUR VIEWS ARE SEEN AS...ECCENTRIC, AND THERE ARE SOME WHO WISH WE WOULD CLOSE OUR DOORS FOREVER.
I FIND IT DIFFICULT TO PINPOINT ONE SUCH PARTY-- AND, IF I MAY, IS THAT NOT *YOUR* JOB? TO FIND CONNECTIONS?
LISTEN, I'M ONLY HERE 'CAUSE I GOTTA BE. FRANKLY, YOU GUYS GIVE ME THE *CREEPS.*
ALL I KNOW IS THAT THERE'S SOMETHING OUT THERE KILLING PEOPLE, AND NO HISTORY LESSON IS GONNA FIX THAT. UNLESS YOU GUYS HAVE BEEN SECRETLY GROWING MONSTERS, I'D SAY WE'RE--
ALL UNITS, PLEASE PROCEED TO THE HANGING GARDENS! ALL UNITS! THERE'S BEEN AN ATTACK!
SPEAK OF THE DEVIL...

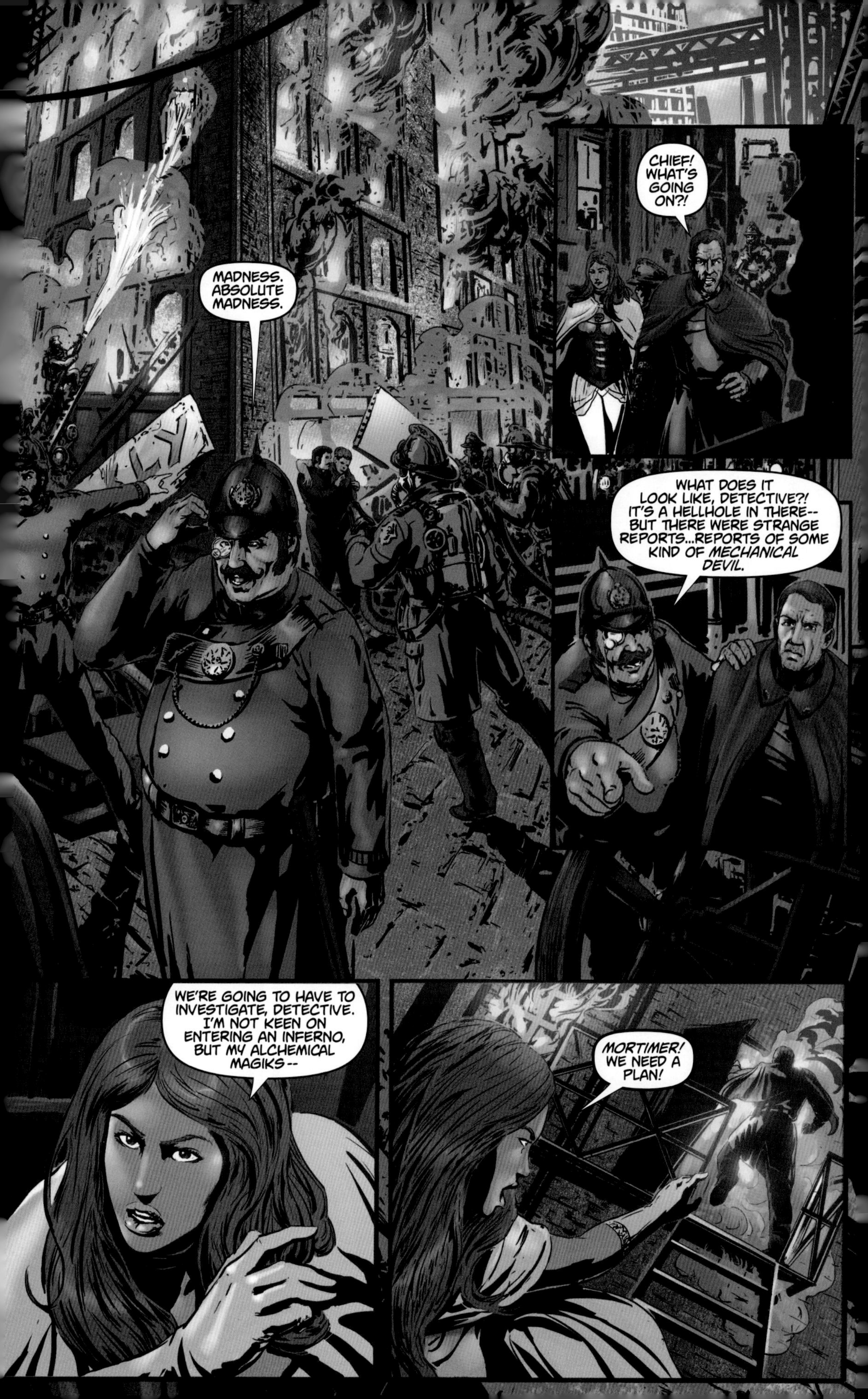
MADNESS. ABSOLUTE MADNESS.
CHIEF! WHAT'S GOING ON?!
WHAT DOES IT LOOK LIKE, DETECTIVE?! IT'S A HELLHOLE IN THERE-- BUT THERE WERE STRANGE REPORTS...REPORTS OF SOME KIND OF *MECHANICAL* DEVIL.
WE'RE GOING TO HAVE TO INVESTIGATE, DETECTIVE. I'M NOT KEEN ON ENTERING AN INFERNO, BUT MY ALCHEMICAL MAGIKS --
MORTIMER! WE NEED A PLAN!

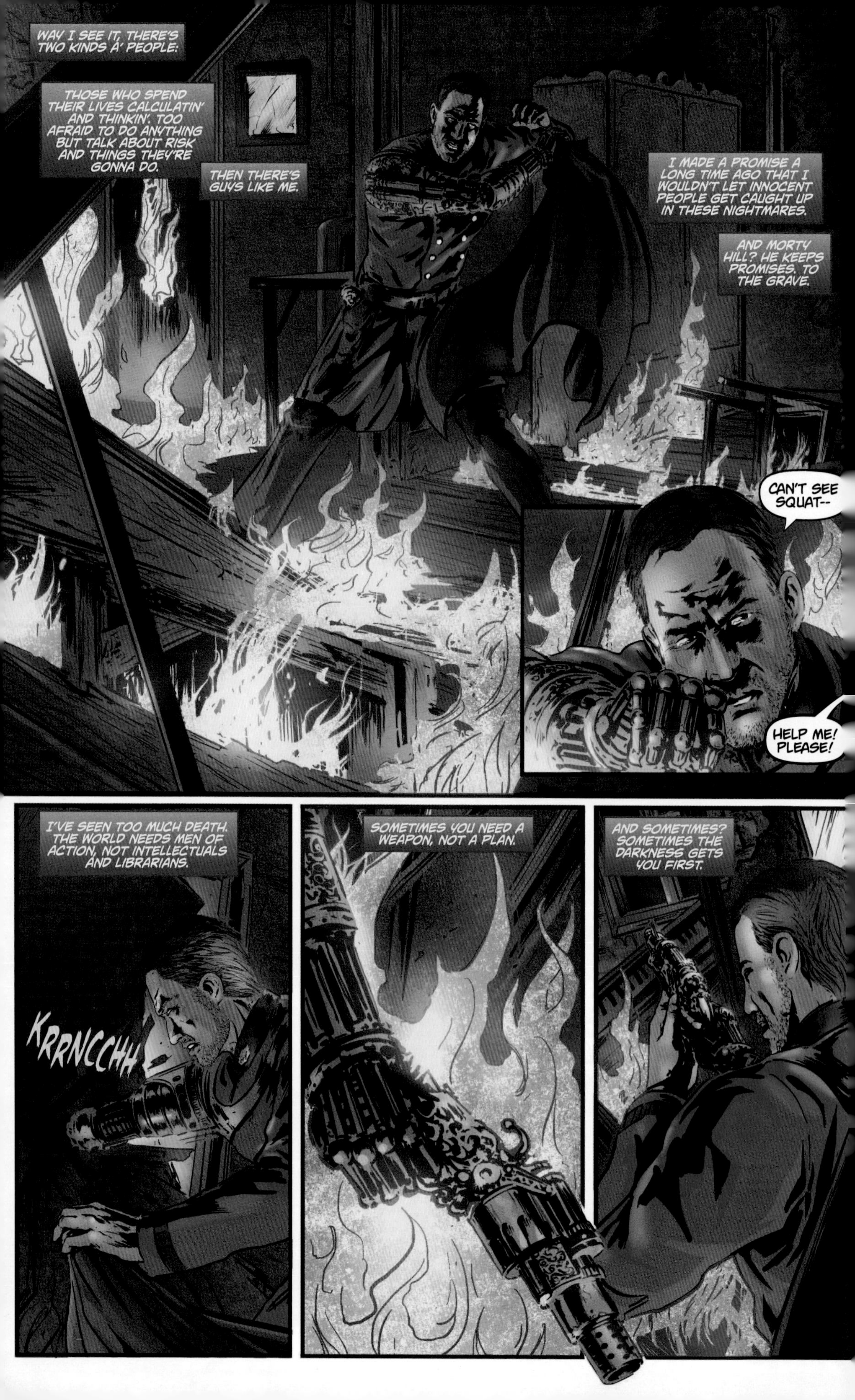
WAY I SEE IT, THERE'S TWO KINDS A' PEOPLE:
THOSE WHO SPEND THEIR LIVES CALCULATIN' AND THINKIN'. TOO AFRAID TO DO ANYTHING BUT TALK ABOUT RISK AND THINGS THEY'RE GONNA DO.
THEN THERE'S GUYS LIKE ME.
I MADE A PROMISE A LONG TIME AGO THAT I WOULDN'T LET INNOCENT PEOPLE GET CAUGHT UP IN THESE NIGHTMARES.
AND MORTY HILL? HE KEEPS PROMISES. TO THE GRAVE.
CAN'T SEE SQUAT--
HELP ME! PLEASE!
I'VE SEEN TOO MUCH DEATH. THE WORLD NEEDS MEN OF ACTION, NOT INTELLECTUALS AND LIBRARIANS.
KRRNCCHH
SOMETIMES YOU NEED A WEAPON, NOT A PLAN.
AND SOMETIMES? SOMETIMES THE DARKNESS GETS YOU FIRST.

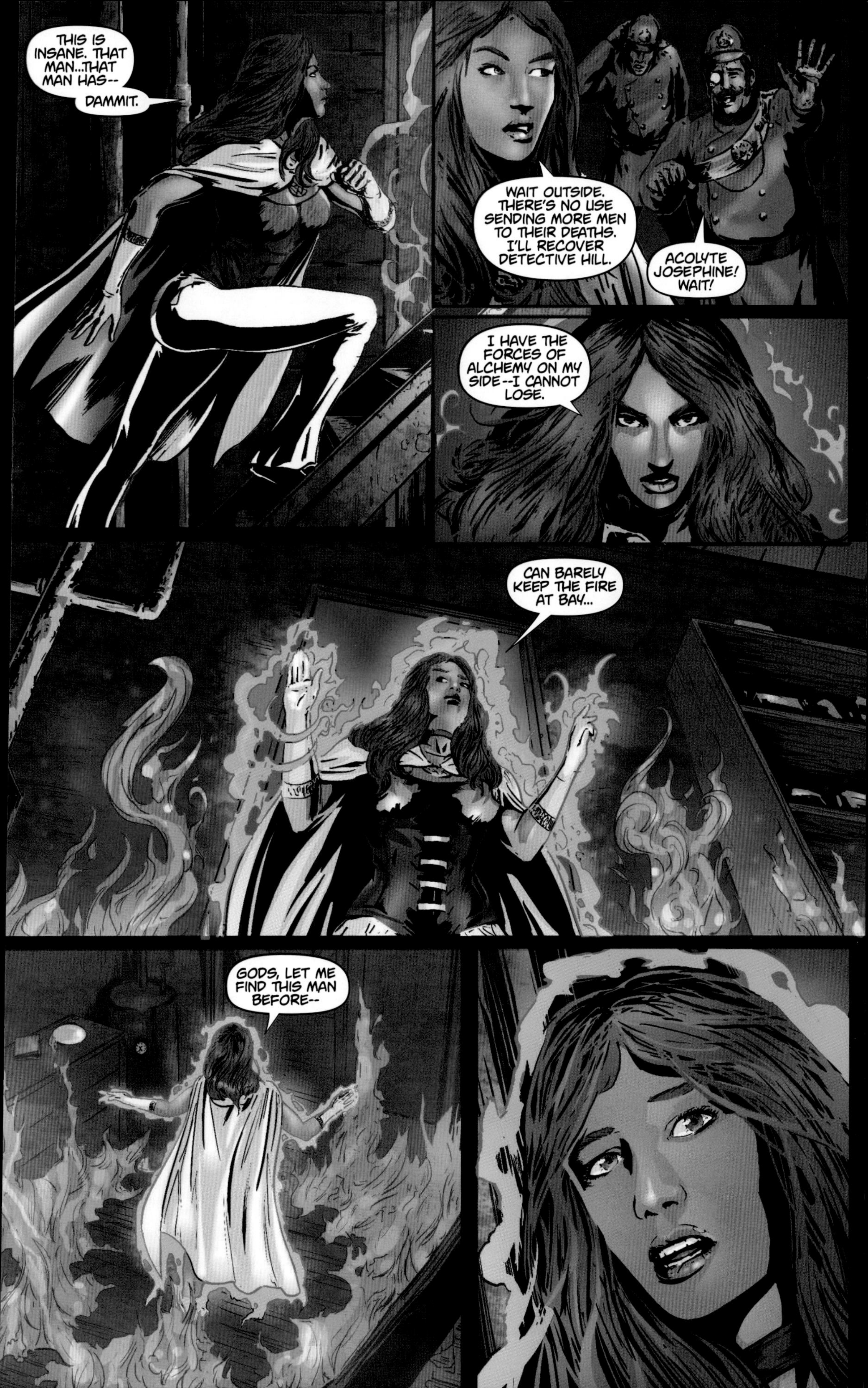
THIS IS INSANE. THAT MAN...THAT MAN HAS--
DAMMIT.
WAIT OUTSIDE. THERE'S NO USE SENDING MORE MEN TO THEIR DEATHS. I'LL RECOVER DETECTIVE HILL.
ACOLYTE JOSEPHINE! WAIT!
I HAVE THE FORCES OF ALCHEMY ON MY SIDE--I CANNOT LOSE.
CAN BARELY KEEP THE FIRE AT BAY...
GODS, LET ME FIND THIS MAN BEFORE--

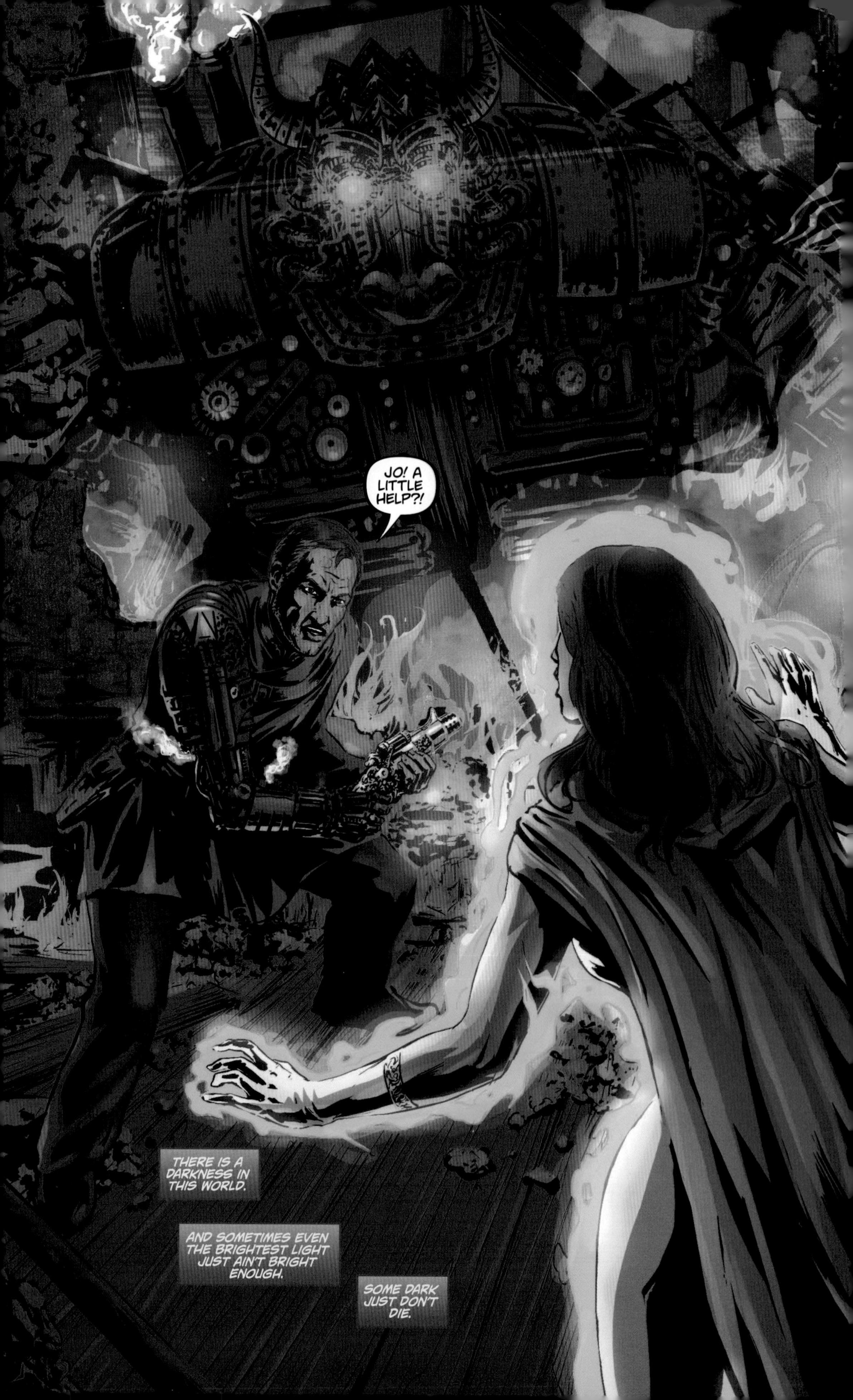
JO! A LITTLE HELP?!
THERE IS A DARKNESS IN THIS WORLD.
AND SOMETIMES EVEN THE BRIGHTEST LIGHT JUST AIN'T BRIGHT ENOUGH.
SOME DARK JUST DON'T DIE.

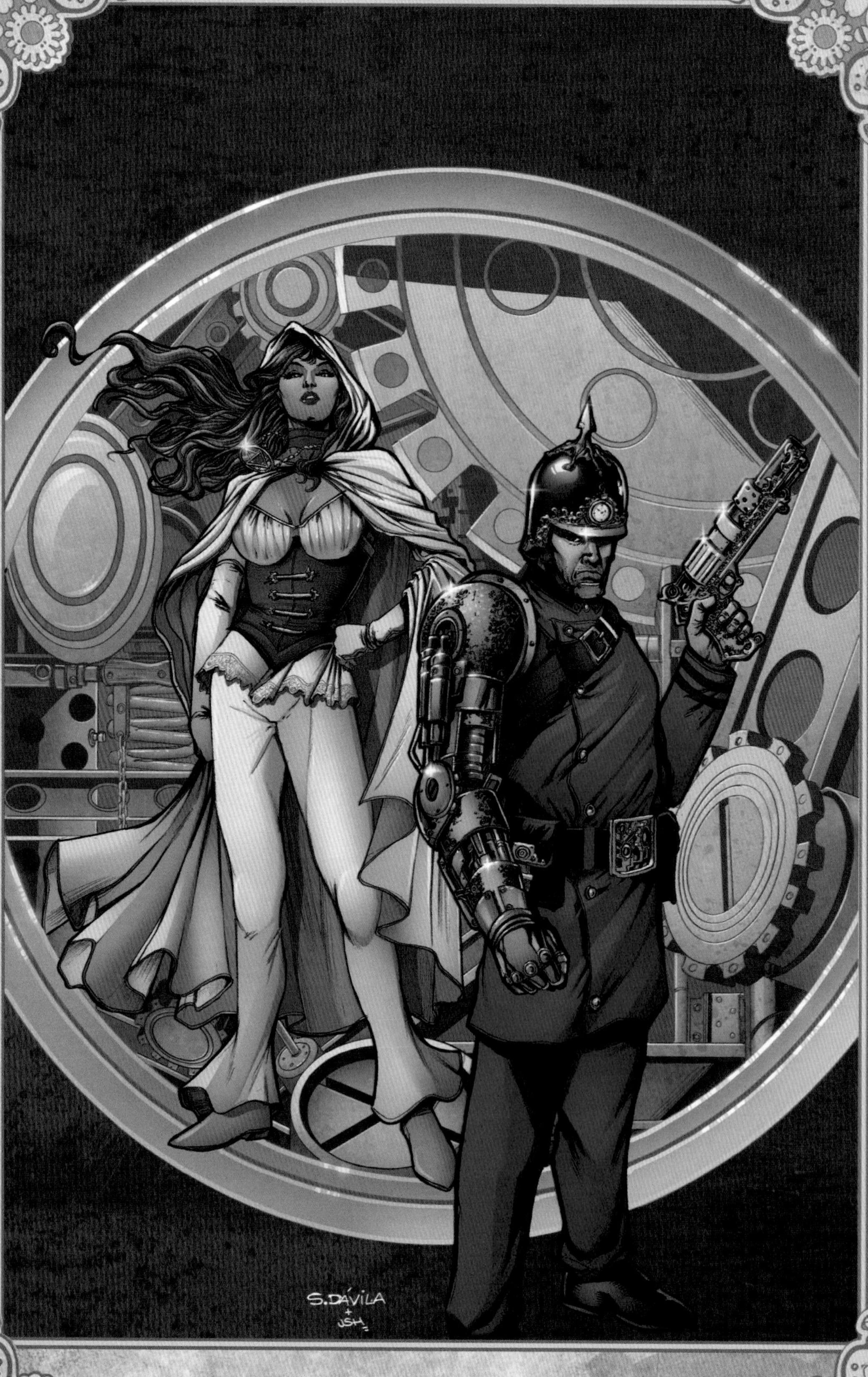
S.DÁVILA

ISSUE TWO

Cover by Sergio Dávila and Jorge Sutil

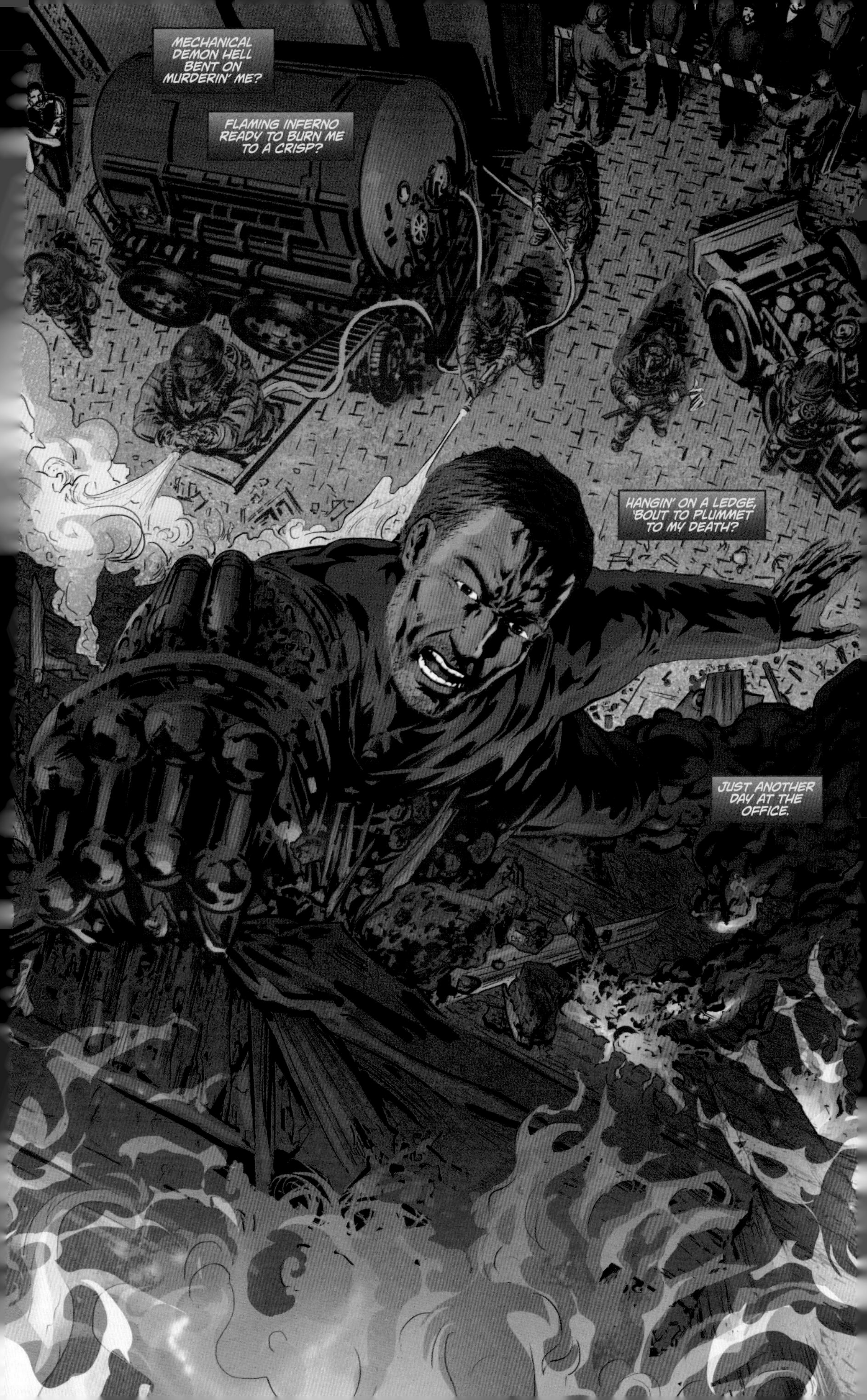
MECHANICAL DEMON HELL BENT ON MURDERIN' ME?
FLAMING INFERNO READY TO BURN ME TO A CRISP?
HANGIN' ON A LEDGE, 'BOUT TO PLUMMET TO MY DEATH?
JUST ANOTHER DAY AT THE OFFICE.

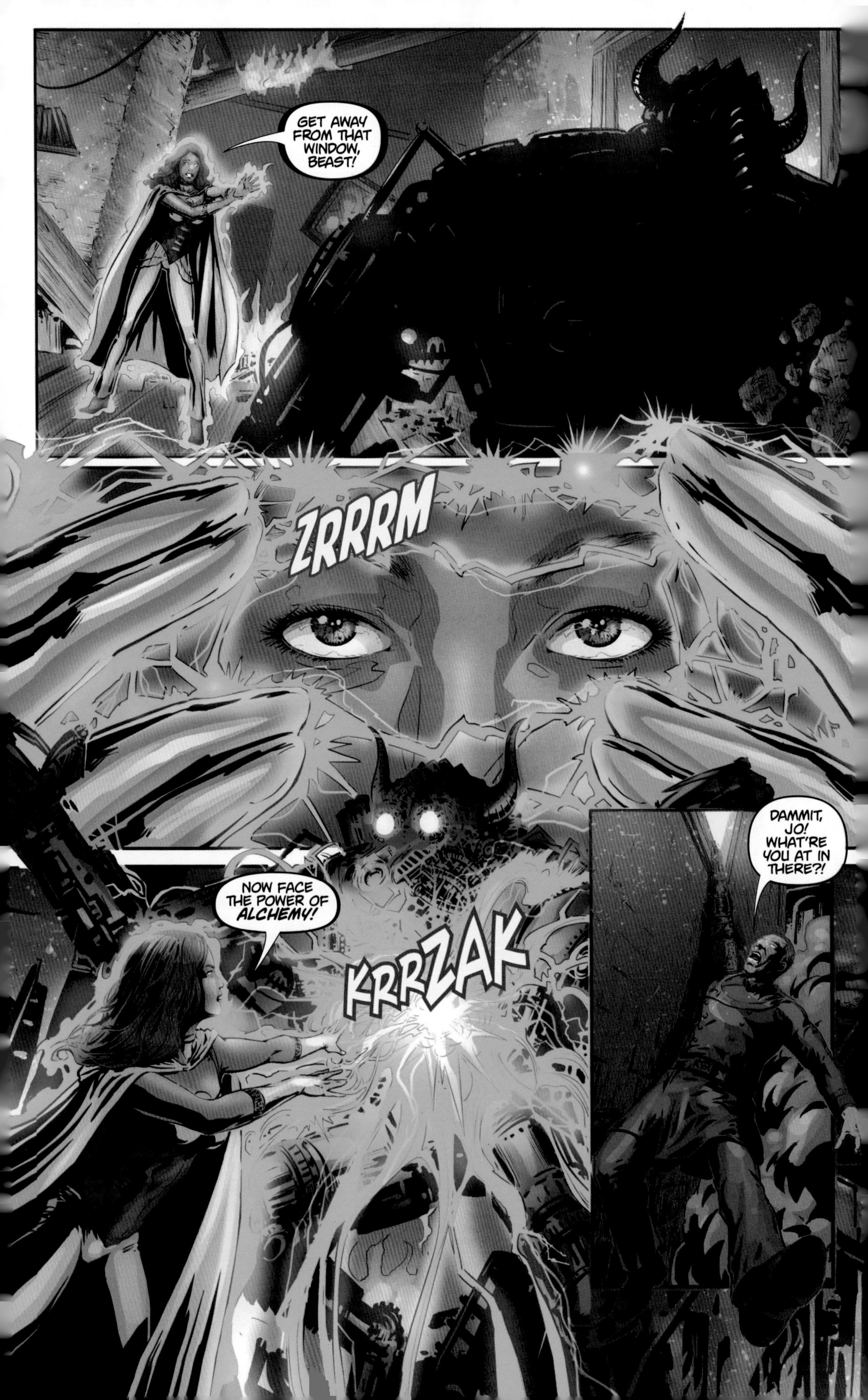
GET AWAY FROM THAT WINDOW, BEAST!
ZRRRM
NOW FACE THE POWER OF ALCHEMY!
KRRZAK
DAMMIT, JO! WHAT'RE YOU AT IN THERE?!

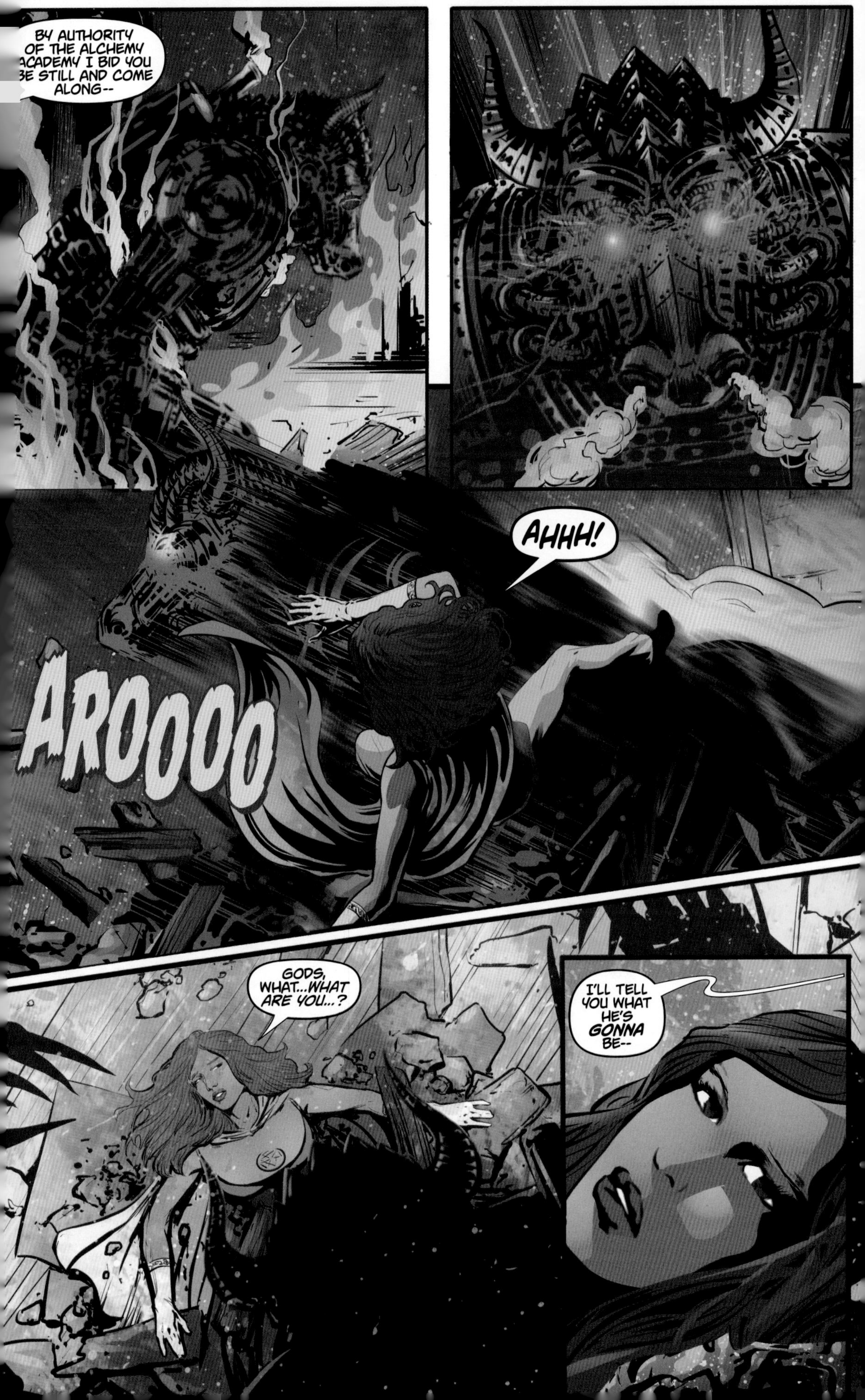
BY AUTHORITY OF THE ALCHEMY ACADEMY I BID YOU BE STILL AND COME ALONG--
AHHH!
AROOOO
GODS, WHAT...WHAT ARE YOU...?
I'LL TELL YOU WHAT HE'S GONNA BE--

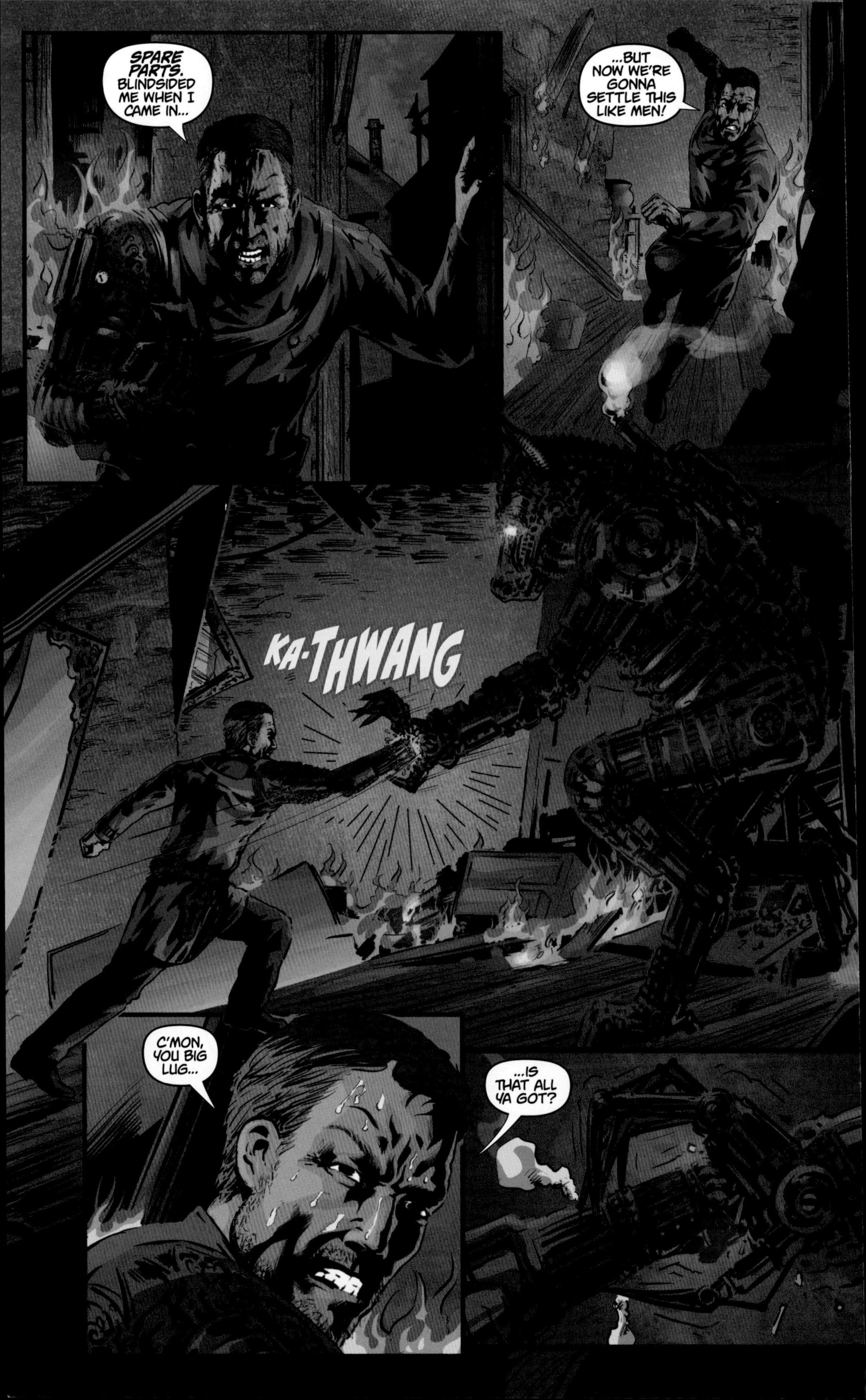
SPARE PARTS. BLINDSIDED ME WHEN I CAME IN...
...BUT NOW WE'RE GONNA SETTLE THIS LIKE MEN!
KA-THWANG
C'MON, YOU BIG LUG...
...IS THAT ALL YA GOT?

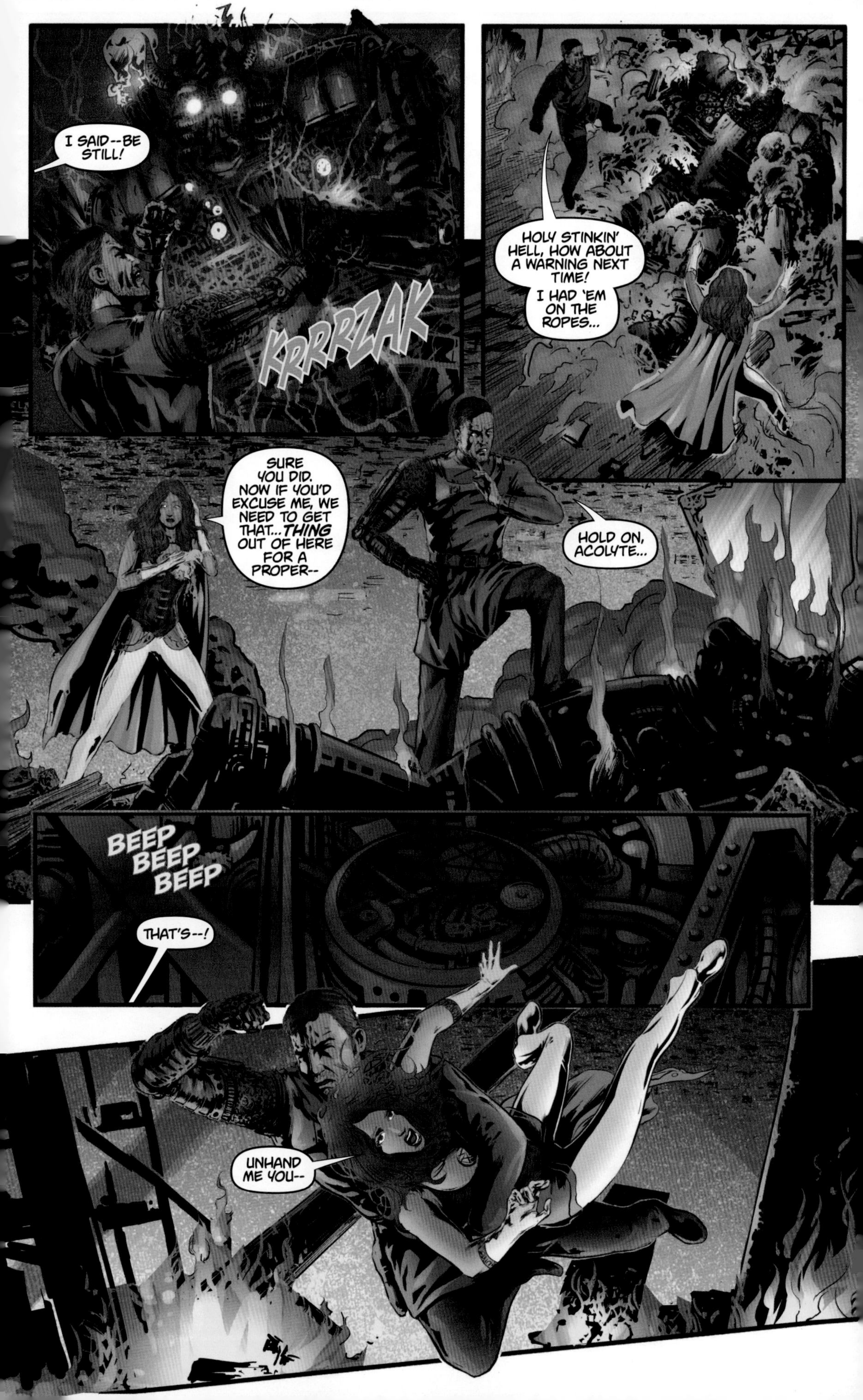
I SAID--BE STILL!
KRRRZAK
HOLY STINKIN' HELL, HOW ABOUT A WARNING NEXT TIME!
I HAD 'EM ON THE ROPES...
SURE YOU DID. NOW IF YOU'D EXCUSE ME, WE NEED TO GET THAT...*THING* OUT OF HERE FOR A PROPER--
HOLD ON, ACOLYTE...
BEEP BEEP BEEP
THAT'S--!
UNHAND ME YOU--

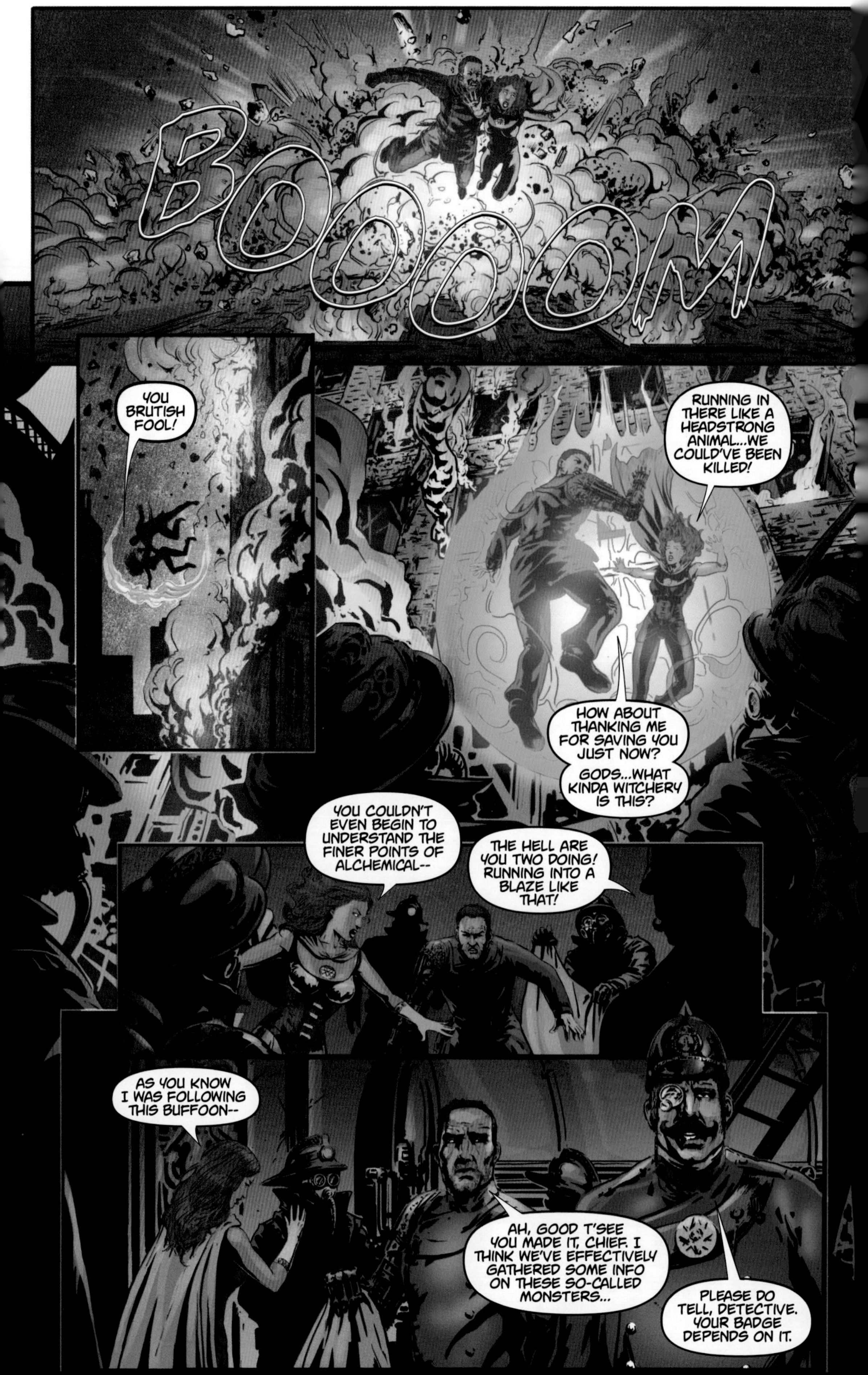
BOOOOOM
YOU BRUTISH FOOL!
RUNNING IN THERE LIKE A HEADSTRONG ANIMAL...WE COULD'VE BEEN KILLED!
HOW ABOUT THANKING ME FOR SAVING YOU JUST NOW?
GODS...WHAT KINDA WITCHERY IS THIS?
YOU COULDN'T EVEN BEGIN TO UNDERSTAND THE FINER POINTS OF ALCHEMICAL--
THE HELL ARE YOU TWO DOING! RUNNING INTO A BLAZE LIKE THAT!
AS YOU KNOW I WAS FOLLOWING THIS BUFFOON--
AH, GOOD T'SEE YOU MADE IT, CHIEF. I THINK WE'VE EFFECTIVELY GATHERED SOME INFO ON THESE SO-CALLED MONSTERS...
PLEASE DO TELL, DETECTIVE. YOUR BADGE DEPENDS ON IT.

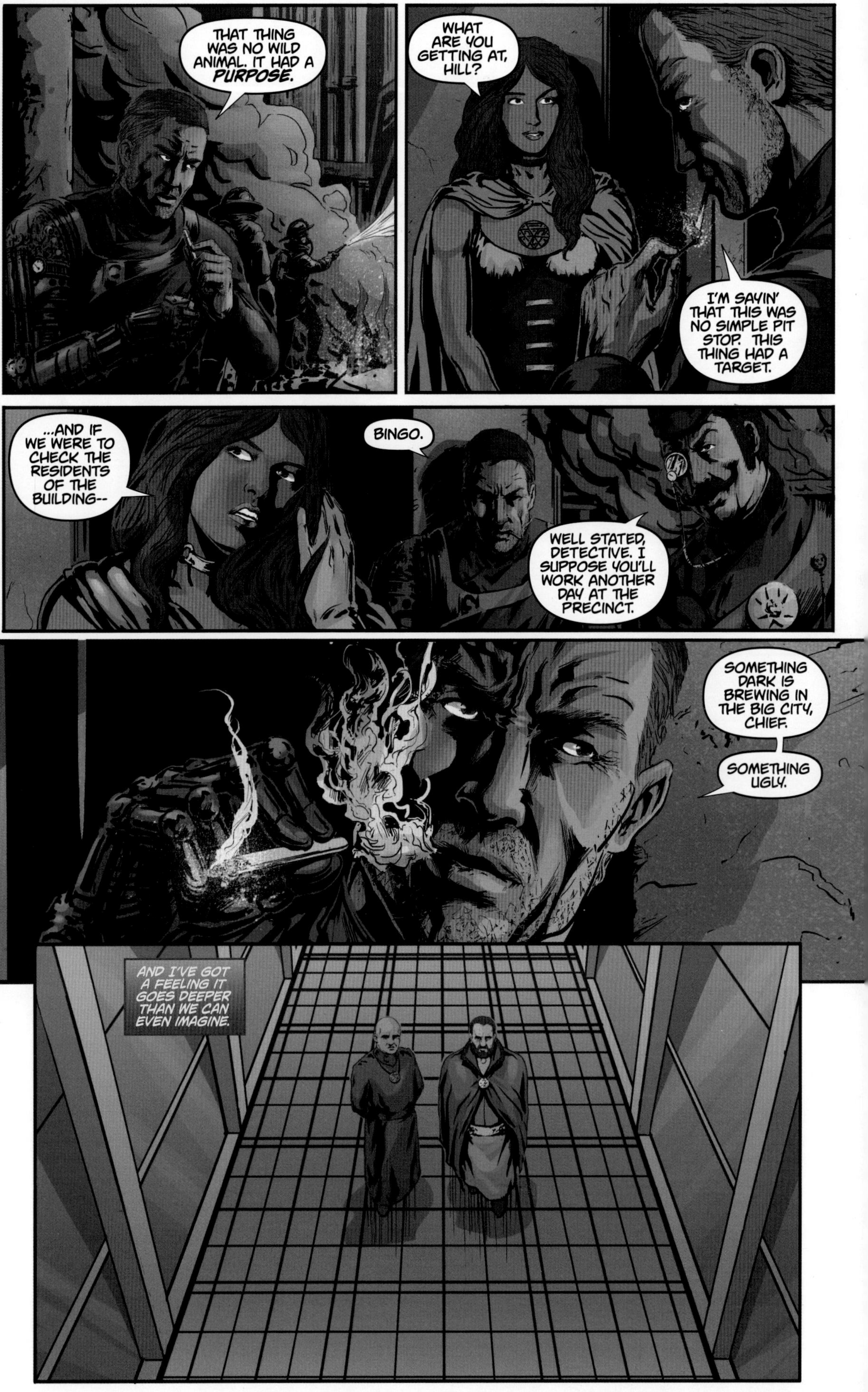
THAT THING WAS NO WILD ANIMAL. IT HAD A PURPOSE.
WHAT ARE YOU GETTING AT, HILL?
I'M SAYIN' THAT THIS WAS NO SIMPLE PIT STOP. THIS THING HAD A TARGET.
...AND IF WE WERE TO CHECK THE RESIDENTS OF THE BUILDING--
BINGO.
WELL STATED, DETECTIVE. I SUPPOSE YOU'LL WORK ANOTHER DAY AT THE PRECINCT.
SOMETHING DARK IS BREWING IN THE BIG CITY, CHIEF.
SOMETHING UGLY.
AND I'VE GOT A FEELING IT GOES DEEPER THAN WE CAN EVEN IMAGINE.

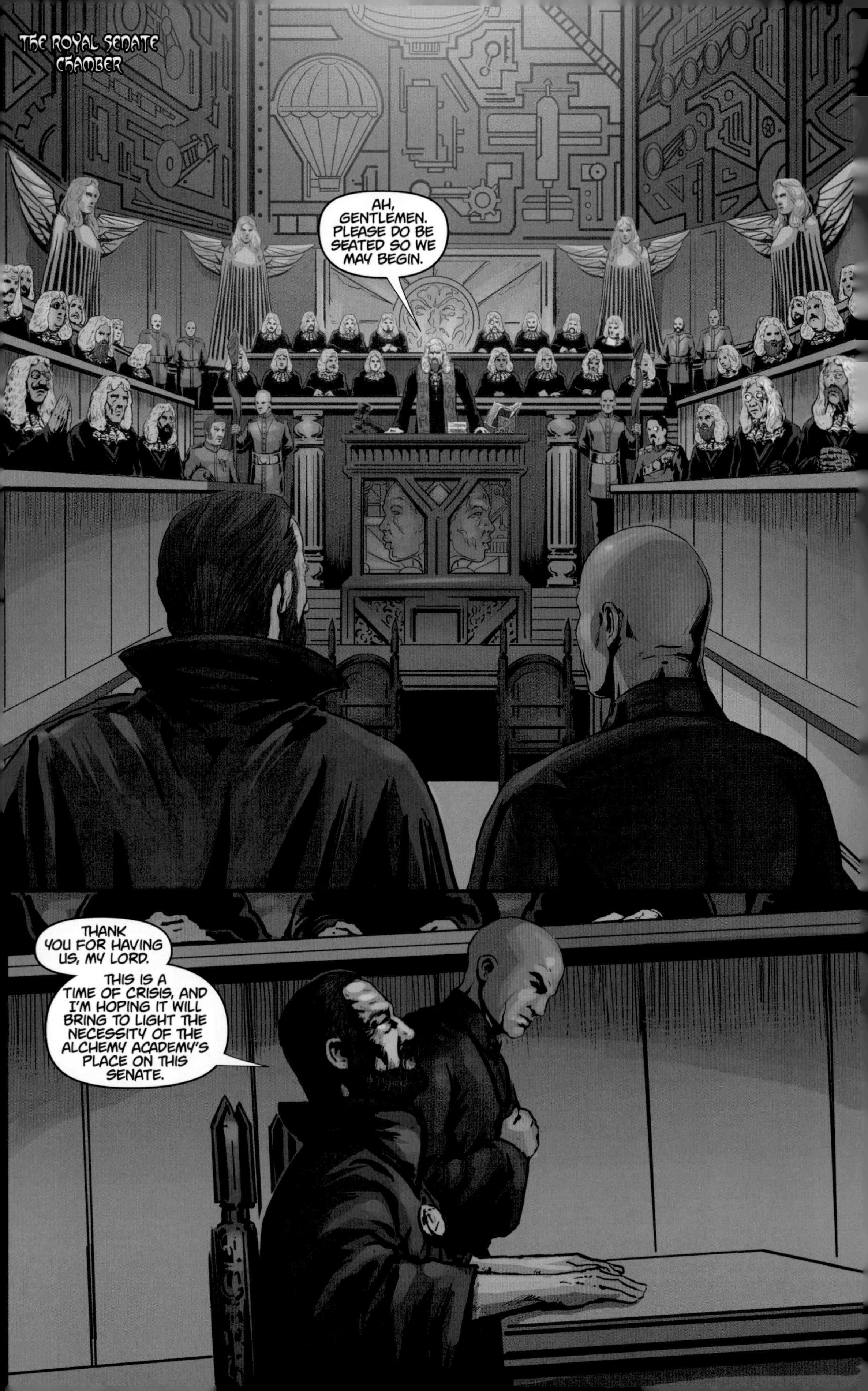
THE ROYAL SENATE CHAMBER
AH, GENTLEMEN. PLEASE DO BE SEATED SO WE MAY BEGIN.
THANK YOU FOR HAVING US, MY LORD.
THIS IS A TIME OF CRISIS, AND I'M HOPING IT WILL BRING TO LIGHT THE NECESSITY OF THE ALCHEMY ACADEMY'S PLACE ON THIS SENATE.

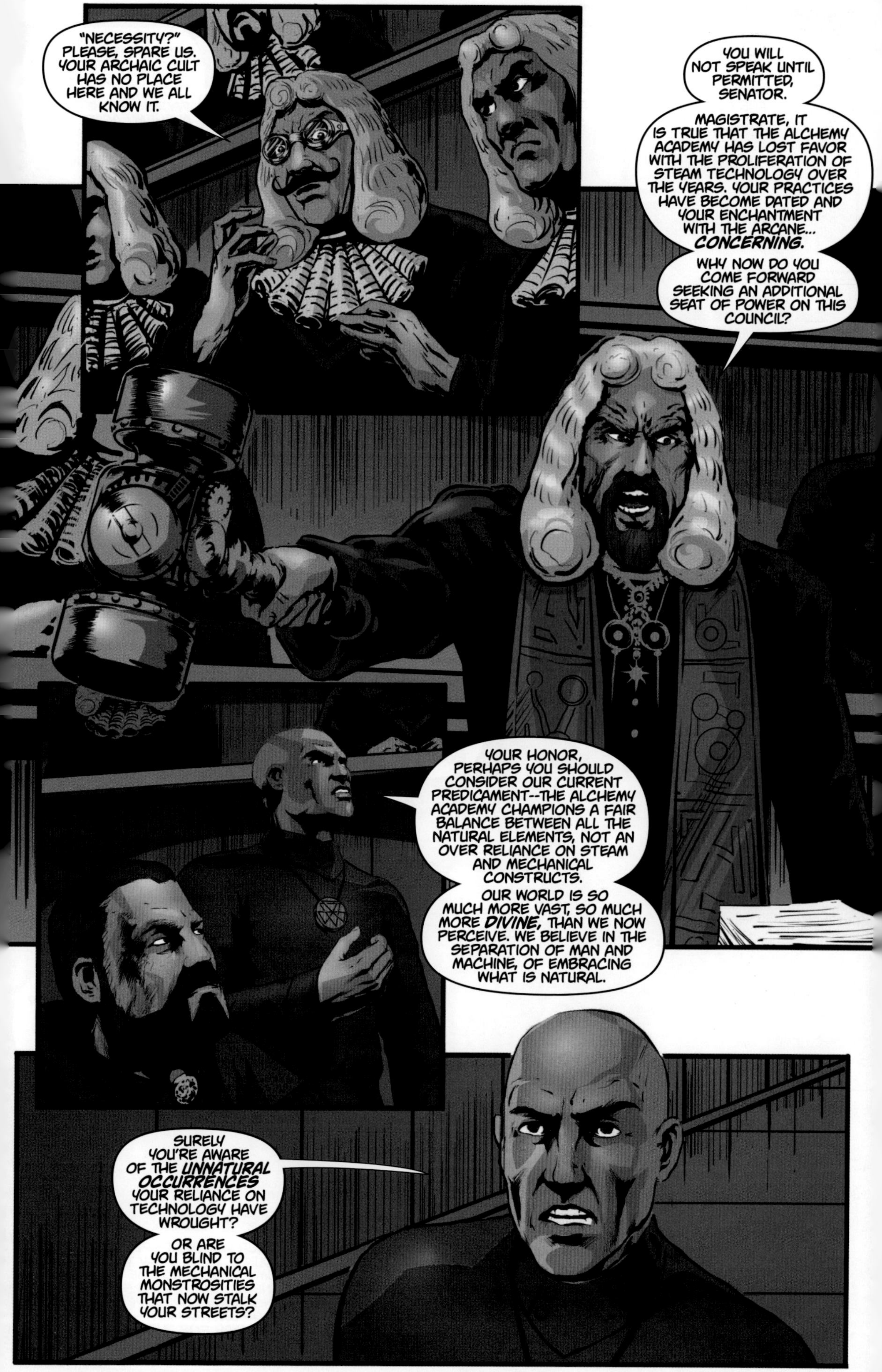
"NECESSITY?" PLEASE, SPARE US. YOUR ARCHAIC CULT HAS NO PLACE HERE AND WE ALL KNOW IT.
YOU WILL NOT SPEAK UNTIL PERMITTED, SENATOR.
MAGISTRATE, IT IS TRUE THAT THE ALCHEMY ACADEMY HAS LOST FAVOR WITH THE PROLIFERATION OF STEAM TECHNOLOGY OVER THE YEARS. YOUR PRACTICES HAVE BECOME DATED AND YOUR ENCHANTMENT WITH THE ARCANE... CONCERNING.
WHY NOW DO YOU COME FORWARD SEEKING AN ADDITIONAL SEAT OF POWER ON THIS COUNCIL?
YOUR HONOR, PERHAPS YOU SHOULD CONSIDER OUR CURRENT PREDICAMENT--THE ALCHEMY ACADEMY CHAMPIONS A FAIR BALANCE BETWEEN ALL THE NATURAL ELEMENTS, NOT AN OVER RELIANCE ON STEAM AND MECHANICAL CONSTRUCTS.
OUR WORLD IS SO MUCH MORE VAST, SO MUCH MORE DIVINE, THAN WE NOW PERCEIVE. WE BELIEVE IN THE SEPARATION OF MAN AND MACHINE, OF EMBRACING WHAT IS NATURAL.
SURELY YOU'RE AWARE OF THE UNNATURAL OCCURRENCES YOUR RELIANCE ON TECHNOLOGY HAVE WROUGHT?
OR ARE YOU BLIND TO THE MECHANICAL MONSTROSITIES THAT NOW STALK YOUR STREETS?

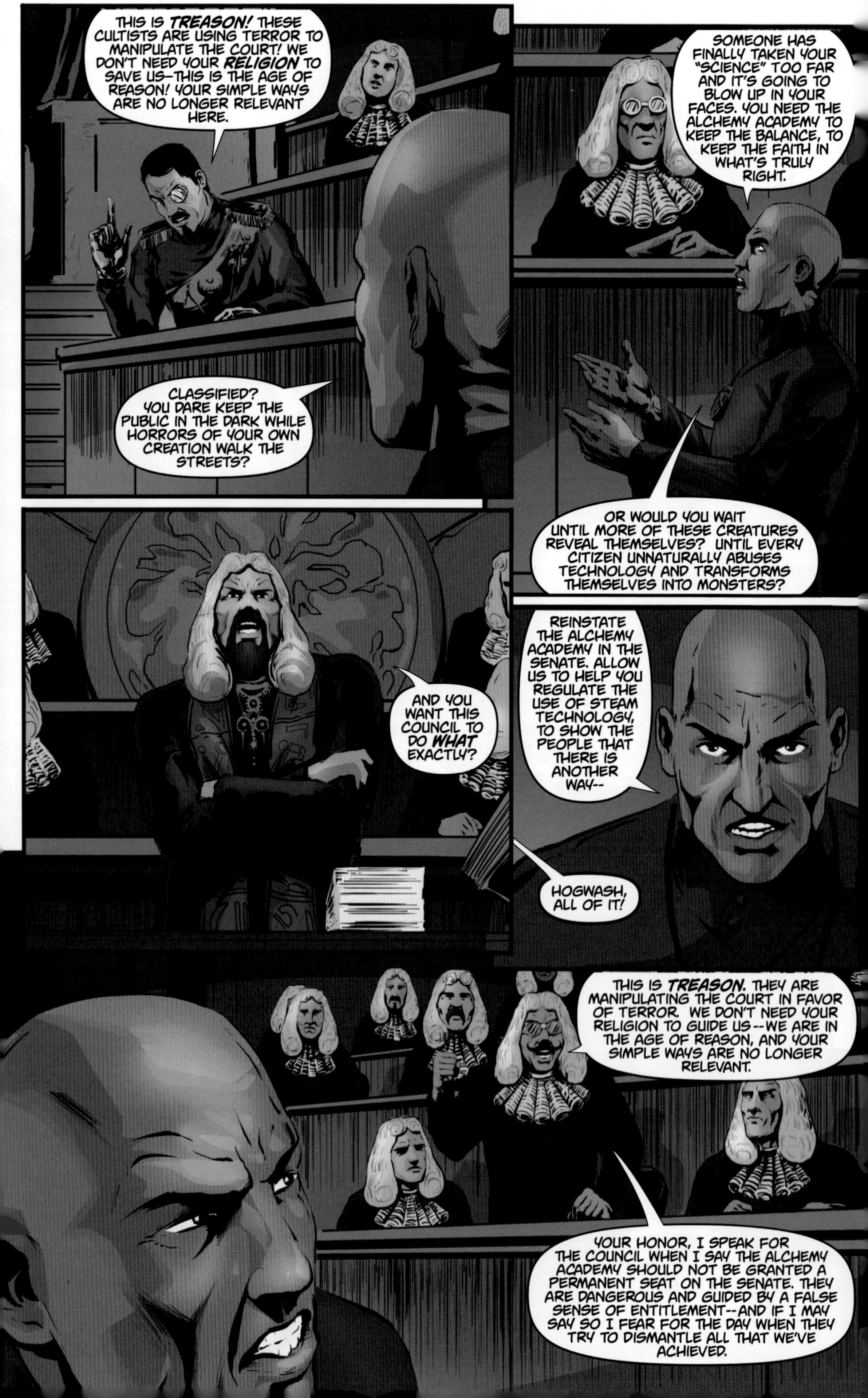

THIS IS *TREASON!* THESE CULTISTS ARE USING TERROR TO MANIPULATE THE COURT! WE DON'T NEED YOUR *RELIGION* TO SAVE US–THIS IS THE AGE OF REASON! YOUR SIMPLE WAYS ARE NO LONGER RELEVANT HERE.
CLASSIFIED? YOU DARE KEEP THE PUBLIC IN THE DARK WHILE HORRORS OF YOUR OWN CREATION WALK THE STREETS?
SOMEONE HAS FINALLY TAKEN YOUR "SCIENCE" TOO FAR AND IT'S GOING TO BLOW UP IN YOUR FACES. YOU NEED THE ALCHEMY ACADEMY TO KEEP THE BALANCE, TO KEEP THE FAITH IN WHAT'S TRULY RIGHT.
OR WOULD YOU WAIT UNTIL MORE OF THESE CREATURES REVEAL THEMSELVES? UNTIL EVERY CITIZEN UNNATURALLY ABUSES TECHNOLOGY AND TRANSFORMS THEMSELVES INTO MONSTERS?
AND YOU WANT THIS COUNCIL TO DO *WHAT* EXACTLY?
REINSTATE THE ALCHEMY ACADEMY IN THE SENATE. ALLOW US TO HELP YOU REGULATE THE USE OF STEAM TECHNOLOGY, TO SHOW THE PEOPLE THAT THERE IS ANOTHER WAY--
HOGWASH, ALL OF IT!
THIS IS *TREASON.* THEY ARE MANIPULATING THE COURT IN FAVOR OF TERROR. WE DON'T NEED YOUR RELIGION TO GUIDE US--WE ARE IN THE AGE OF REASON, AND YOUR SIMPLE WAYS ARE NO LONGER RELEVANT.
YOUR HONOR, I SPEAK FOR THE COUNCIL WHEN I SAY THE ALCHEMY ACADEMY SHOULD NOT BE GRANTED A PERMANENT SEAT ON THE SENATE. THEY ARE DANGEROUS AND GUIDED BY A FALSE SENSE OF ENTITLEMENT--AND IF I MAY SAY SO I FEAR FOR THE DAY WHEN THEY TRY TO DISMANTLE ALL THAT WE'VE ACHIEVED.

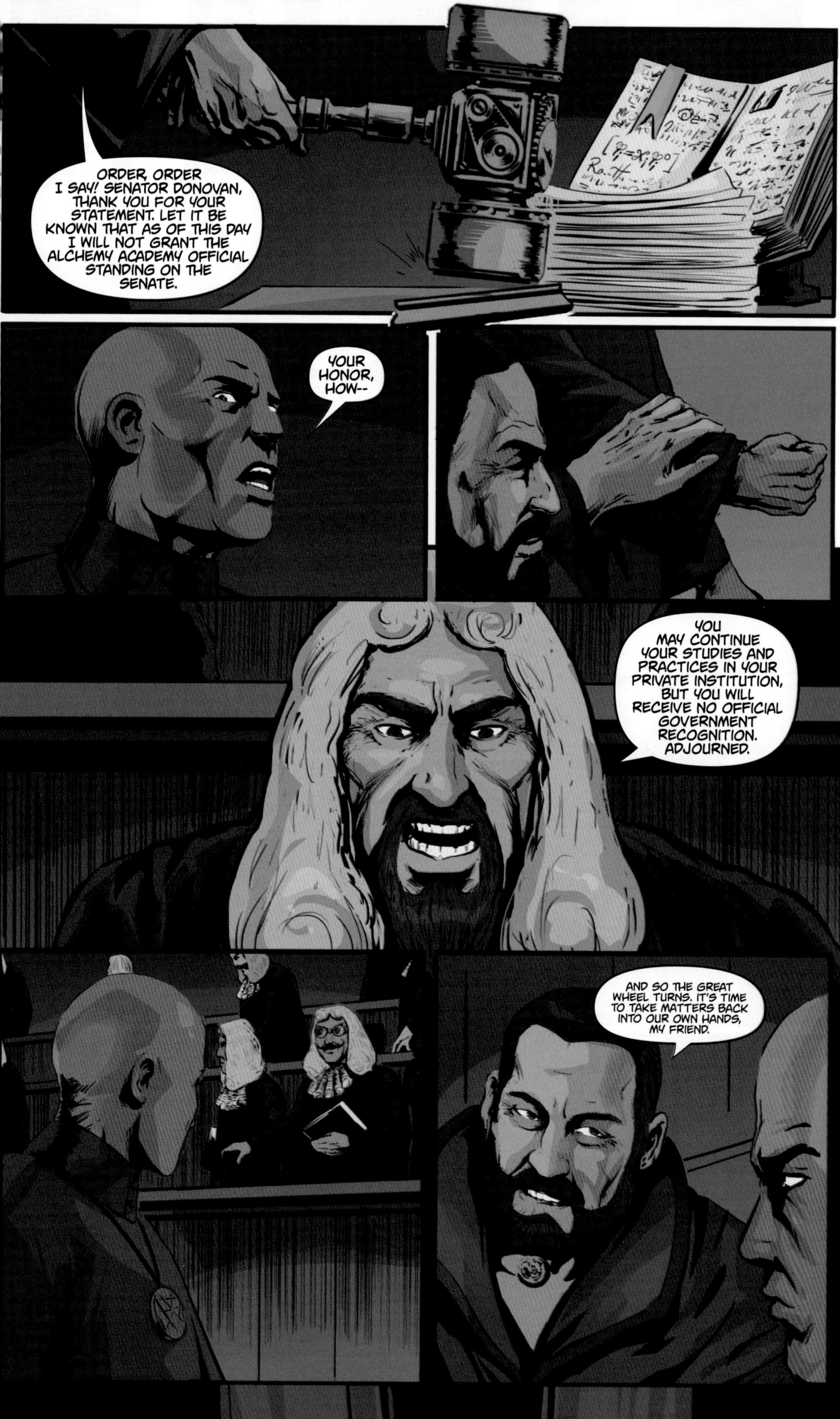
ORDER, ORDER I SAY! SENATOR DONOVAN, THANK YOU FOR YOUR STATEMENT. LET IT BE KNOWN THAT AS OF THIS DAY I WILL NOT GRANT THE ALCHEMY ACADEMY OFFICIAL STANDING ON THE SENATE.
YOUR HONOR, HOW--
YOU MAY CONTINUE YOUR STUDIES AND PRACTICES IN YOUR PRIVATE INSTITUTION, BUT YOU WILL RECEIVE NO OFFICIAL GOVERNMENT RECOGNITION. ADJOURNED.
AND SO THE GREAT WHEEL TURNS. IT'S TIME TO TAKE MATTERS BACK INTO OUR OWN HANDS, MY FRIEND.

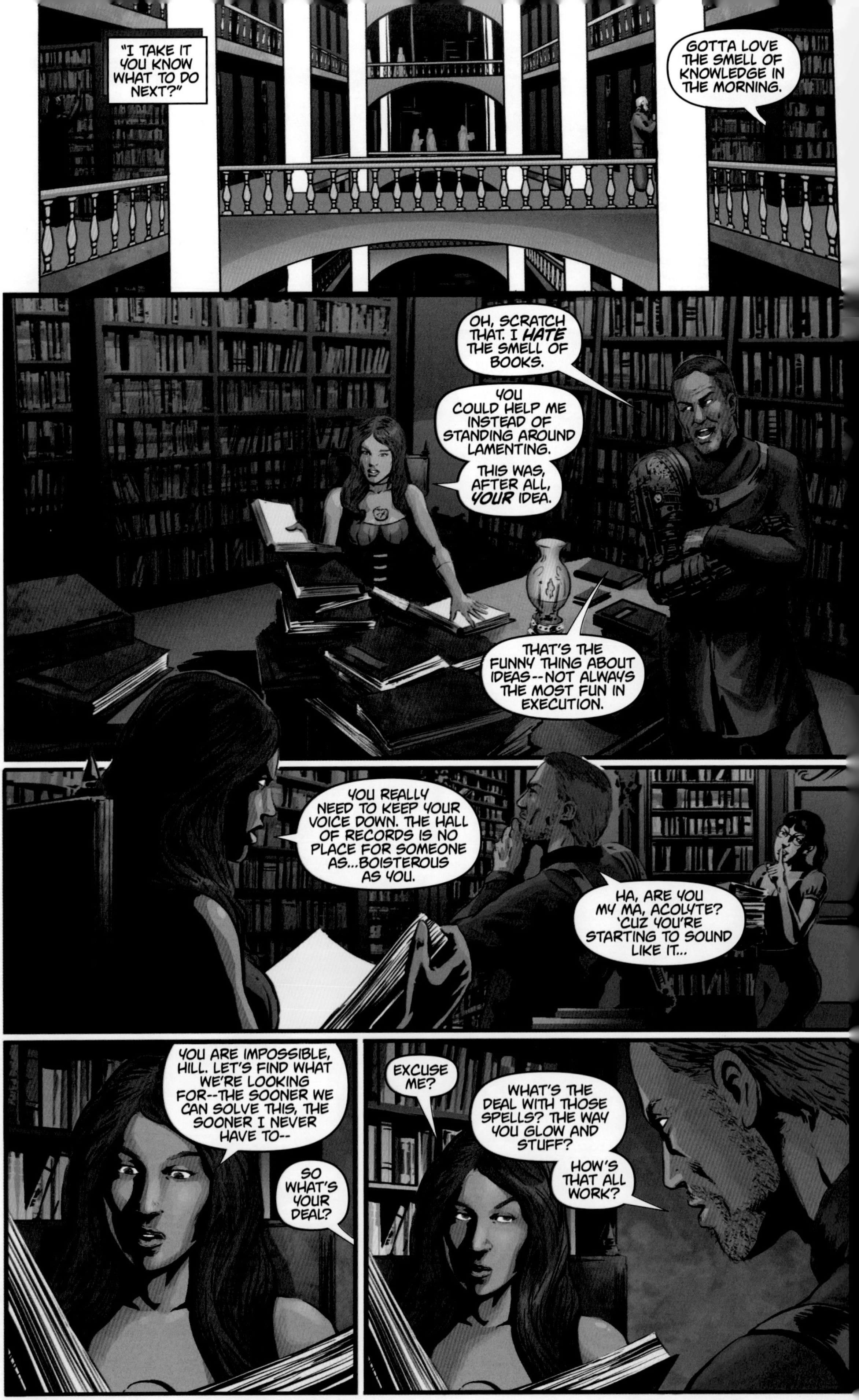

"I TAKE IT YOU KNOW WHAT TO DO NEXT?"
GOTTA LOVE THE SMELL OF KNOWLEDGE IN THE MORNING.
OH, SCRATCH THAT. I HATE THE SMELL OF BOOKS.
YOU COULD HELP ME INSTEAD OF STANDING AROUND LAMENTING.
THIS WAS, AFTER ALL, YOUR IDEA.
THAT'S THE FUNNY THING ABOUT IDEAS--NOT ALWAYS THE MOST FUN IN EXECUTION.
YOU REALLY NEED TO KEEP YOUR VOICE DOWN. THE HALL OF RECORDS IS NO PLACE FOR SOMEONE AS...BOISTEROUS AS YOU.
HA, ARE YOU MY MA, ACOLYTE? 'CUZ YOU'RE STARTING TO SOUND LIKE IT...
YOU ARE IMPOSSIBLE, HILL. LET'S FIND WHAT WE'RE LOOKING FOR--THE SOONER WE CAN SOLVE THIS, THE SOONER I NEVER HAVE TO--
SO WHAT'S YOUR DEAL?
EXCUSE ME?
WHAT'S THE DEAL WITH THOSE SPELLS? THE WAY YOU GLOW AND STUFF?
HOW'S THAT ALL WORK?

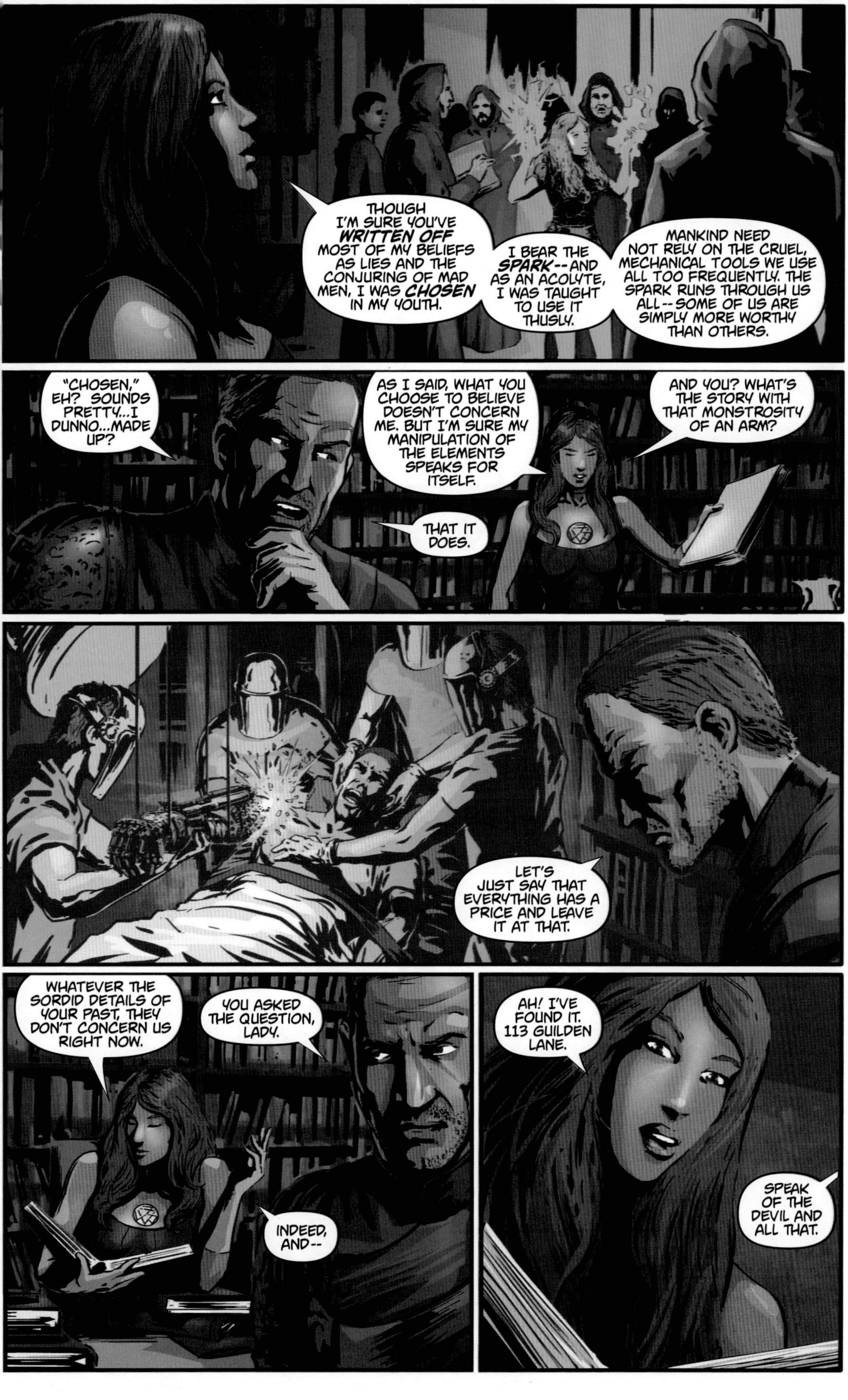
THOUGH I'M SURE YOU'VE WRITTEN OFF MOST OF MY BELIEFS AS LIES AND THE CONJURING OF MAD MEN, I WAS CHOSEN IN MY YOUTH.
I BEAR THE SPARK-- AND AS AN ACOLYTE, I WAS TAUGHT TO USE IT THUSLY.
MANKIND NEED NOT RELY ON THE CRUEL, MECHANICAL TOOLS WE USE ALL TOO FREQUENTLY. THE SPARK RUNS THROUGH US ALL-- SOME OF US ARE SIMPLY MORE WORTHY THAN OTHERS.
"CHOSEN," EH? SOUNDS PRETTY...I DUNNO...MADE UP?
AS I SAID, WHAT YOU CHOOSE TO BELIEVE DOESN'T CONCERN ME. BUT I'M SURE MY MANIPULATION OF THE ELEMENTS SPEAKS FOR ITSELF.
THAT IT DOES.
AND YOU? WHAT'S THE STORY WITH THAT MONSTROSITY OF AN ARM?
LET'S JUST SAY THAT EVERYTHING HAS A PRICE AND LEAVE IT AT THAT.
WHATEVER THE SORDID DETAILS OF YOUR PAST, THEY DON'T CONCERN US RIGHT NOW.
YOU ASKED THE QUESTION, LADY.
INDEED, AND--
AH! I'VE FOUND IT. 113 GUILDEN LANE.
SPEAK OF THE DEVIL AND ALL THAT.

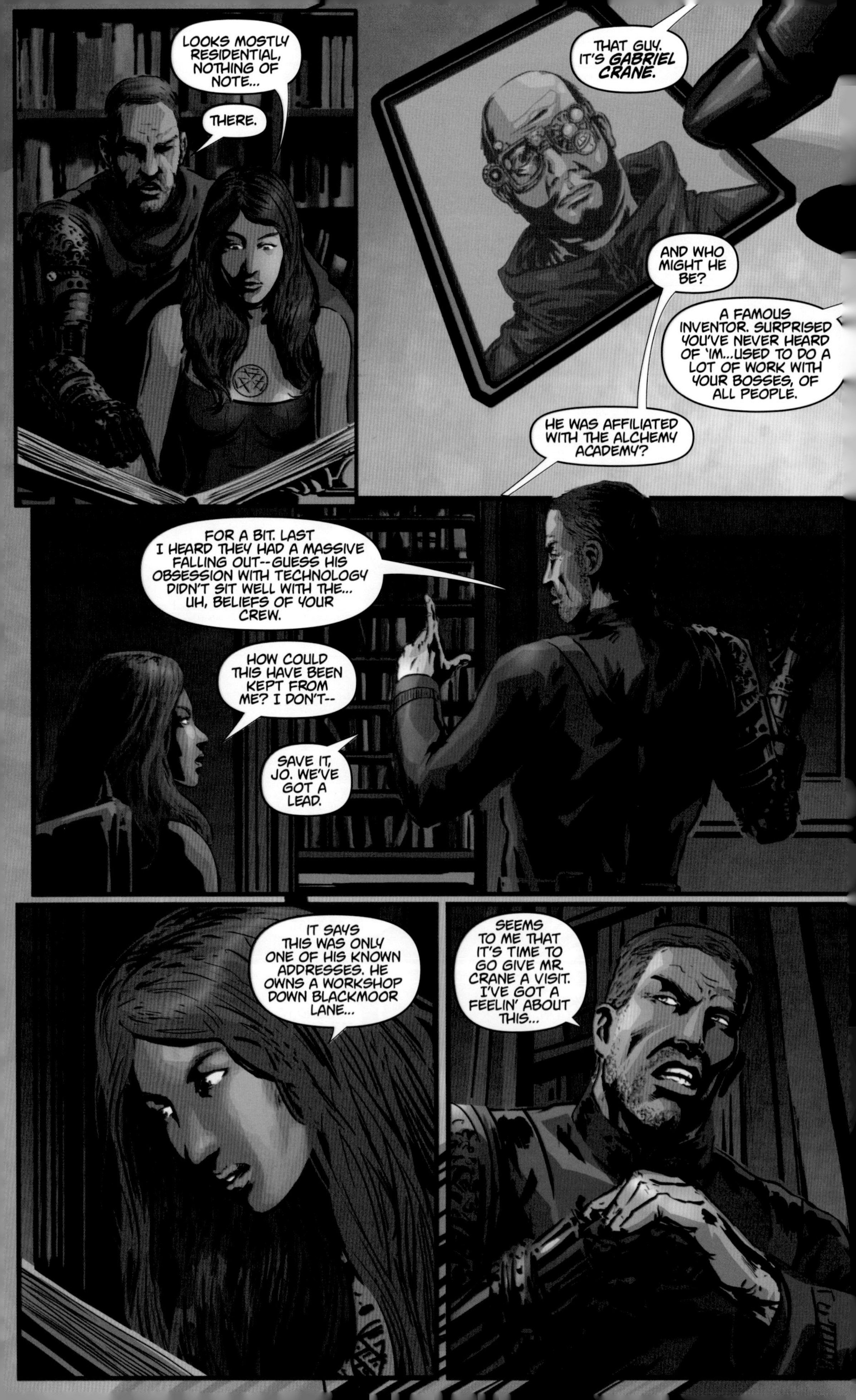
LOOKS MOSTLY RESIDENTIAL, NOTHING OF NOTE...
THERE.
THAT GUY. IT'S *GABRIEL CRANE.*
AND WHO MIGHT HE BE?
A FAMOUS INVENTOR. SURPRISED YOU'VE NEVER HEARD OF 'IM...USED TO DO A LOT OF WORK WITH YOUR BOSSES, OF ALL PEOPLE.
HE WAS AFFILIATED WITH THE ALCHEMY ACADEMY?
FOR A BIT. LAST I HEARD THEY HAD A MASSIVE FALLING OUT--GUESS HIS OBSESSION WITH TECHNOLOGY DIDN'T SIT WELL WITH THE... UH, BELIEFS OF YOUR CREW.
HOW COULD THIS HAVE BEEN KEPT FROM ME? I DON'T--
SAVE IT, JO. WE'VE GOT A LEAD.
IT SAYS THIS WAS ONLY ONE OF HIS KNOWN ADDRESSES. HE OWNS A WORKSHOP DOWN BLACKMOOR LANE...
SEEMS TO ME THAT IT'S TIME TO GO GIVE MR. CRANE A VISIT. I'VE GOT A FEELIN' ABOUT THIS...

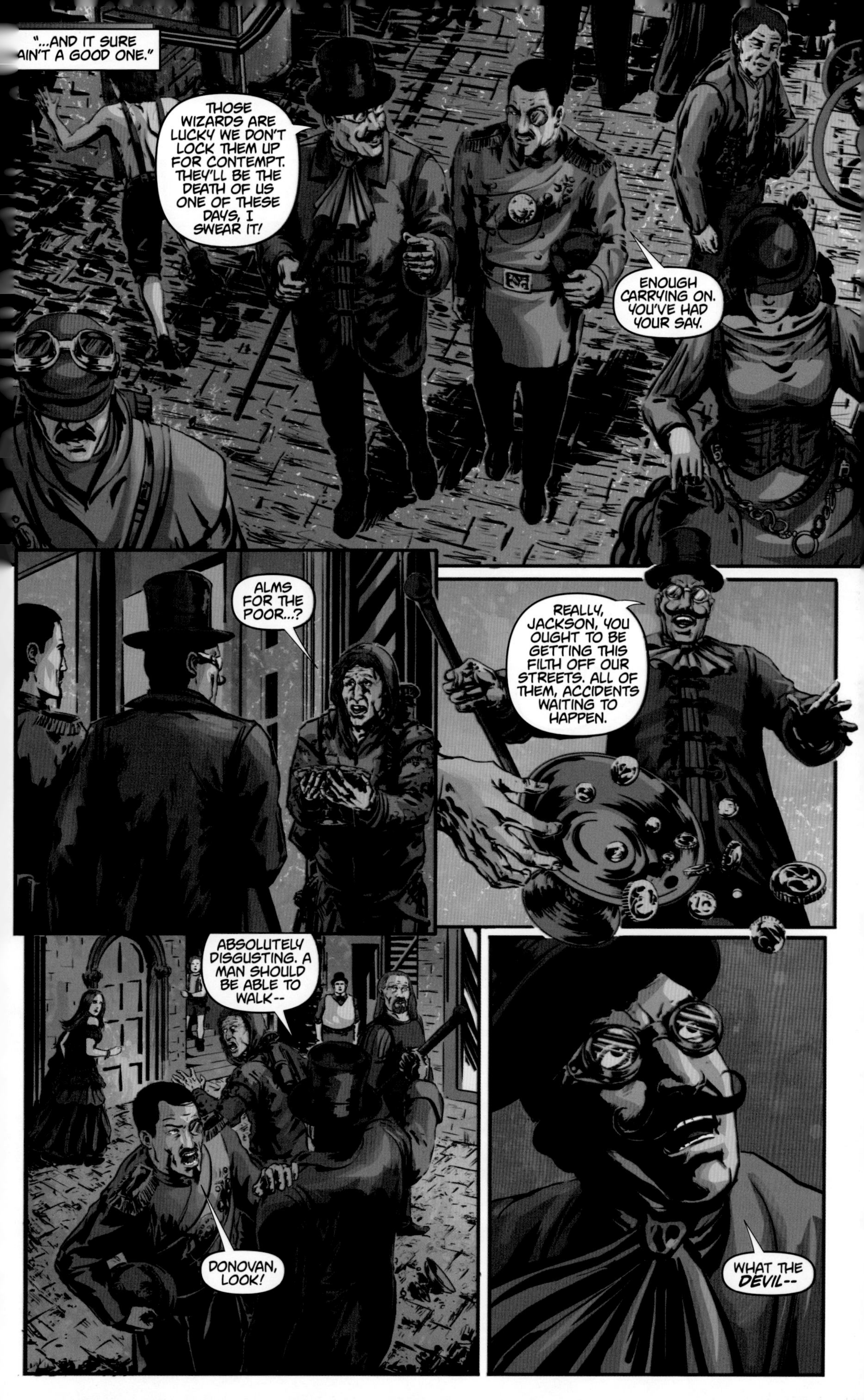
"...AND IT SURE AIN'T A GOOD ONE."
THOSE WIZARDS ARE LUCKY WE DON'T LOCK THEM UP FOR CONTEMPT. THEY'LL BE THE DEATH OF US ONE OF THESE DAYS, I SWEAR IT!
ENOUGH CARRYING ON. YOU'VE HAD YOUR SAY.
ALMS FOR THE POOR...?
REALLY, JACKSON, YOU OUGHT TO BE GETTING THIS FILTH OFF OUR STREETS. ALL OF THEM, ACCIDENTS WAITING TO HAPPEN.
ABSOLUTELY DISGUSTING. A MAN SHOULD BE ABLE TO WALK--
DONOVAN, LOOK!
WHAT THE *DEVIL*--

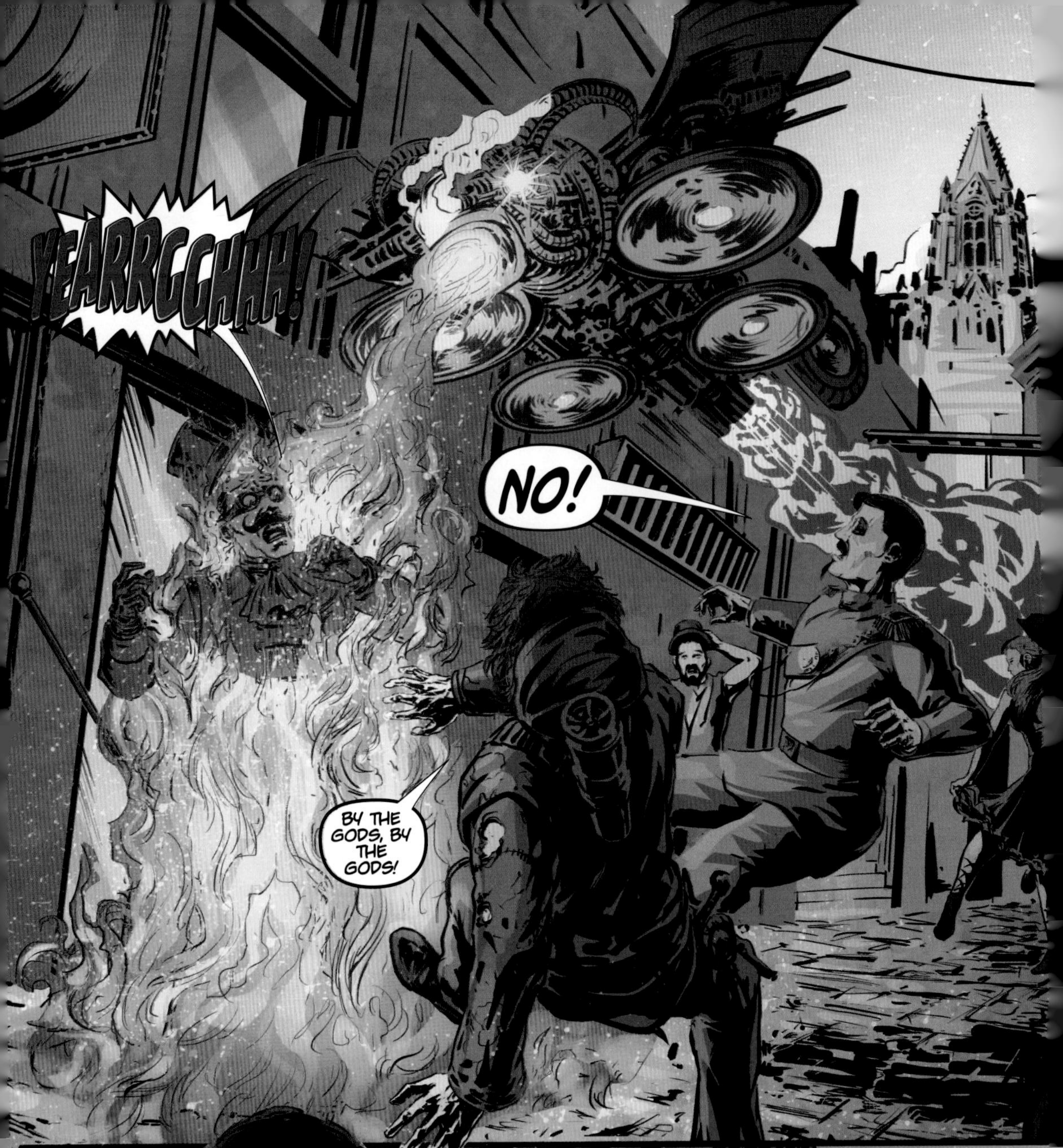
YEARRGGHHH!
NO!
BY THE GODS, BY THE GODS!

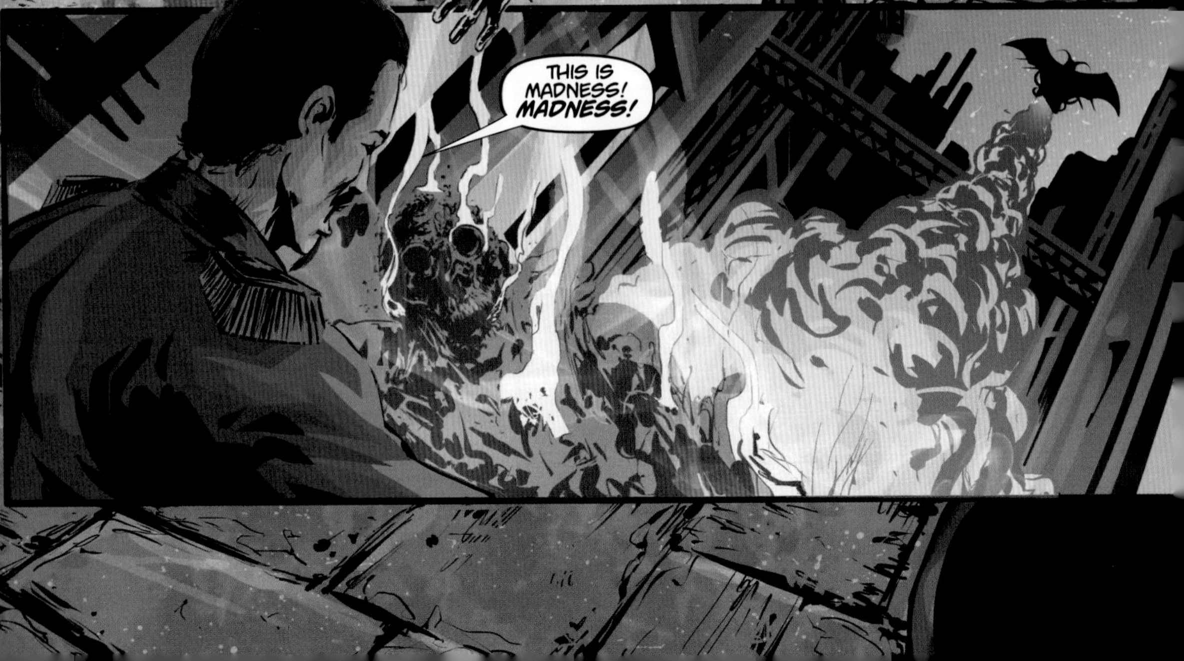
THIS IS MADNESS! MADNESS!

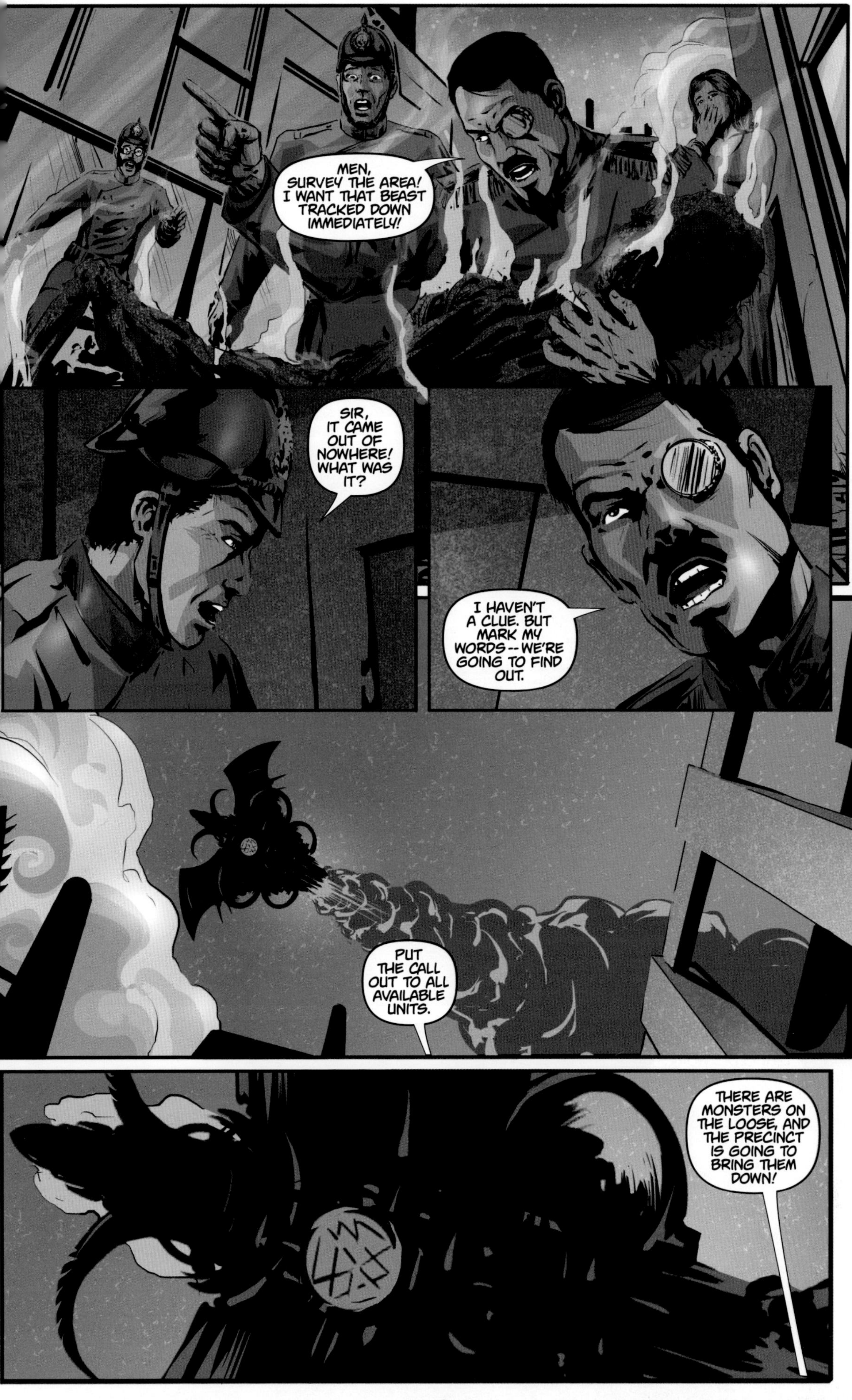
MEN, SURVEY THE AREA! I WANT THAT BEAST TRACKED DOWN IMMEDIATELY!
SIR, IT CAME OUT OF NOWHERE! WHAT WAS IT?
I HAVEN'T A CLUE. BUT MARK MY WORDS-- WE'RE GOING TO FIND OUT.
PUT THE CALL OUT TO ALL AVAILABLE UNITS.
THERE ARE MONSTERS ON THE LOOSE, AND THE PRECINCT IS GOING TO BRING THEM DOWN!

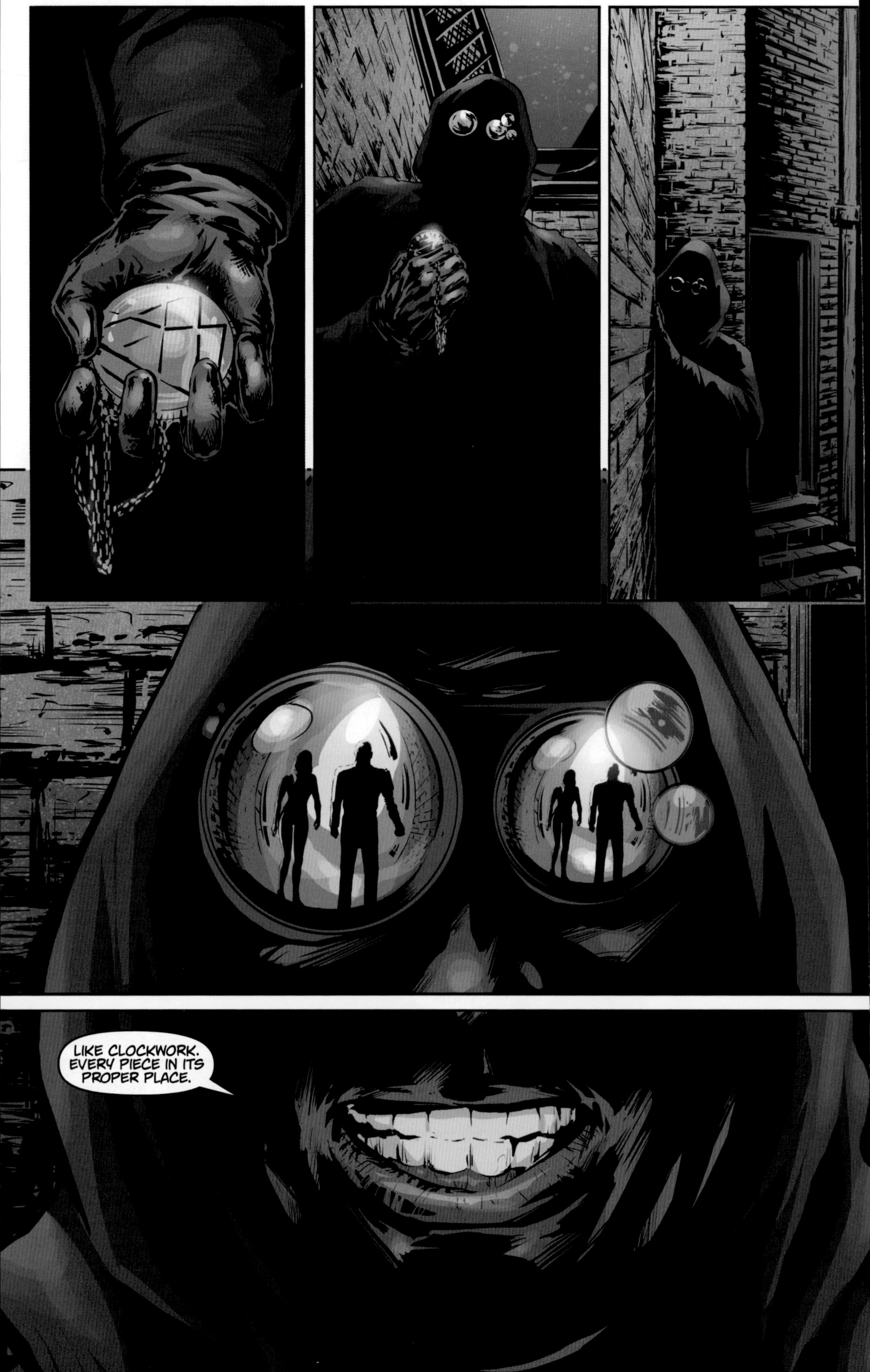
LIKE CLOCKWORK. EVERY PIECE IN ITS PROPER PLACE.

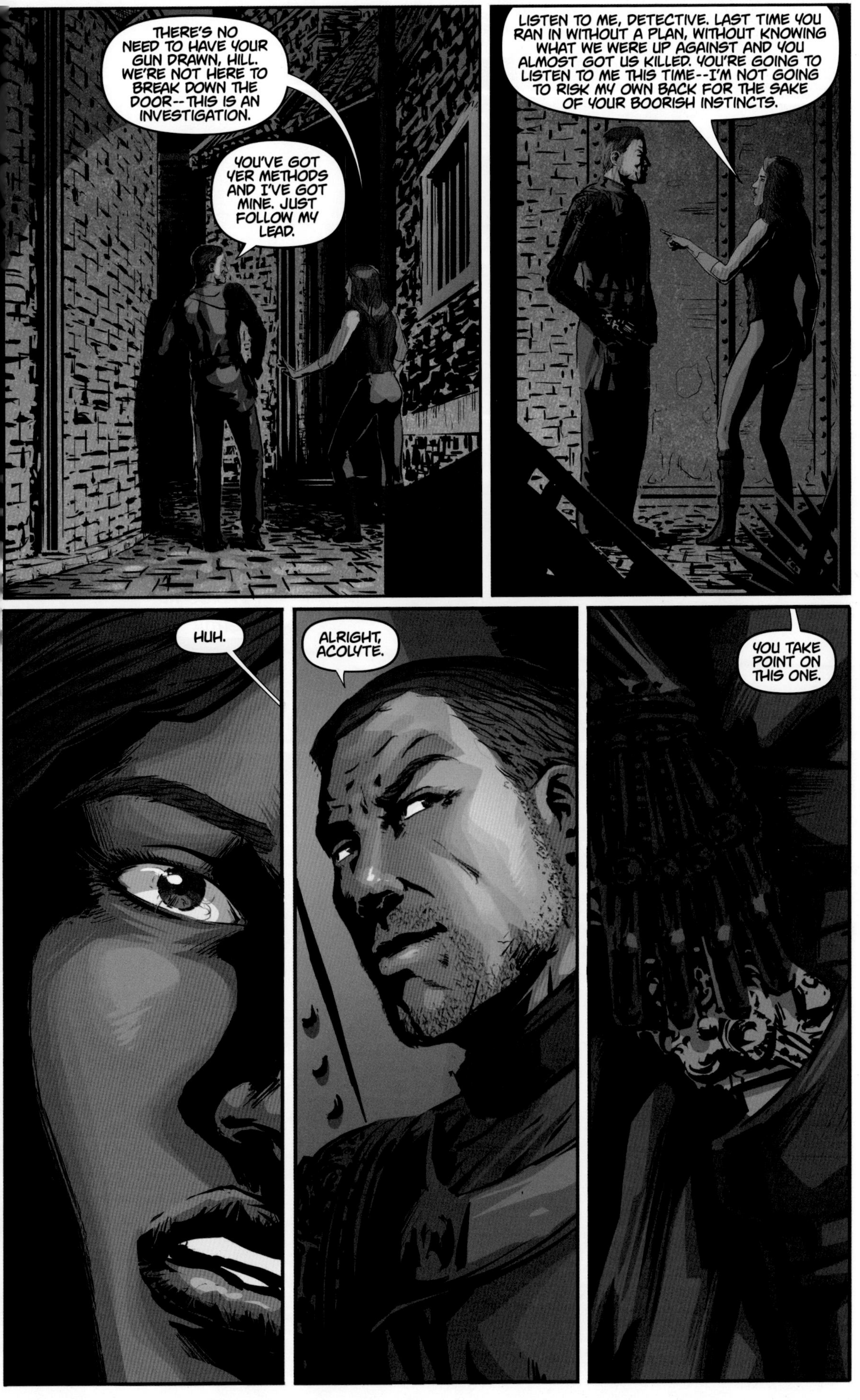
THERE'S NO NEED TO HAVE YOUR GUN DRAWN, HILL. WE'RE NOT HERE TO BREAK DOWN THE DOOR--THIS IS AN INVESTIGATION.
YOU'VE GOT YER METHODS AND I'VE GOT MINE. JUST FOLLOW MY LEAD.
LISTEN TO ME, DETECTIVE. LAST TIME YOU RAN IN WITHOUT A PLAN, WITHOUT KNOWING WHAT WE WERE UP AGAINST AND YOU ALMOST GOT US KILLED. YOU'RE GOING TO LISTEN TO ME THIS TIME--I'M NOT GOING TO RISK MY OWN BACK FOR THE SAKE OF YOUR BOORISH INSTINCTS.
HUH.
ALRIGHT, ACOLYTE.
YOU TAKE POINT ON THIS ONE.

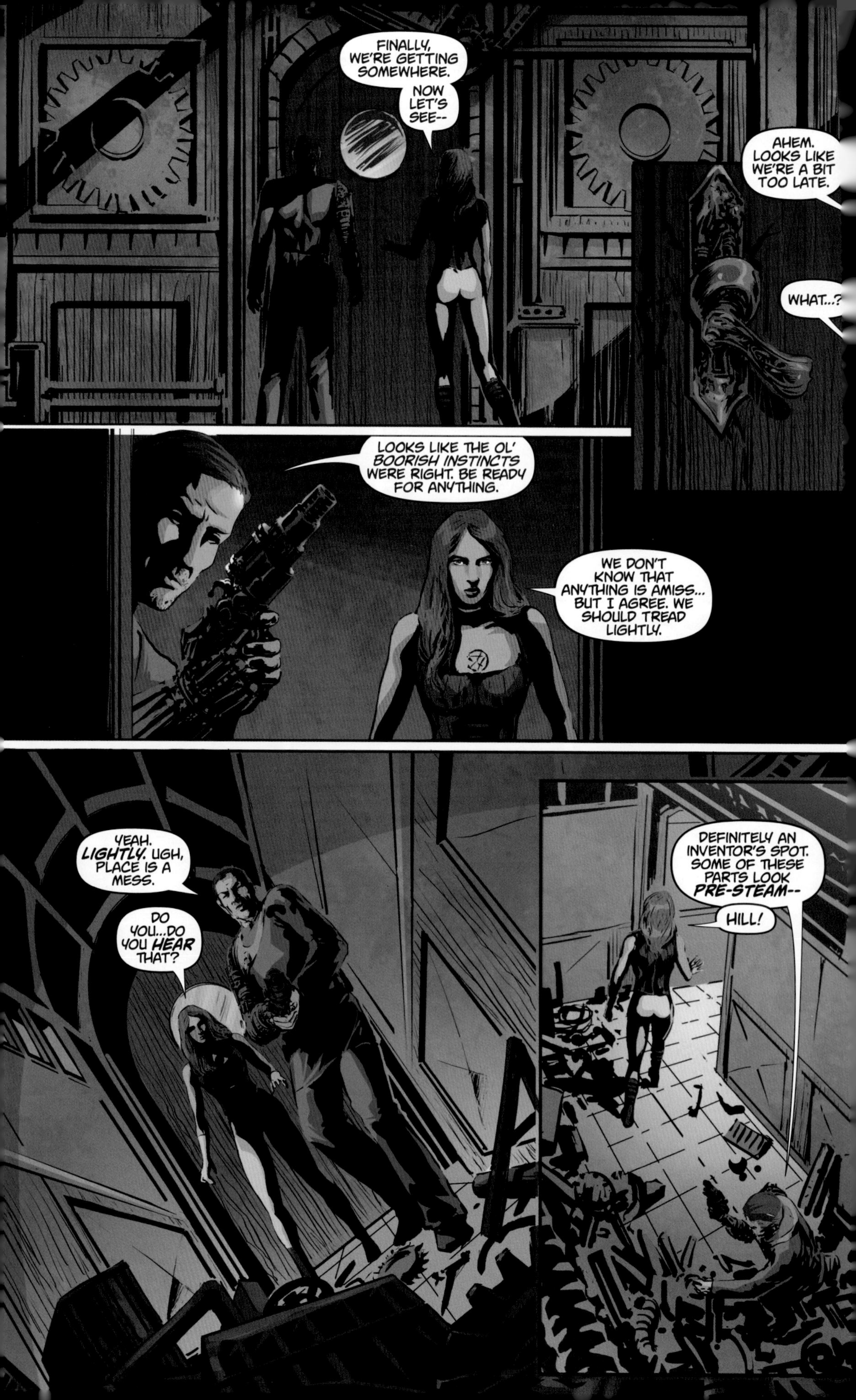
FINALLY, WE'RE GETTING SOMEWHERE.
NOW LET'S SEE--
AHEM. LOOKS LIKE WE'RE A BIT TOO LATE.
WHAT...?
LOOKS LIKE THE OL' BOORISH INSTINCTS WERE RIGHT. BE READY FOR ANYTHING.
WE DON'T KNOW THAT ANYTHING IS AMISS... BUT I AGREE. WE SHOULD TREAD LIGHTLY.
YEAH. LIGHTLY. UGH, PLACE IS A MESS.
DO YOU...DO YOU HEAR THAT?
DEFINITELY AN INVENTOR'S SPOT. SOME OF THESE PARTS LOOK PRE-STEAM--
HILL!

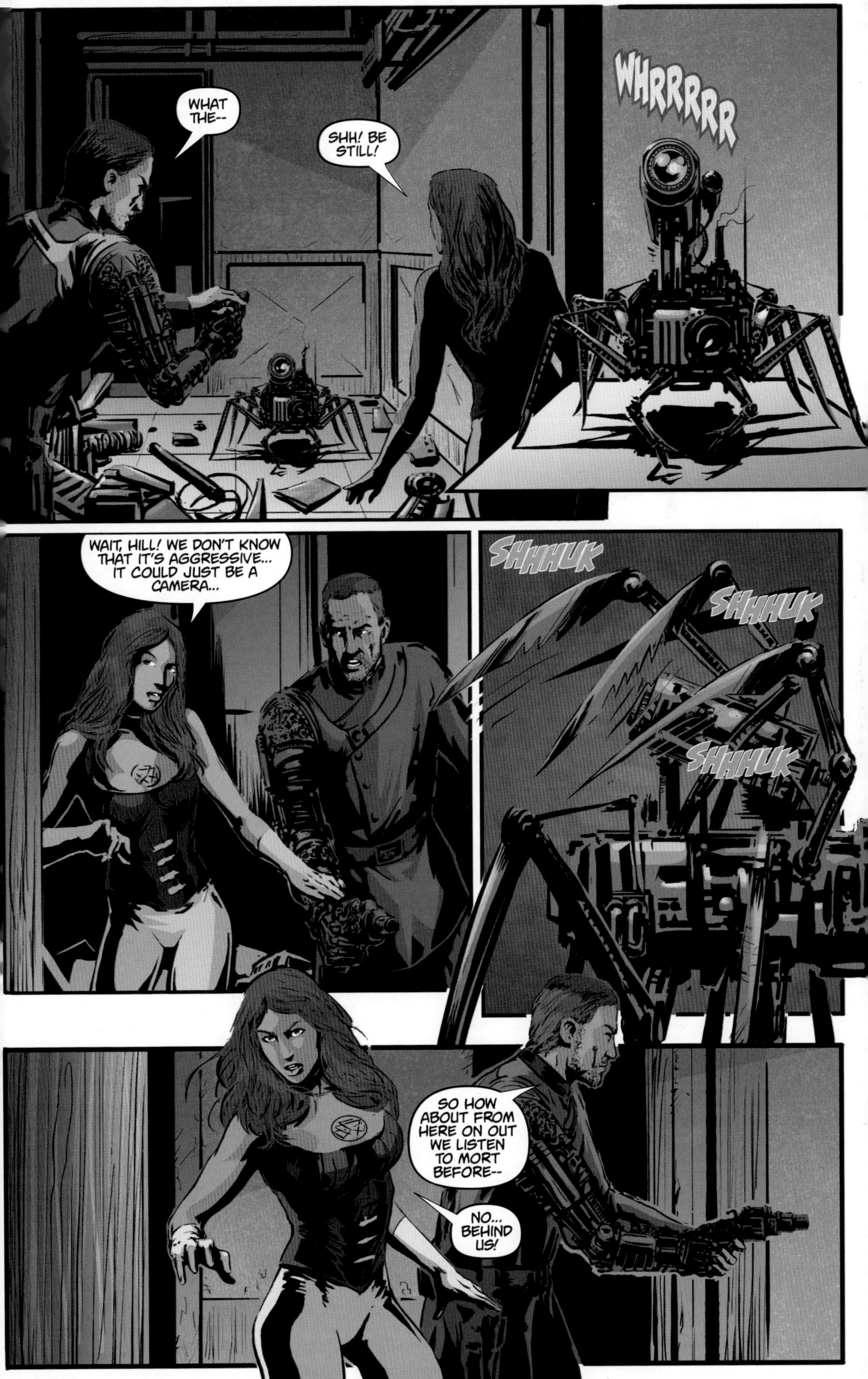
WHAT THE--
SHH! BE STILL!
WHRRRRR
WAIT, HILL! WE DON'T KNOW THAT IT'S AGGRESSIVE... IT COULD JUST BE A CAMERA...
SHHHUK
SHHHUK
SHHHUK
SO HOW ABOUT FROM HERE ON OUT WE LISTEN TO MORT BEFORE--
NO... BEHIND US!

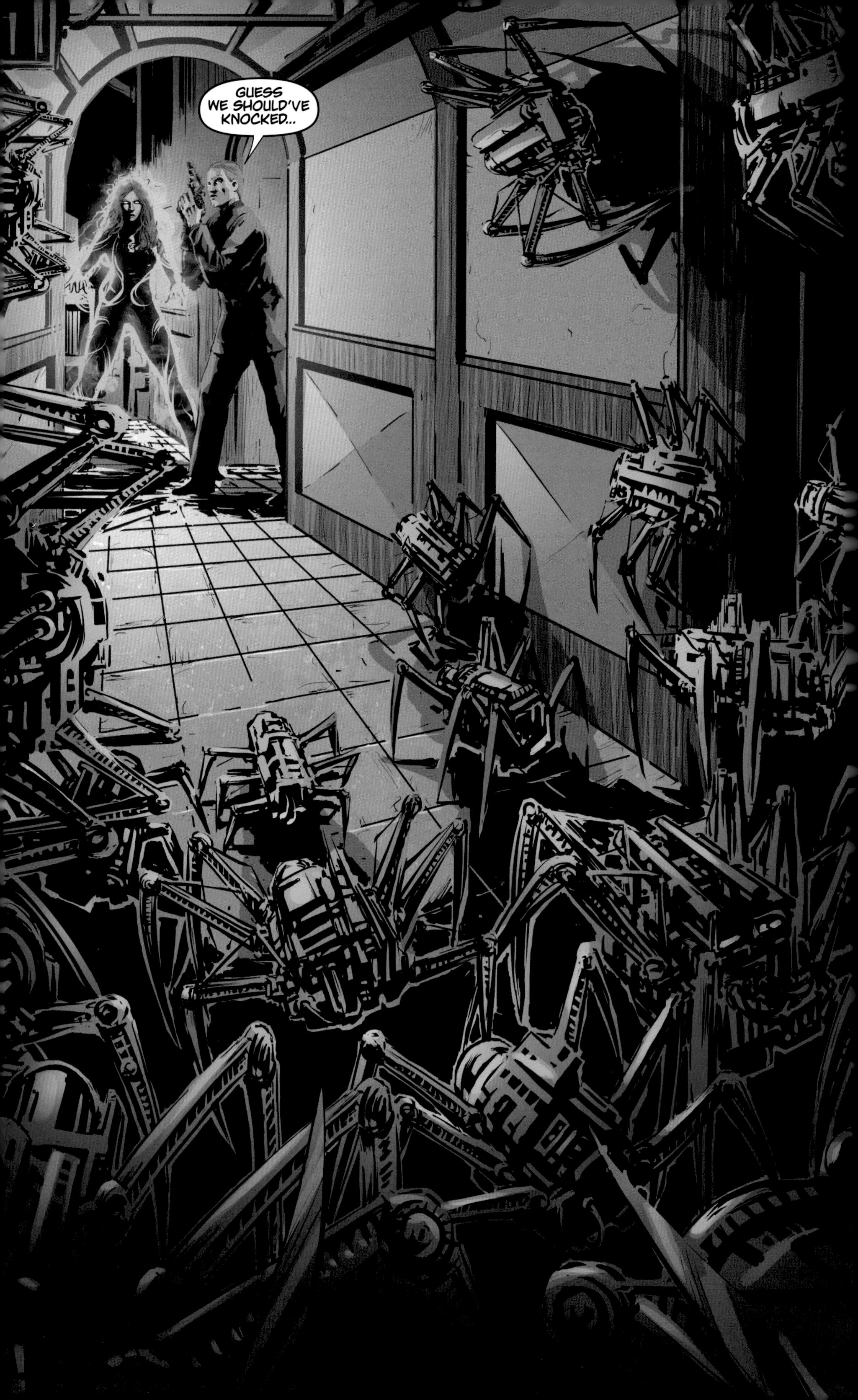
GUESS WE SHOULD'VE KNOCKED...

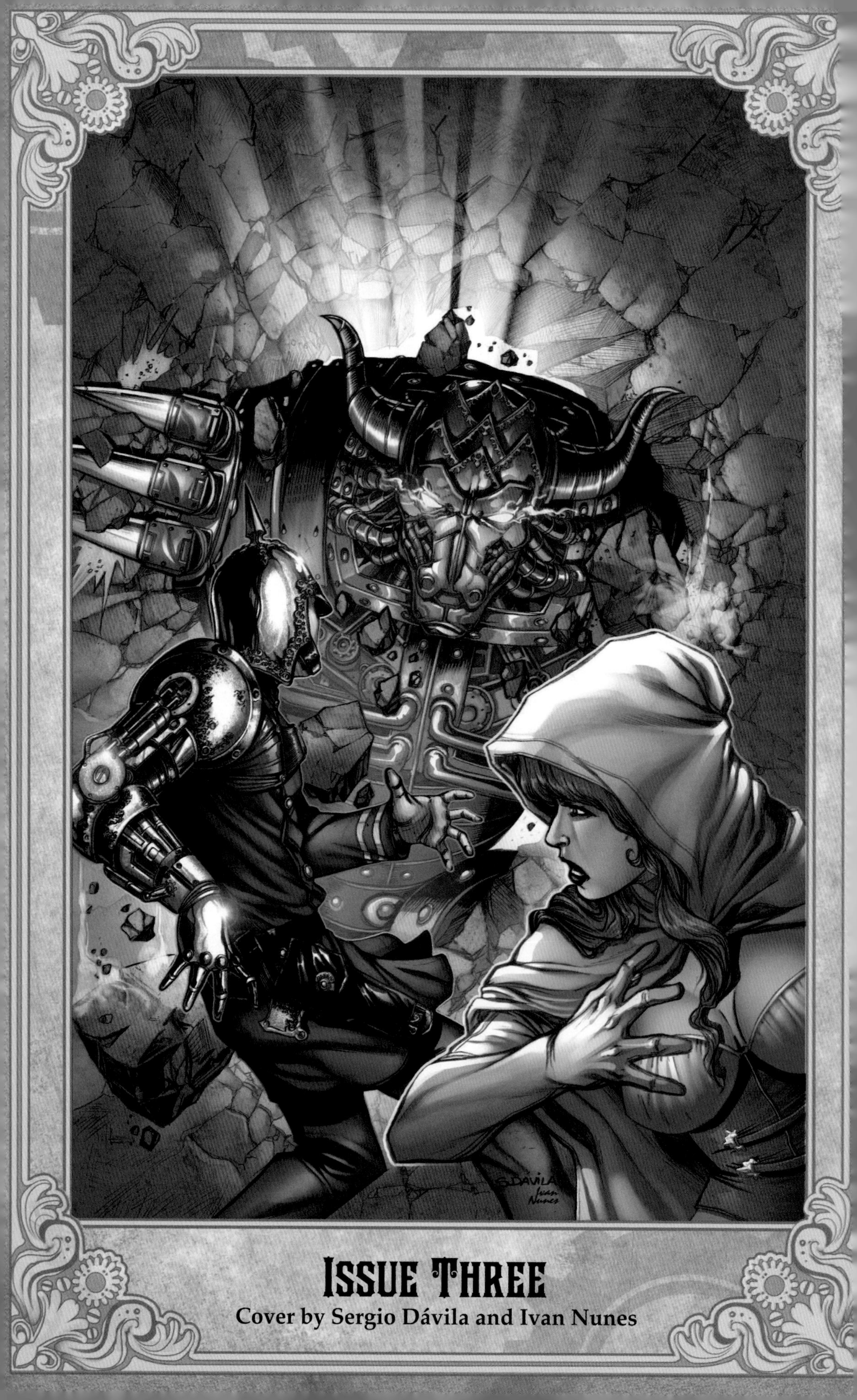
S.DÁVILA
Ivan Nunes

ISSUE THREE

Cover by Sergio Dávila and Ivan Nunes

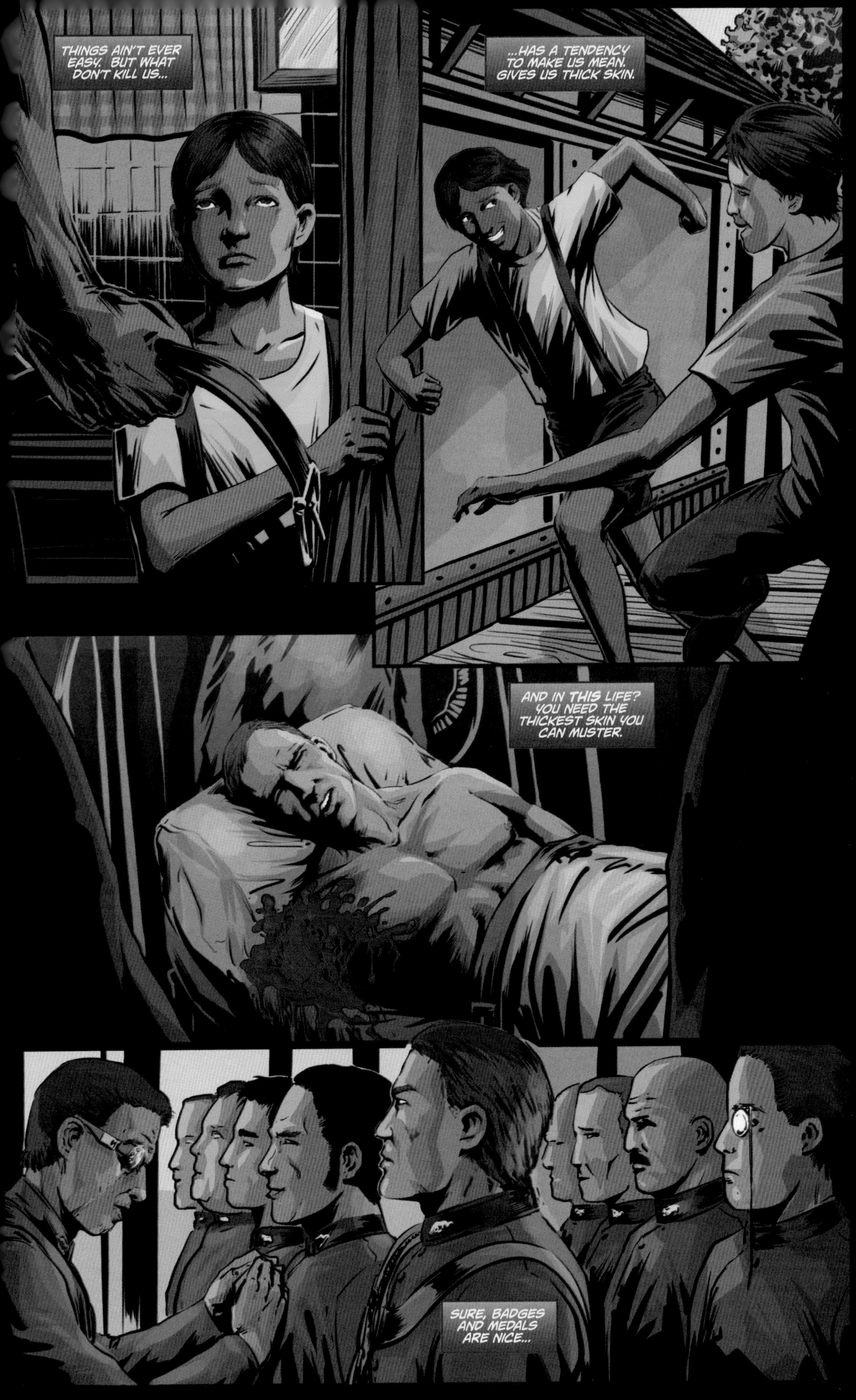
THINGS AIN'T EVER EASY. BUT WHAT DON'T KILL US...
...HAS A TENDENCY TO MAKE US MEAN. GIVES US THICK SKIN.
AND IN THIS LIFE? YOU NEED THE THICKEST SKIN YOU CAN MUSTER.
SURE, BADGES AND MEDALS ARE NICE...

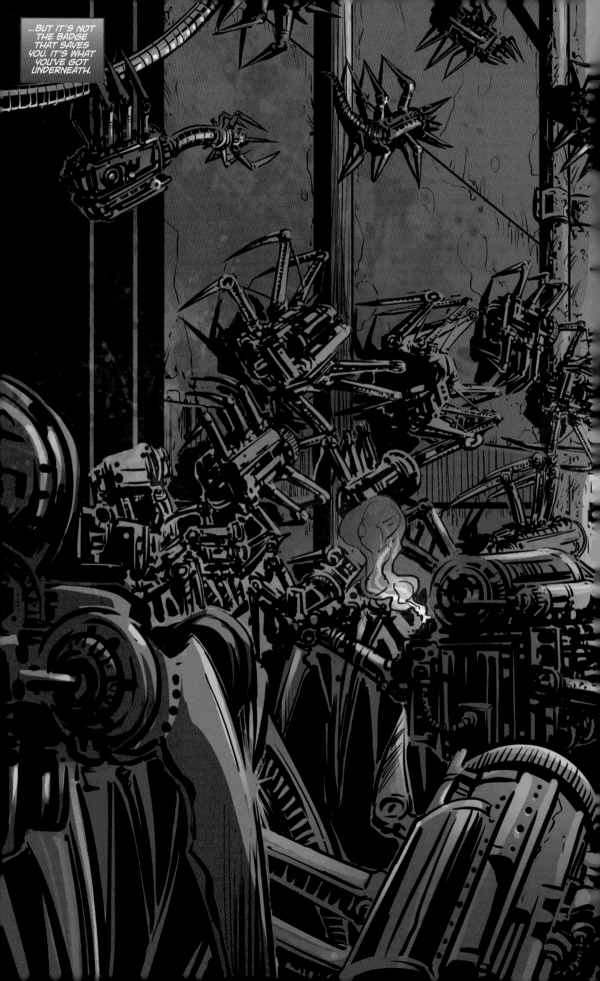

...BUT IT'S NOT THE BADGE THAT SAVES YOU. IT'S WHAT YOU'VE GOT UNDERNEATH.

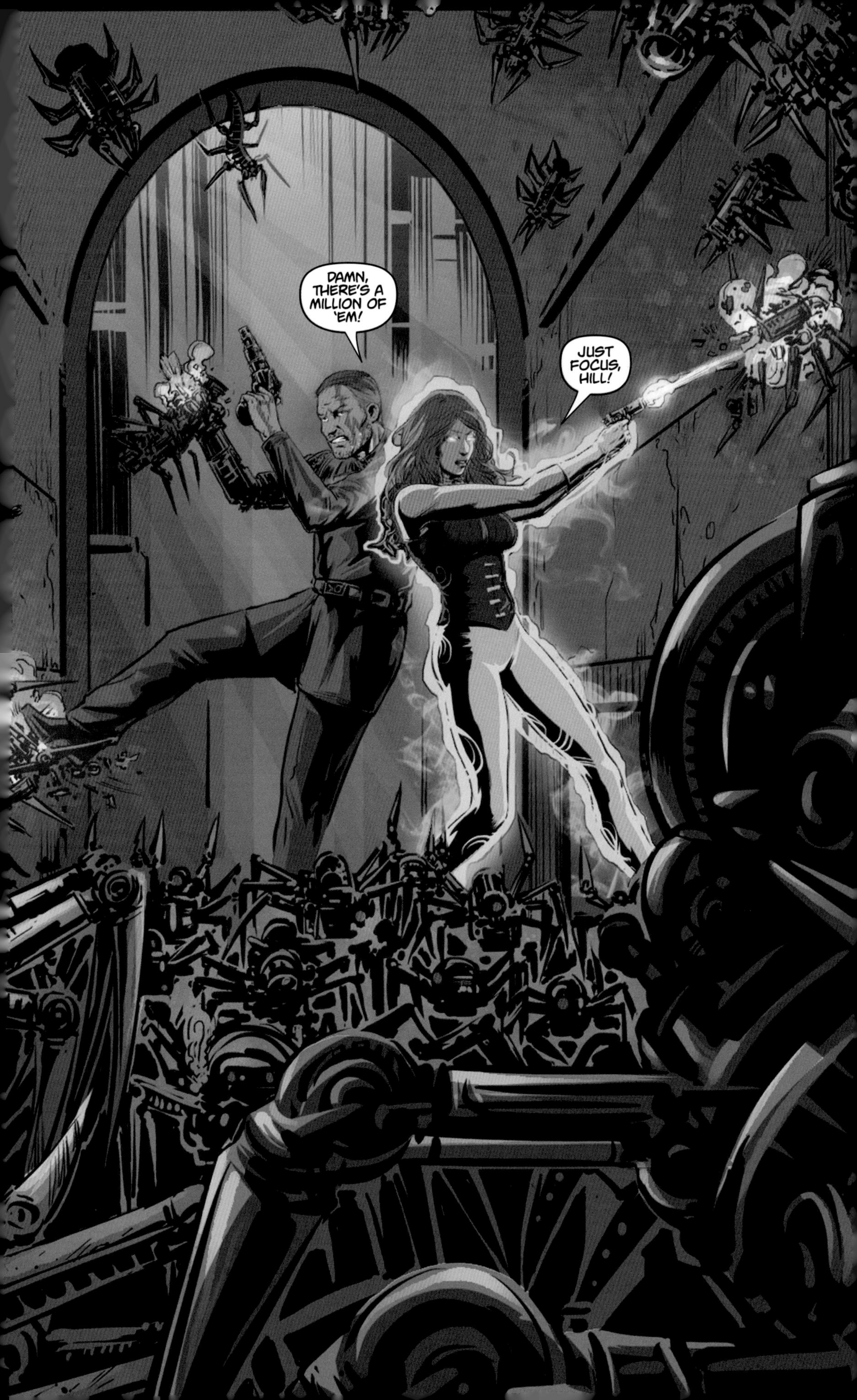
DAMN, THERE'S A MILLION OF 'EM!
JUST FOCUS, HILL!

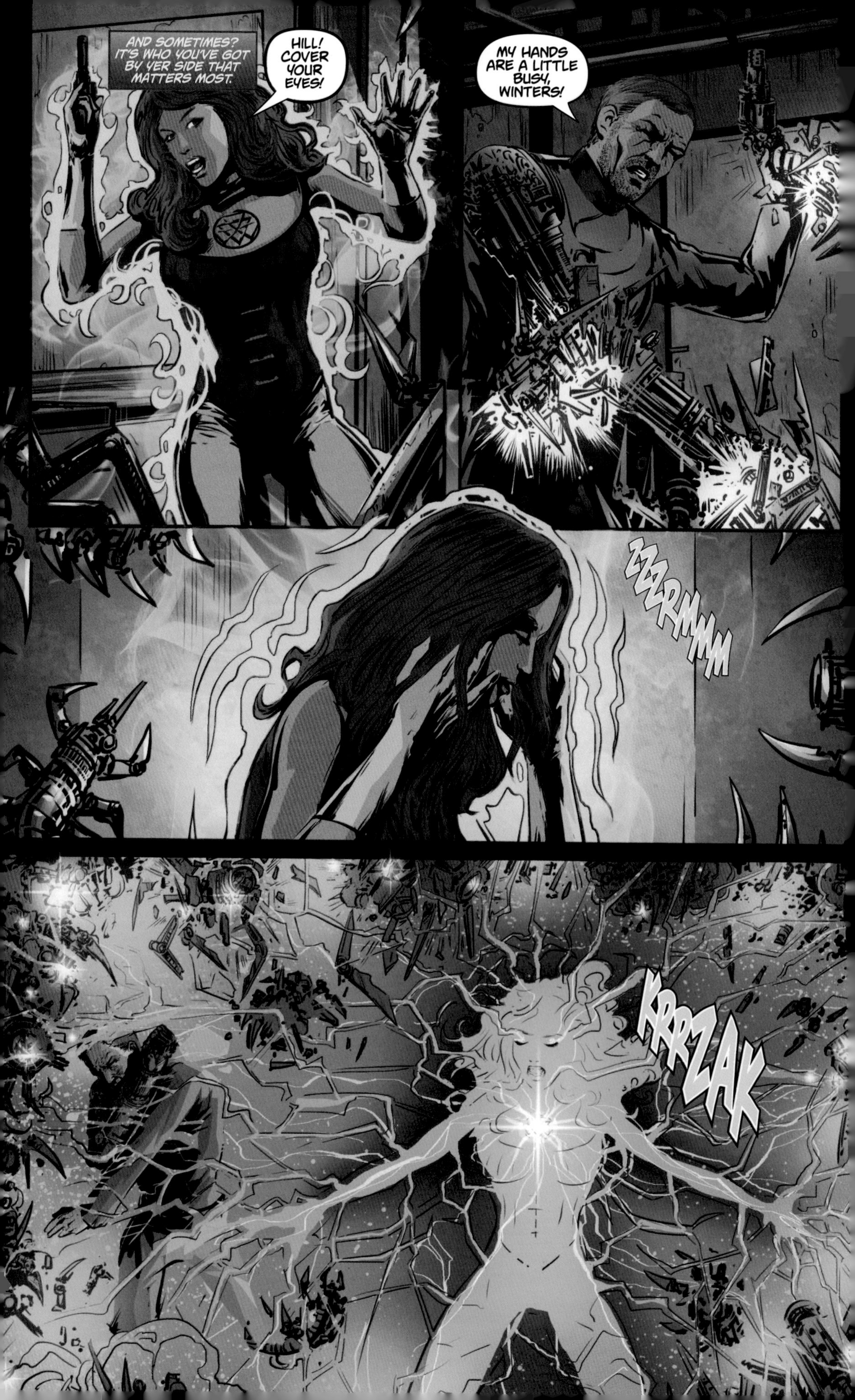
AND SOMETIMES? IT'S WHO YOU'VE GOT BY YER SIDE THAT MATTERS MOST.
HILL! COVER YOUR EYES!
MY HANDS ARE A LITTLE BUSY, WINTERS!
ZZZRMMMM
KRRZAK

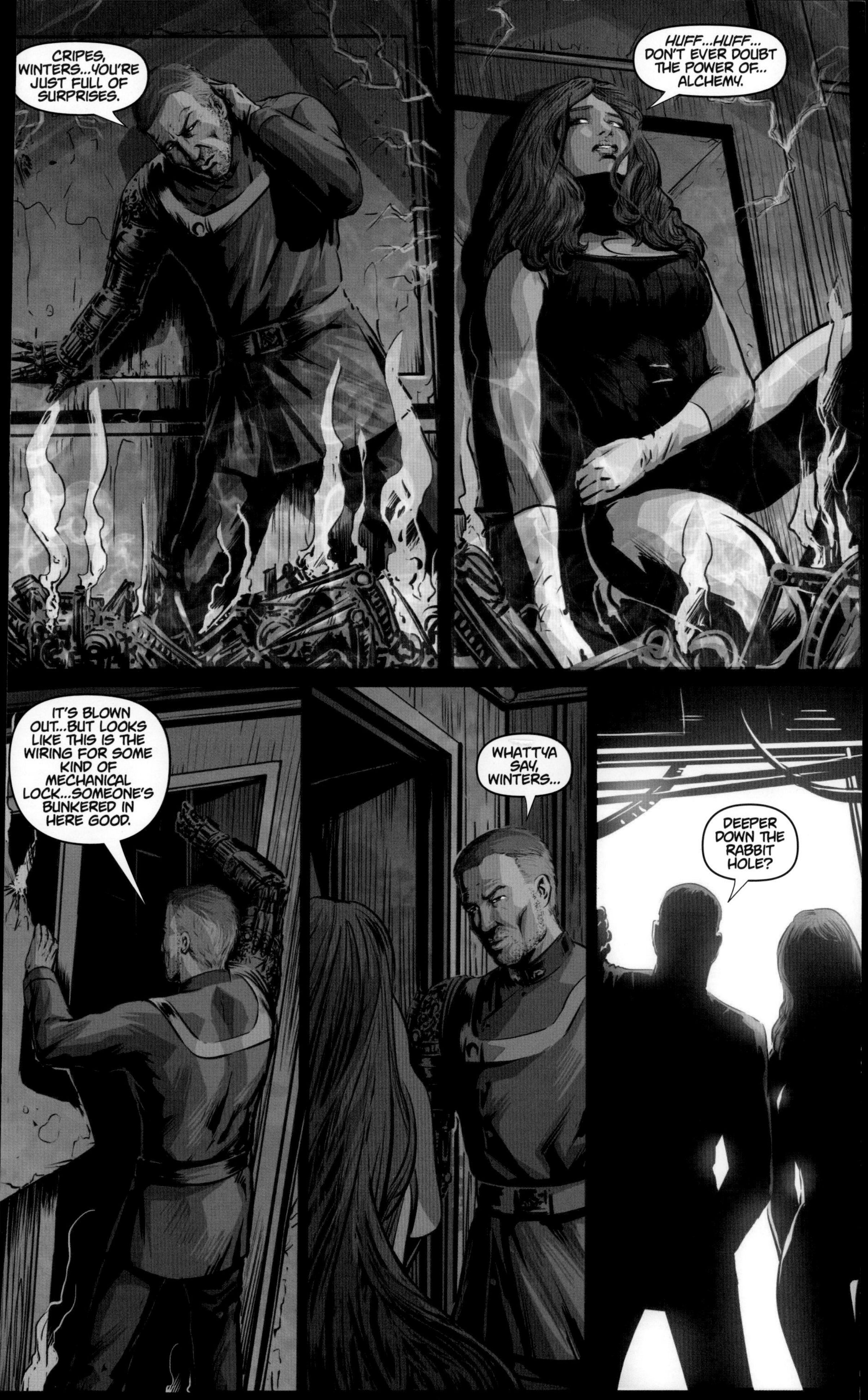
CRIPES, WINTERS...YOU'RE JUST FULL OF SURPRISES.
HUFF...HUFF... DON'T EVER DOUBT THE POWER OF... ALCHEMY.
IT'S BLOWN OUT...BUT LOOKS LIKE THIS IS THE WIRING FOR SOME KIND OF MECHANICAL LOCK...SOMEONE'S BUNKERED IN HERE GOOD.
WHATTYA SAY, WINTERS...
DEEPER DOWN THE RABBIT HOLE?

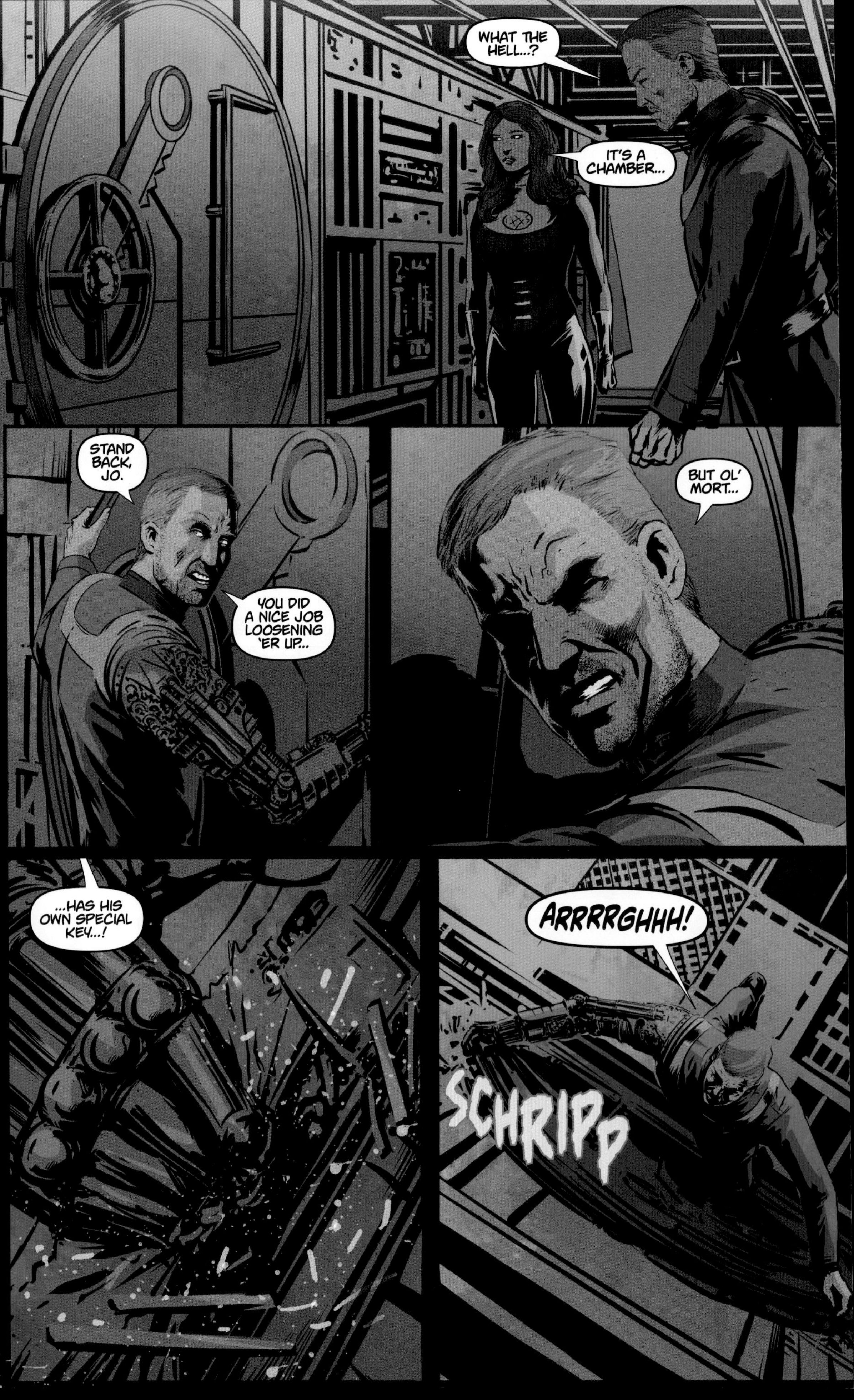
WHAT THE HELL...?
IT'S A CHAMBER...
STAND BACK, JO.
YOU DID A NICE JOB LOOSENING 'ER UP...
BUT OL' MORT...
...HAS HIS OWN SPECIAL KEY...!
ARRRRGHHH!
SCHRIPP

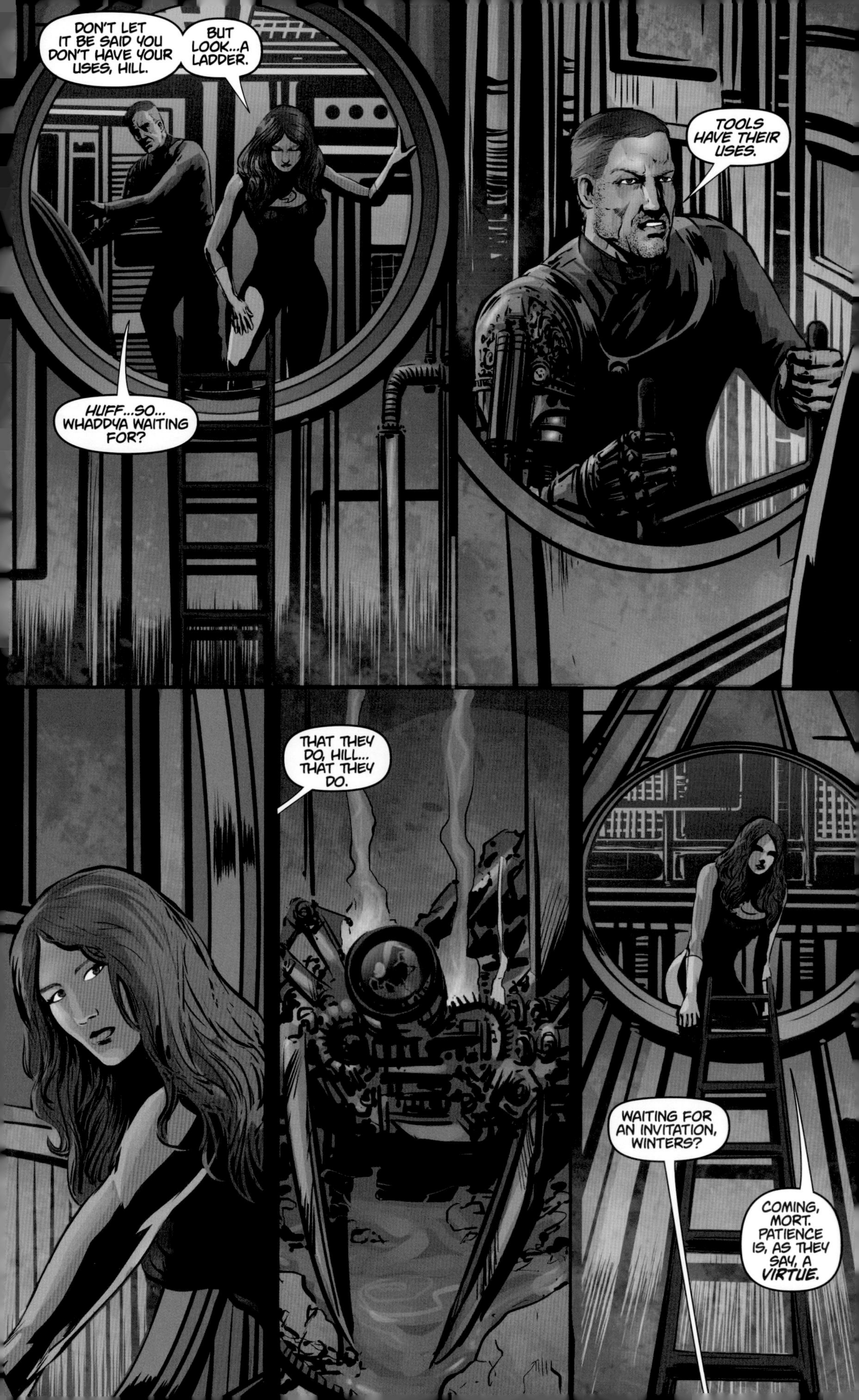
DON'T LET IT BE SAID YOU DON'T HAVE YOUR USES, HILL.
BUT LOOK...A LADDER.
HUFF...SO... WHADDYA WAITING FOR?
TOOLS HAVE THEIR USES.
THAT THEY DO, HILL... THAT THEY DO.
WAITING FOR AN INVITATION, WINTERS?
COMING, MORT. PATIENCE IS, AS THEY SAY, A VIRTUE.

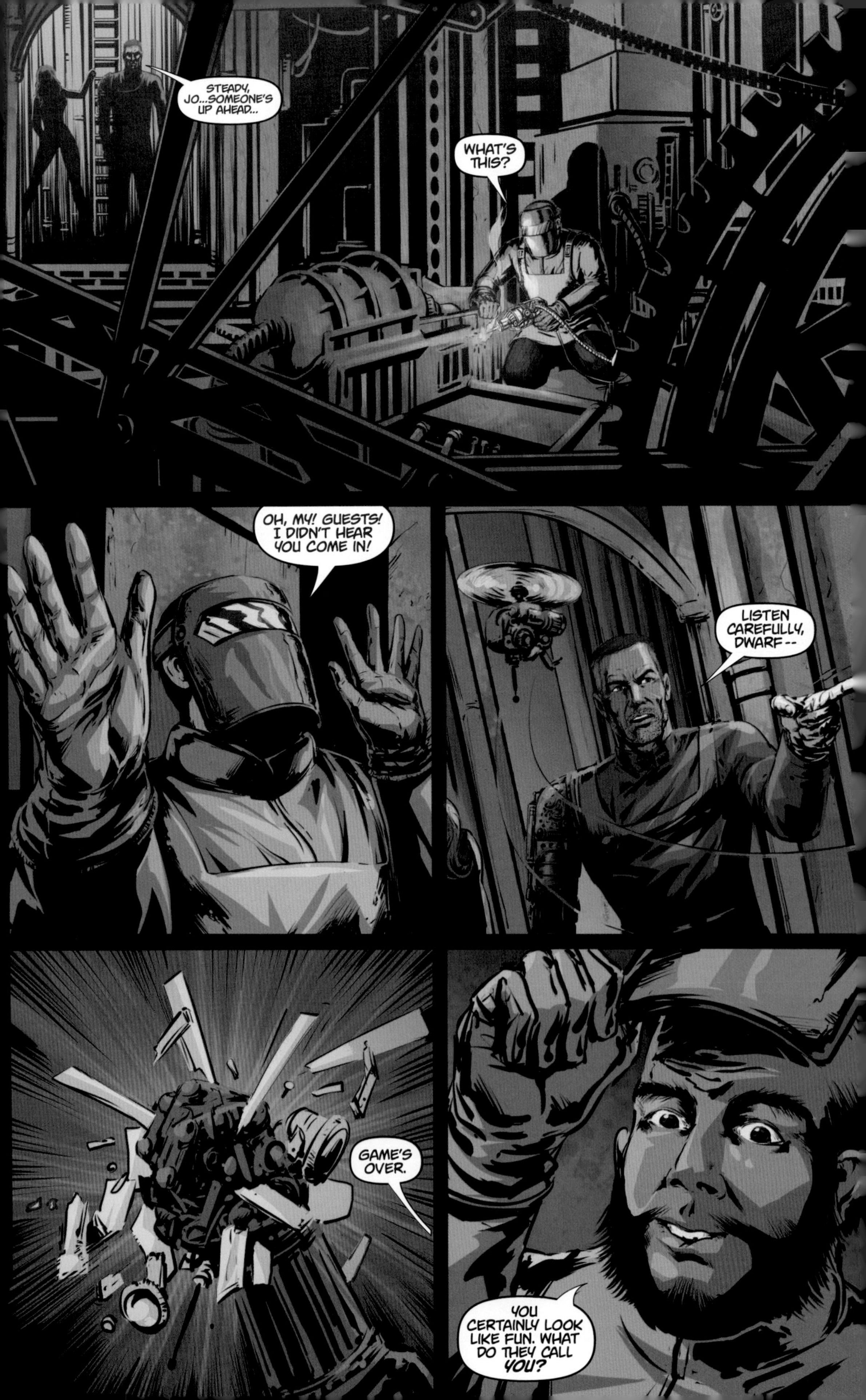
STEADY, JO...SOMEONE'S UP AHEAD...
WHAT'S THIS?
OH, MY! GUESTS! I DIDN'T HEAR YOU COME IN!
LISTEN CAREFULLY, DWARF --
GAME'S OVER.
YOU CERTAINLY LOOK LIKE FUN. WHAT DO THEY CALL YOU?

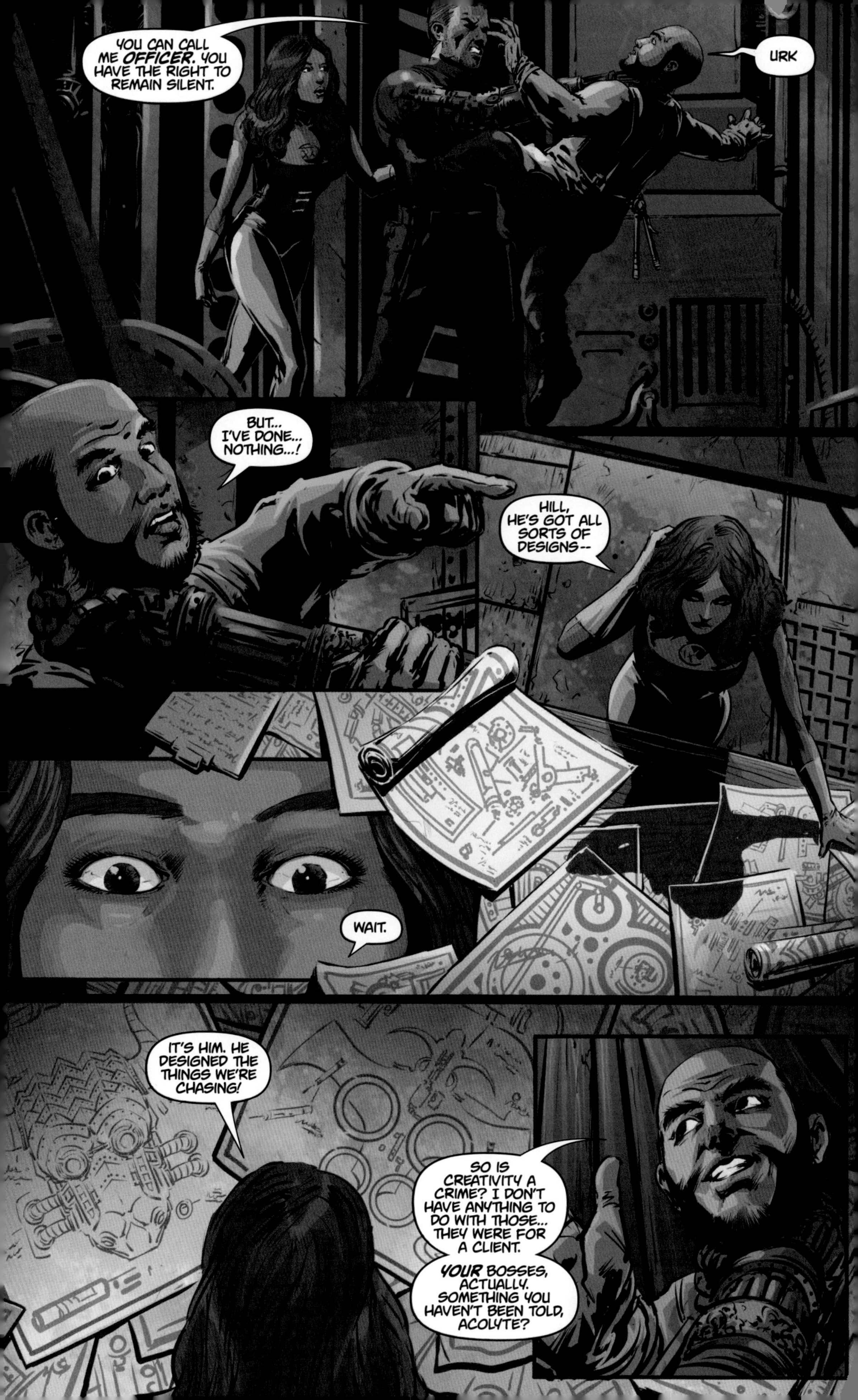
YOU CAN CALL ME *OFFICER.* YOU HAVE THE RIGHT TO REMAIN SILENT.
URK
BUT... I'VE DONE... NOTHING...!
HILL, HE'S GOT ALL SORTS OF DESIGNS--
WAIT.
IT'S HIM. HE DESIGNED THE THINGS WE'RE CHASING!
SO IS CREATIVITY A CRIME? I DON'T HAVE ANYTHING TO DO WITH THOSE... THEY WERE FOR A CLIENT.
YOUR BOSSES, ACTUALLY. SOMETHING YOU HAVEN'T BEEN TOLD, ACOLYTE?

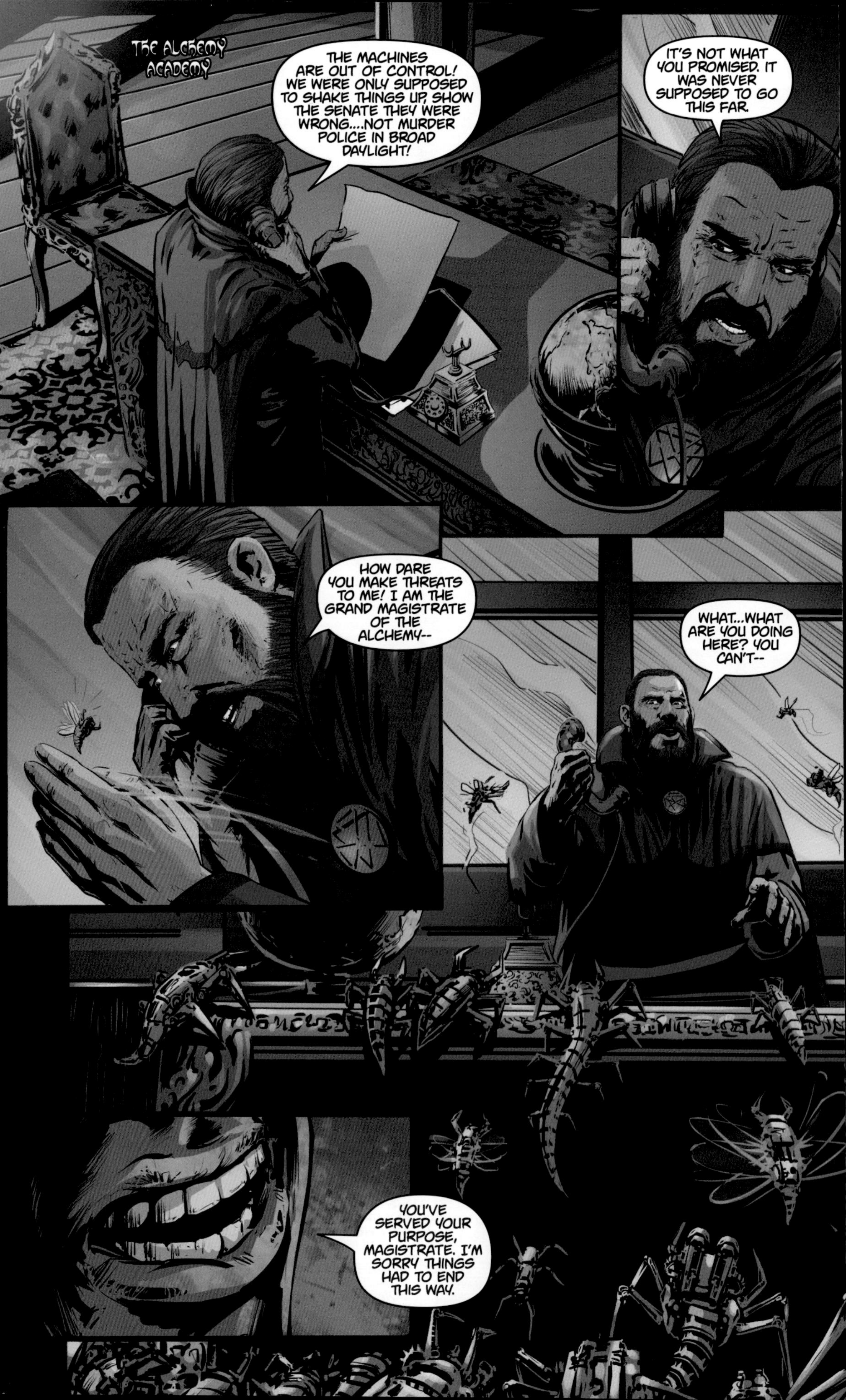
THE ALCHEMY ACADEMY
THE MACHINES ARE OUT OF CONTROL! WE WERE ONLY SUPPOSED TO SHAKE THINGS UP, SHOW THE SENATE THEY WERE WRONG....NOT MURDER POLICE IN BROAD DAYLIGHT!
IT'S NOT WHAT YOU PROMISED. IT WAS NEVER SUPPOSED TO GO THIS FAR.
HOW DARE YOU MAKE THREATS TO ME! I AM THE GRAND MAGISTRATE OF THE ALCHEMY--
WHAT...WHAT ARE YOU DOING HERE? YOU CAN'T--
YOU'VE SERVED YOUR PURPOSE, MAGISTRATE. I'M SORRY THINGS HAD TO END THIS WAY.

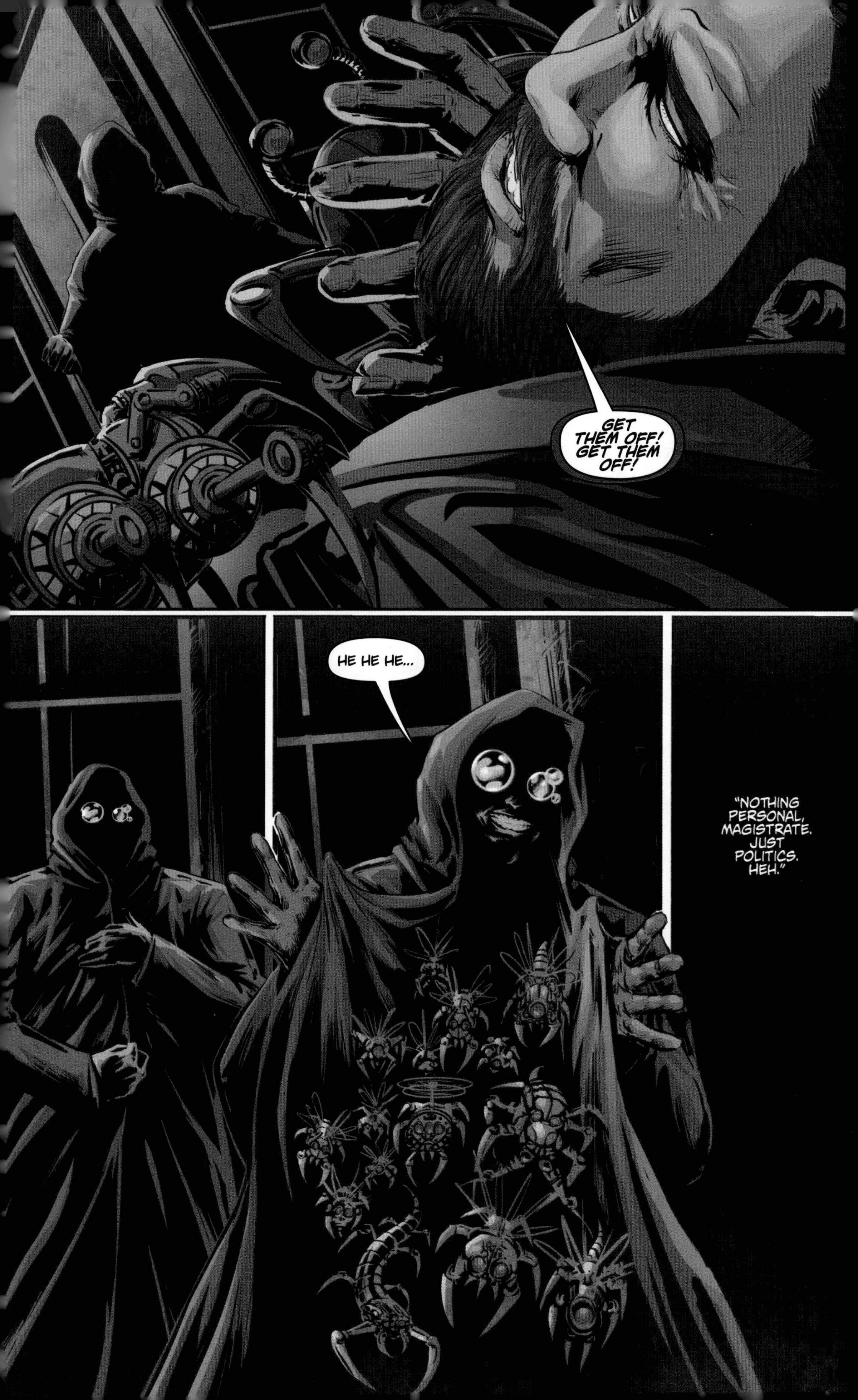
GET THEM OFF! GET THEM OFF!
HE HE HE...
"NOTHING PERSONAL, MAGISTRATE. JUST POLITICS. HEH."

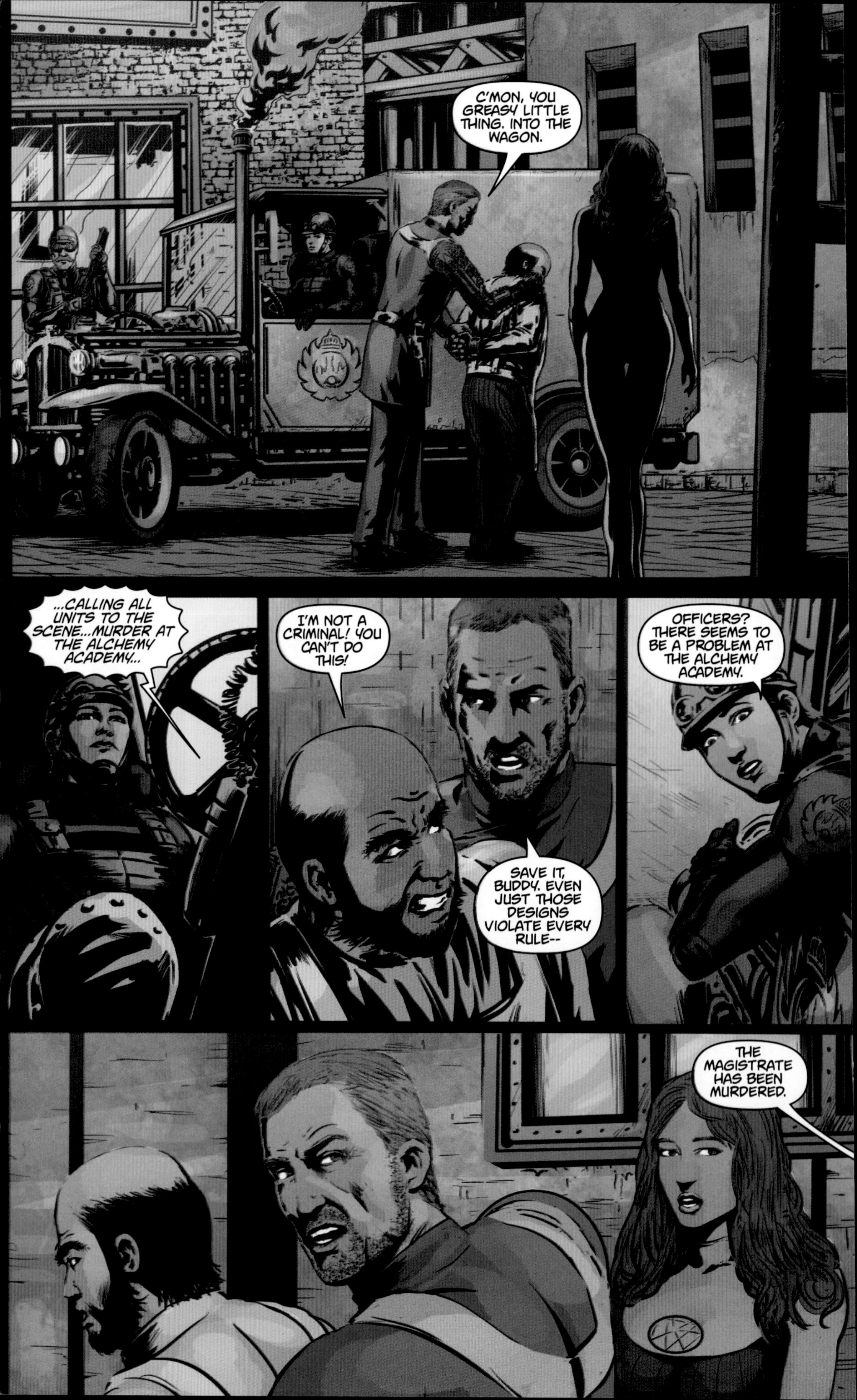
C'MON, YOU GREASY LITTLE THING. INTO THE WAGON.
...CALLING ALL UNITS TO THE SCENE...MURDER AT THE ALCHEMY ACADEMY...
I'M NOT A CRIMINAL! YOU CAN'T DO THIS!
SAVE IT, BUDDY. EVEN JUST THOSE DESIGNS VIOLATE EVERY RULE--
OFFICERS? THERE SEEMS TO BE A PROBLEM AT THE ALCHEMY ACADEMY.
THE MAGISTRATE HAS BEEN MURDERED.

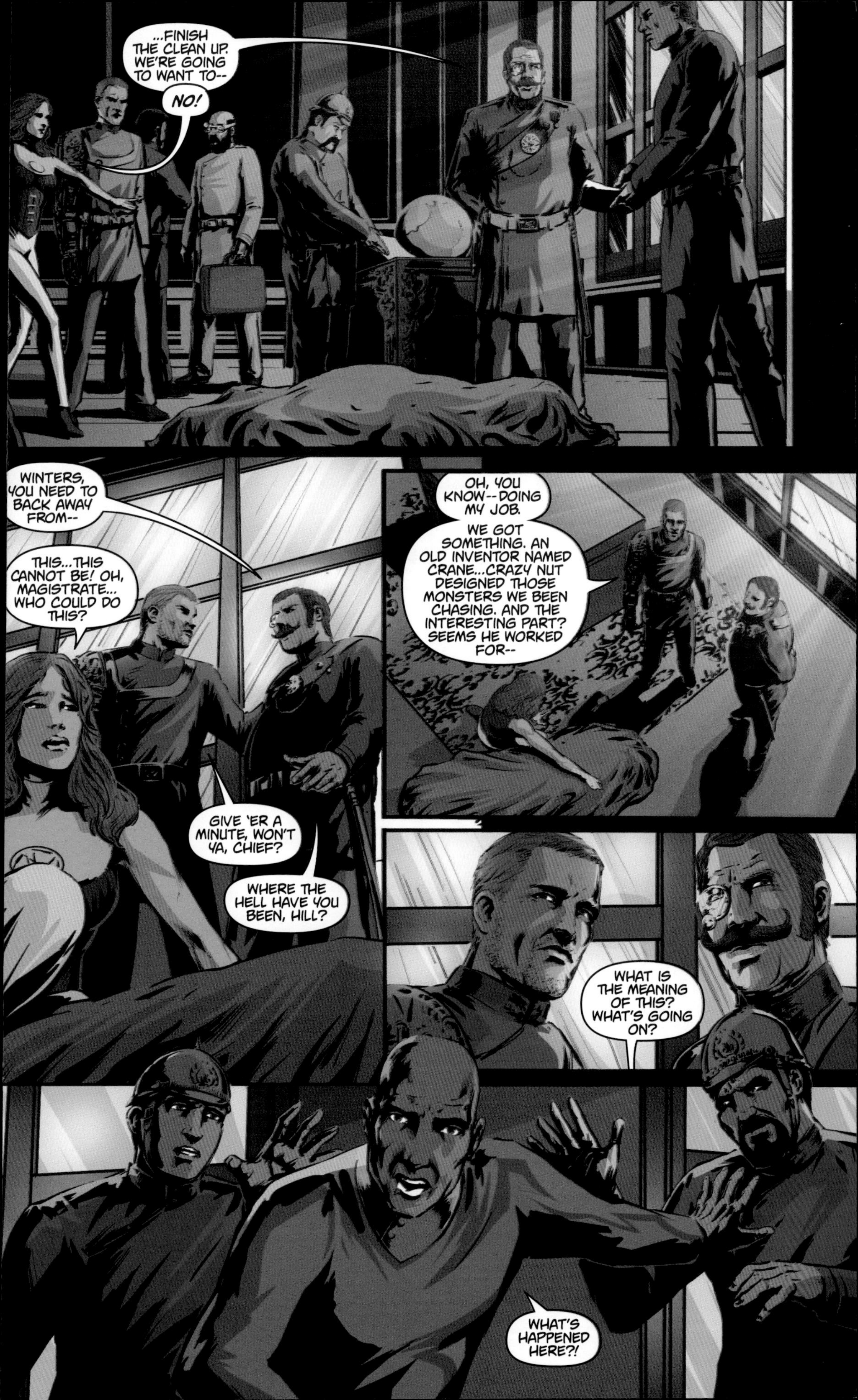
...FINISH THE CLEAN UP. WE'RE GOING TO WANT TO--
NO!
WINTERS, YOU NEED TO BACK AWAY FROM--
THIS...THIS CANNOT BE! OH, MAGISTRATE... WHO COULD DO THIS?
GIVE 'ER A MINUTE, WON'T YA, CHIEF?
WHERE THE HELL HAVE YOU BEEN, HILL?
OH, YOU KNOW--DOING MY JOB.
WE GOT SOMETHING. AN OLD INVENTOR NAMED CRANE...CRAZY NUT DESIGNED THOSE MONSTERS WE BEEN CHASING. AND THE INTERESTING PART? SEEMS HE WORKED FOR--
WHAT IS THE MEANING OF THIS? WHAT'S GOING ON?
WHAT'S HAPPENED HERE?!

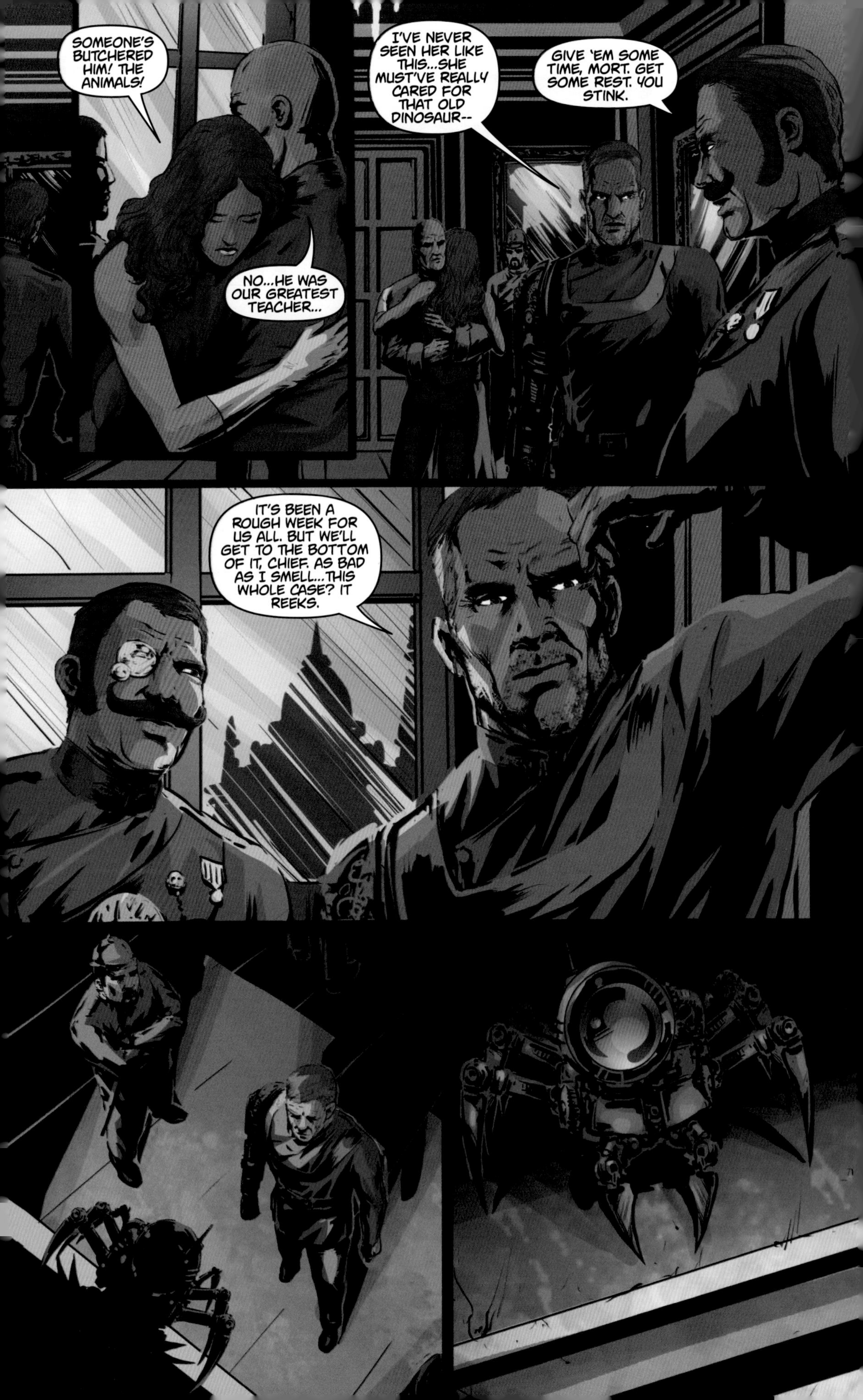
SOMEONE'S BUTCHERED HIM! THE ANIMALS!
NO...HE WAS OUR GREATEST TEACHER...
I'VE NEVER SEEN HER LIKE THIS...SHE MUST'VE REALLY CARED FOR THAT OLD DINOSAUR--
GIVE 'EM SOME TIME, MORT. GET SOME REST. YOU STINK.
IT'S BEEN A ROUGH WEEK FOR US ALL. BUT WE'LL GET TO THE BOTTOM OF IT, CHIEF. AS BAD AS I SMELL...THIS WHOLE CASE? IT REEKS.

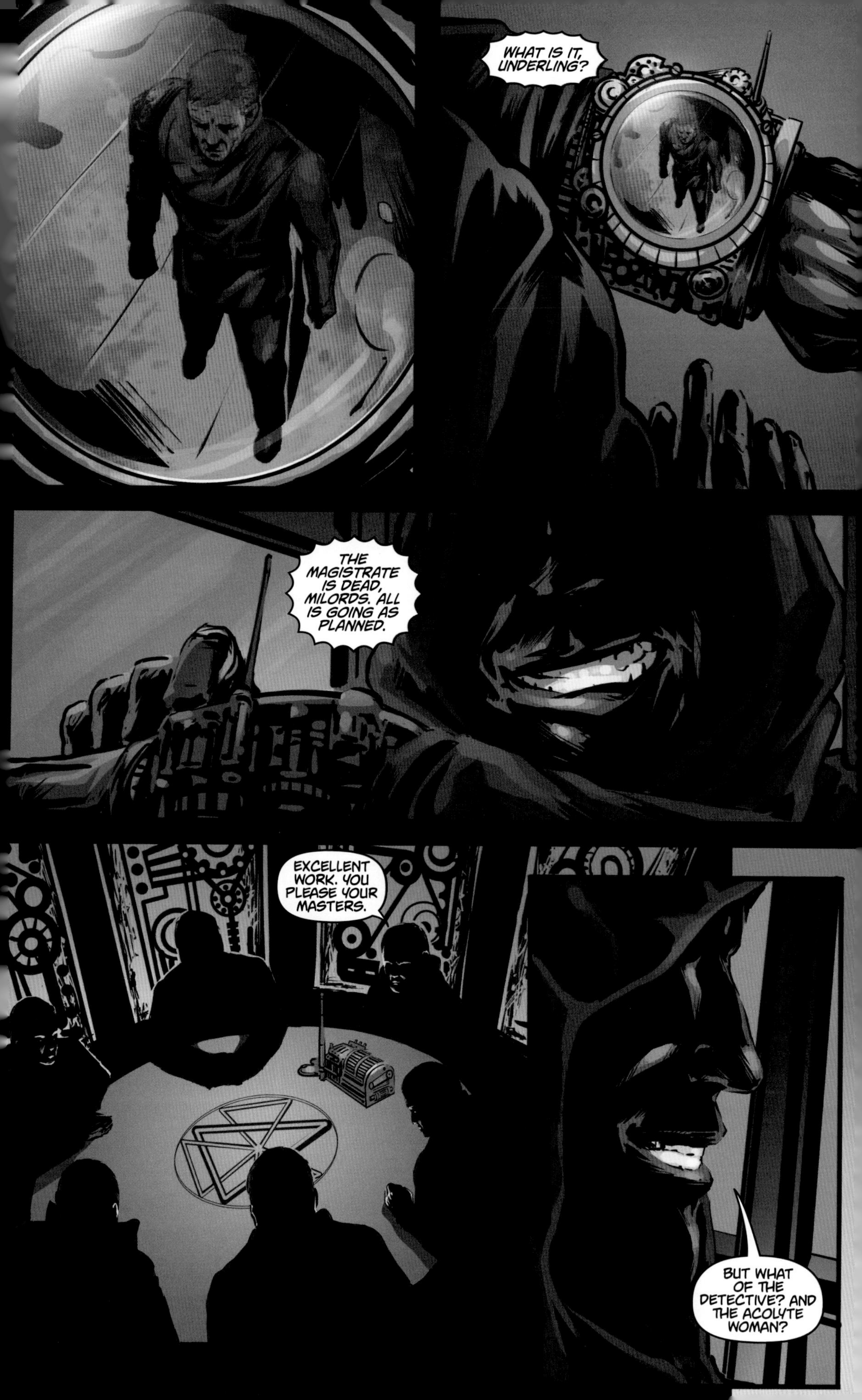
WHAT IS IT, UNDERLING?
THE MAGISTRATE IS DEAD, MILORDS. ALL IS GOING AS PLANNED.
EXCELLENT WORK. YOU PLEASE YOUR MASTERS.
BUT WHAT OF THE DETECTIVE? AND THE ACOLYTE WOMAN?

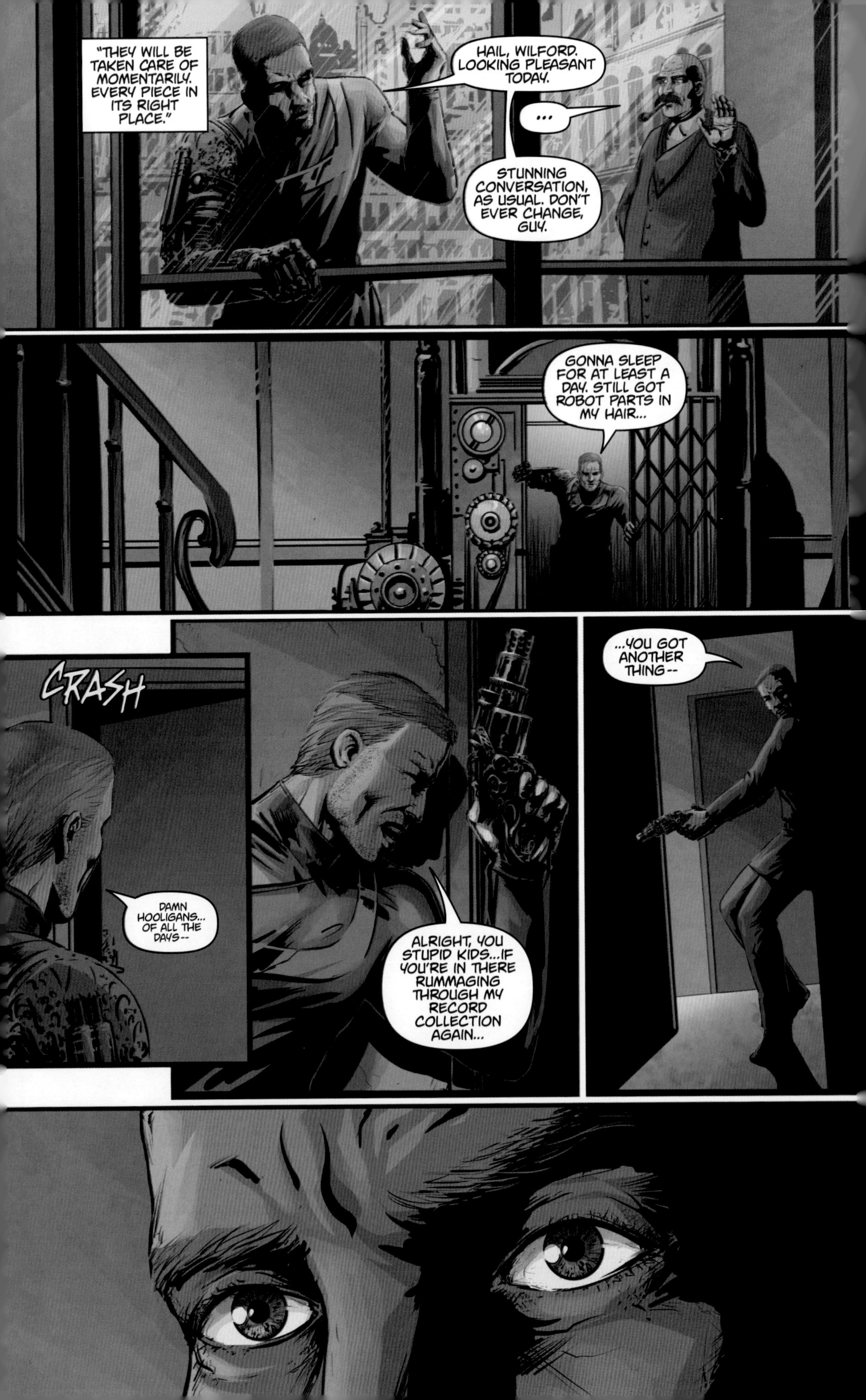
"THEY WILL BE TAKEN CARE OF MOMENTARILY. EVERY PIECE IN ITS RIGHT PLACE."
HAIL, WILFORD. LOOKING PLEASANT TODAY.
...
STUNNING CONVERSATION, AS USUAL. DON'T EVER CHANGE, GUY.
GONNA SLEEP FOR AT LEAST A DAY. STILL GOT ROBOT PARTS IN MY HAIR...
CRASH
DAMN HOOLIGANS... OF ALL THE DAYS--
ALRIGHT, YOU STUPID KIDS...IF YOU'RE IN THERE RUMMAGING THROUGH MY RECORD COLLECTION AGAIN...
...YOU GOT ANOTHER THING--

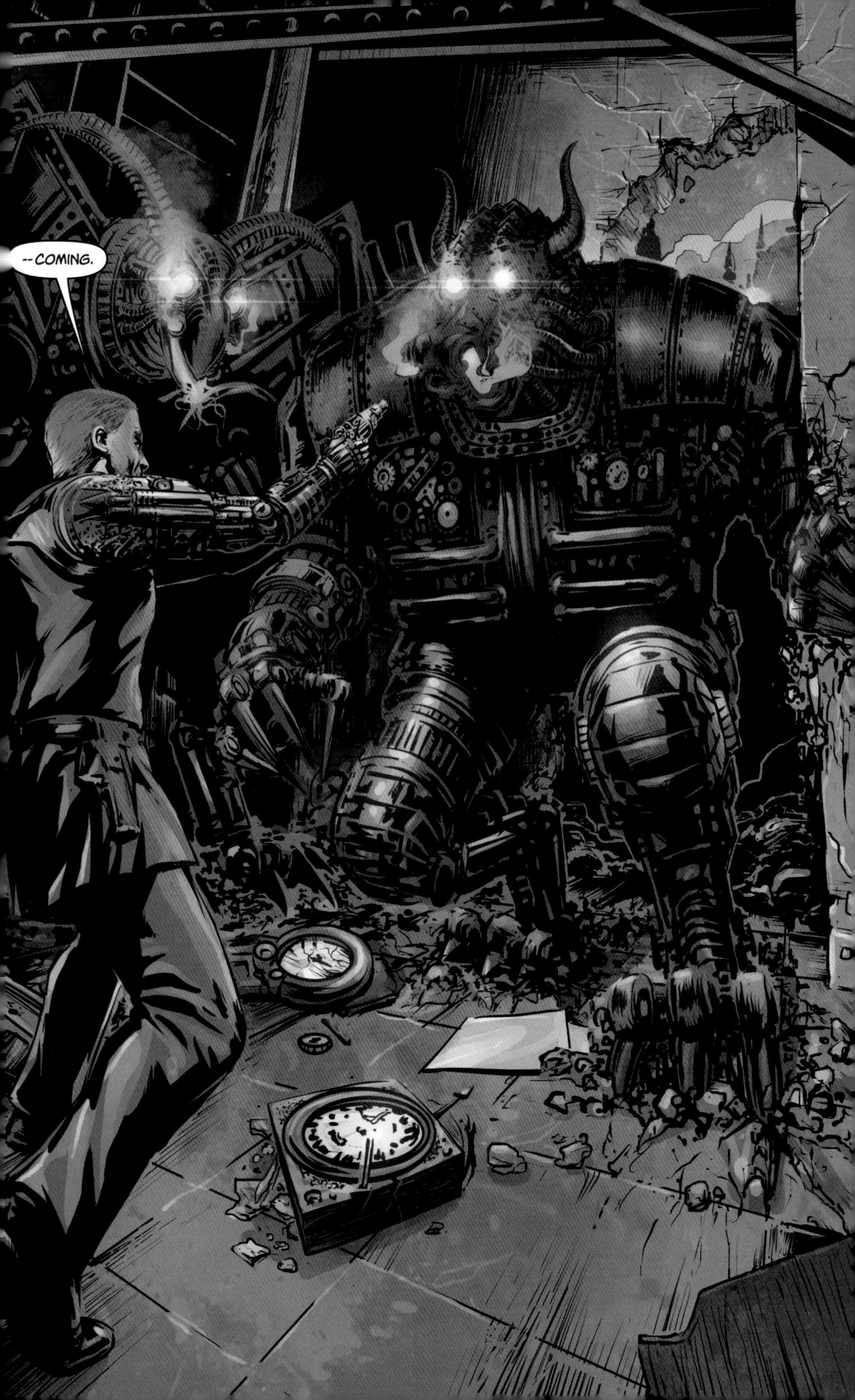
--COMING.

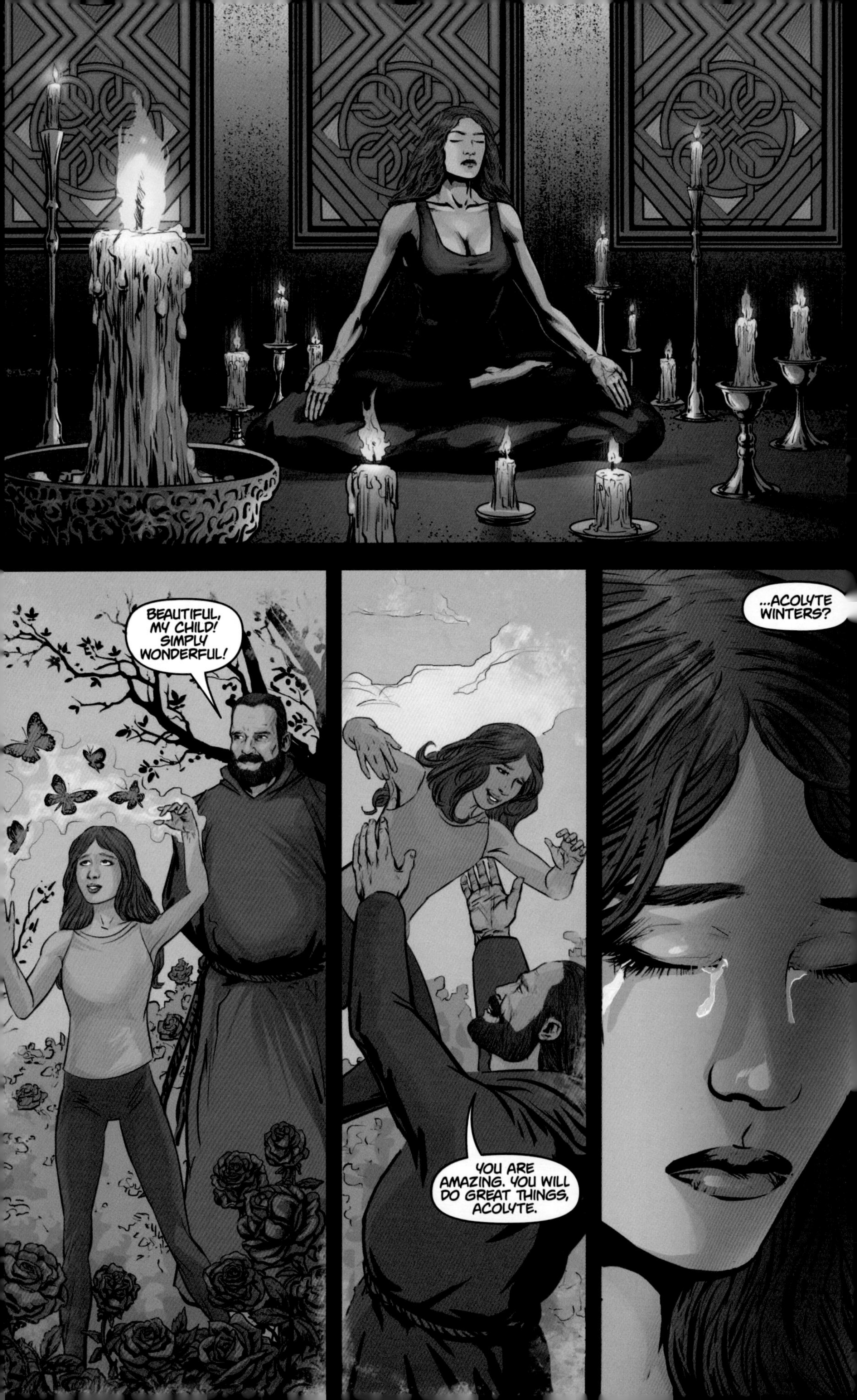
BEAUTIFUL, MY CHILD! SIMPLY WONDERFUL!
YOU ARE AMAZING. YOU WILL DO GREAT THINGS, ACOLYTE.
...ACOLYTE WINTERS?

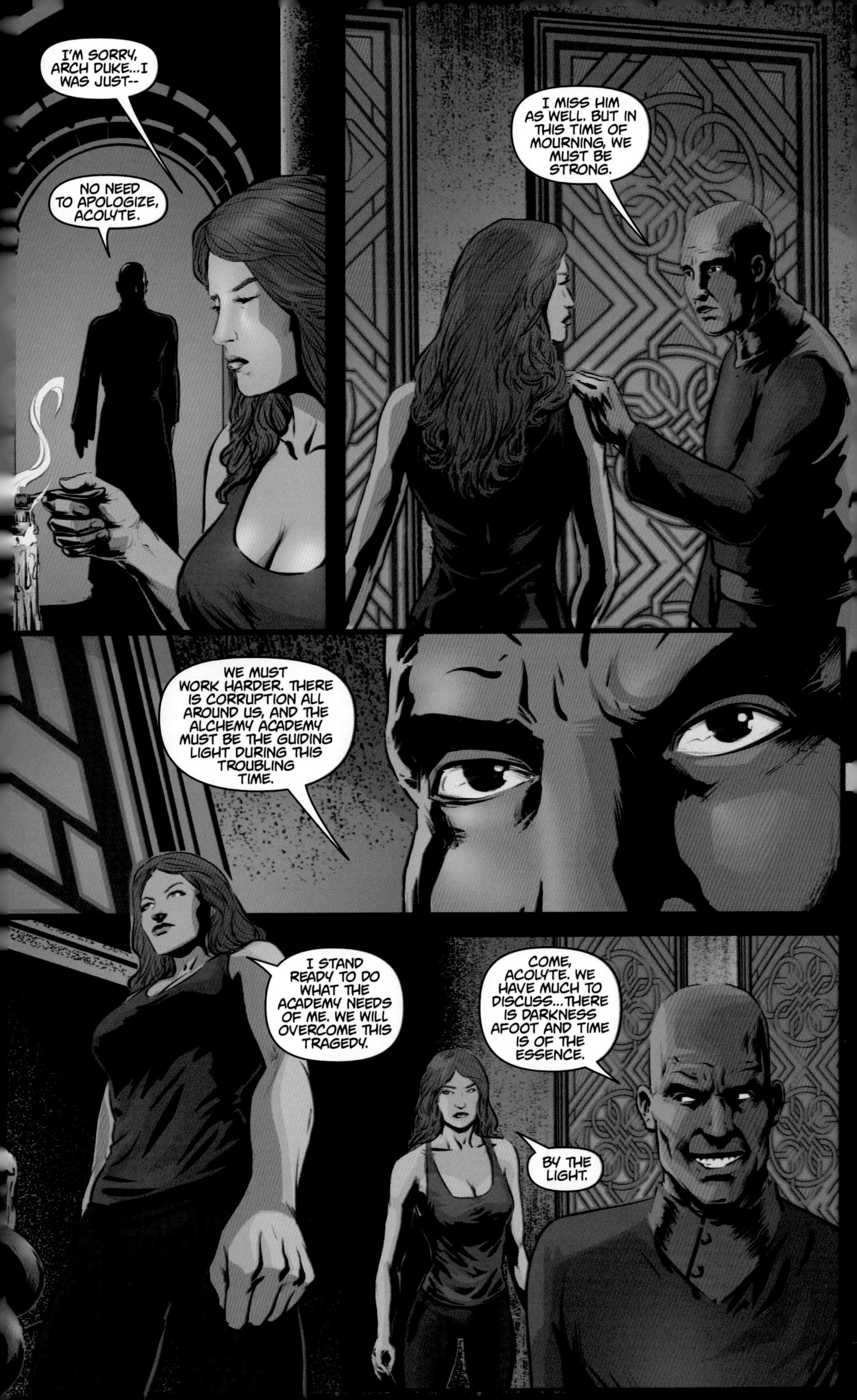
I'M SORRY, ARCH DUKE...I WAS JUST--
NO NEED TO APOLOGIZE, ACOLYTE.
I MISS HIM AS WELL. BUT IN THIS TIME OF MOURNING, WE MUST BE STRONG.
WE MUST WORK HARDER. THERE IS CORRUPTION ALL AROUND US, AND THE ALCHEMY ACADEMY MUST BE THE GUIDING LIGHT DURING THIS TROUBLING TIME.
I STAND READY TO DO WHAT THE ACADEMY NEEDS OF ME. WE WILL OVERCOME THIS TRAGEDY.
COME, ACOLYTE. WE HAVE MUCH TO DISCUSS...THERE IS DARKNESS AFOOT AND TIME IS OF THE ESSENCE.
BY THE LIGHT.

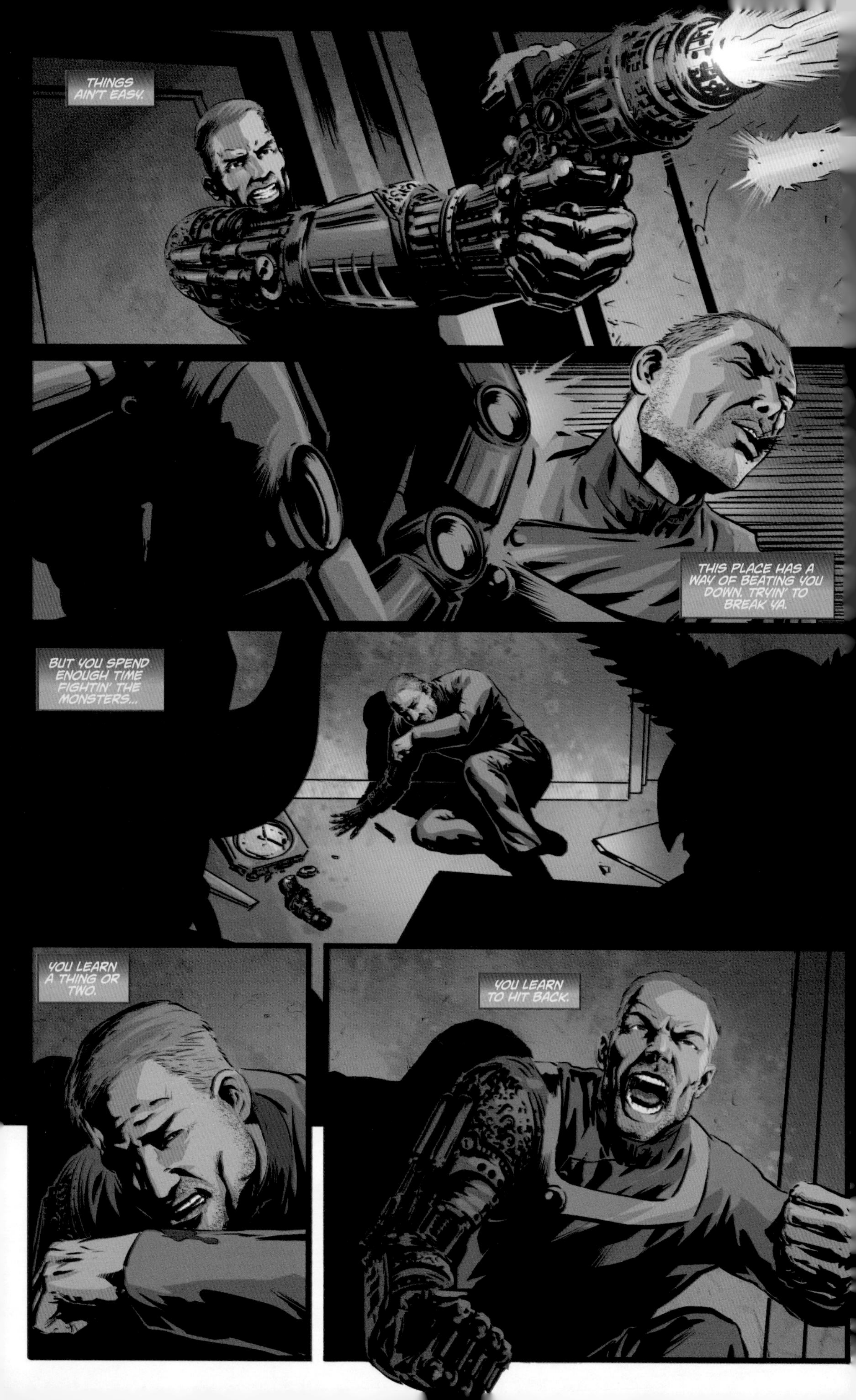
THINGS AIN'T EASY.
THIS PLACE HAS A WAY OF BEATING YOU DOWN. TRYIN' TO BREAK YA.
BUT YOU SPEND ENOUGH TIME FIGHTIN' THE MONSTERS...
YOU LEARN A THING OR TWO.
YOU LEARN TO HIT BACK.

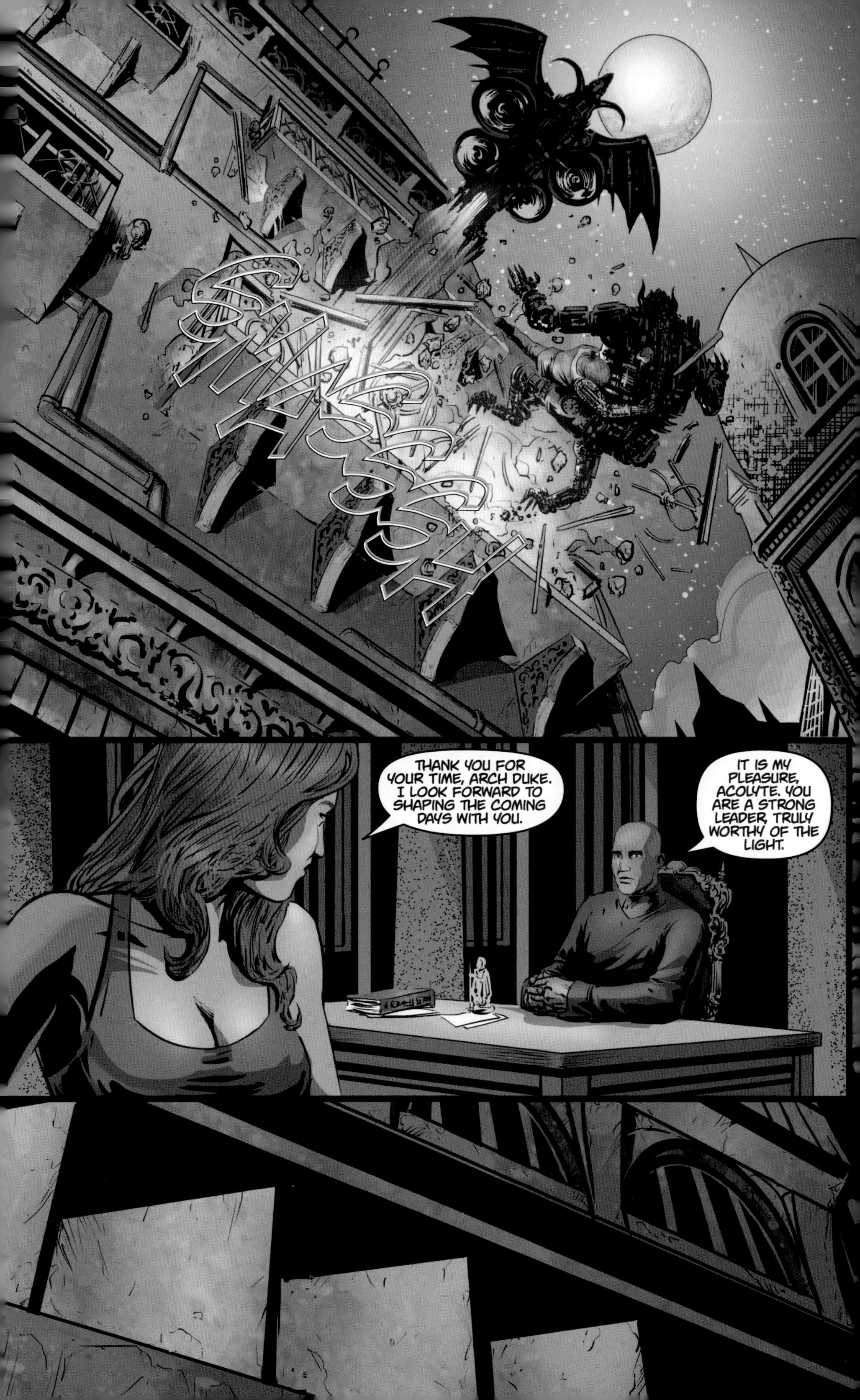
SMASSSSH
THANK YOU FOR YOUR TIME, ARCH DUKE. I LOOK FORWARD TO SHAPING THE COMING DAYS WITH YOU.
IT IS MY PLEASURE, ACOLYTE. YOU ARE A STRONG LEADER, TRULY WORTHY OF THE LIGHT.

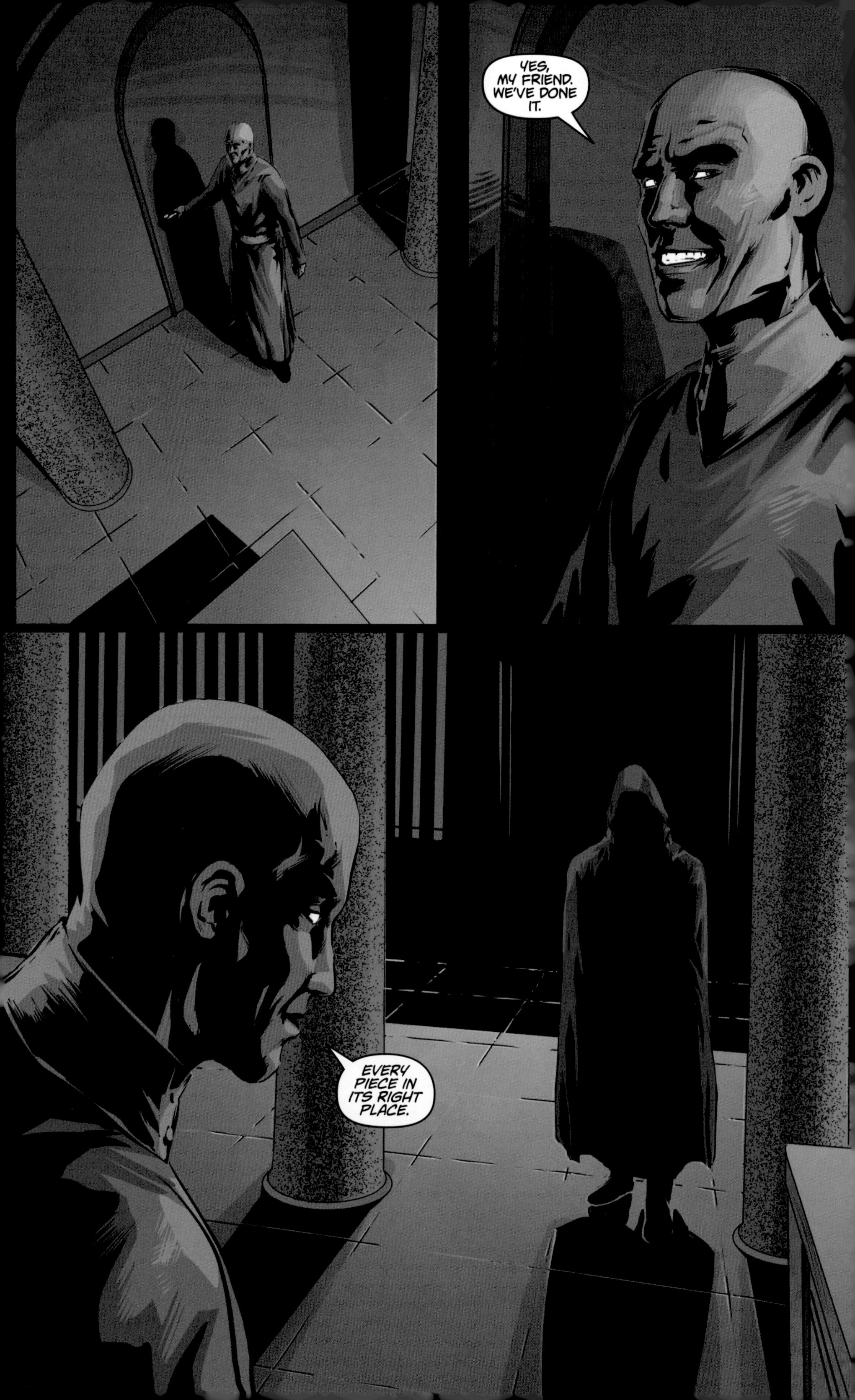
YES, MY FRIEND. WE'VE DONE IT.
EVERY PIECE IN ITS RIGHT PLACE.

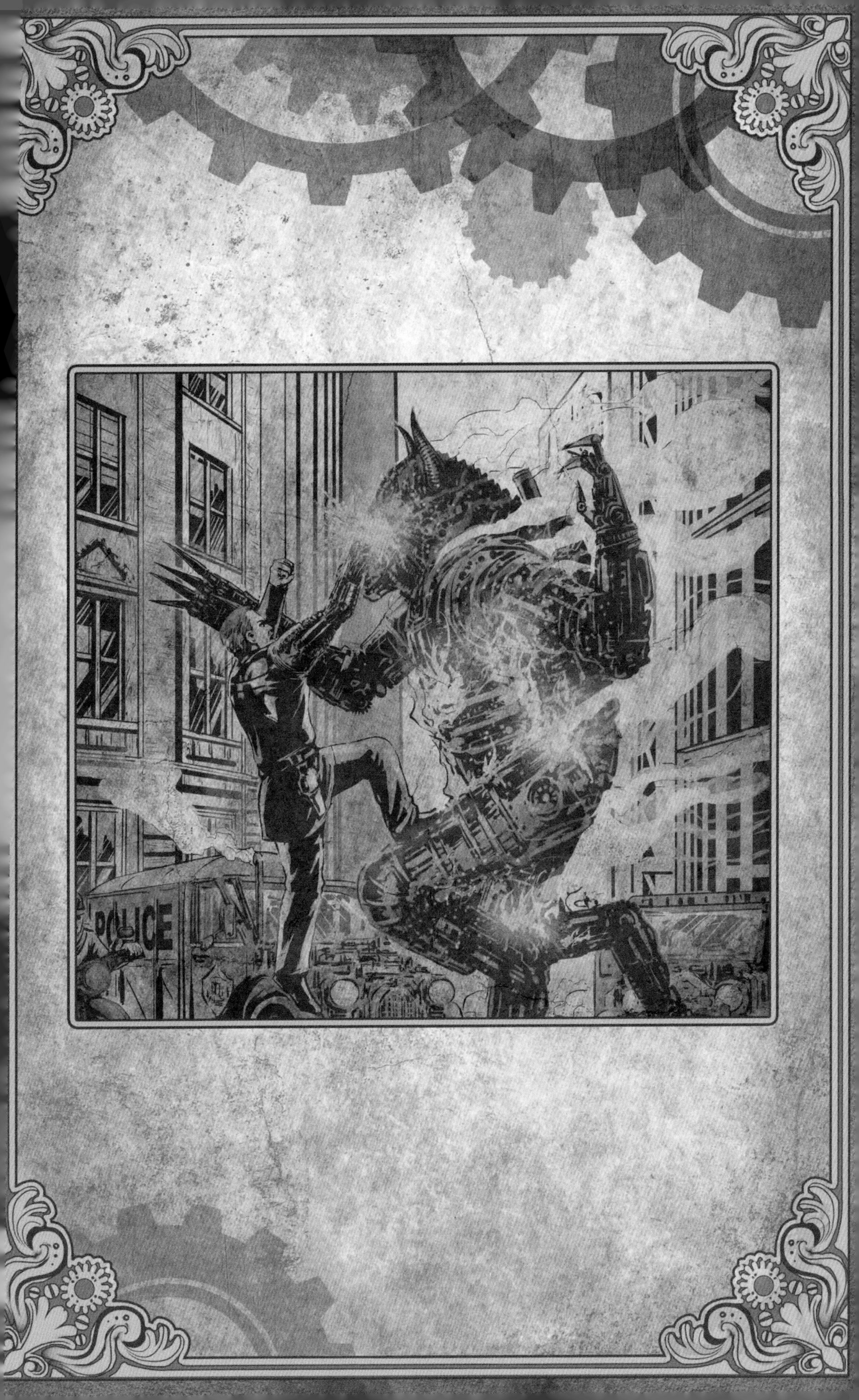
POLICE

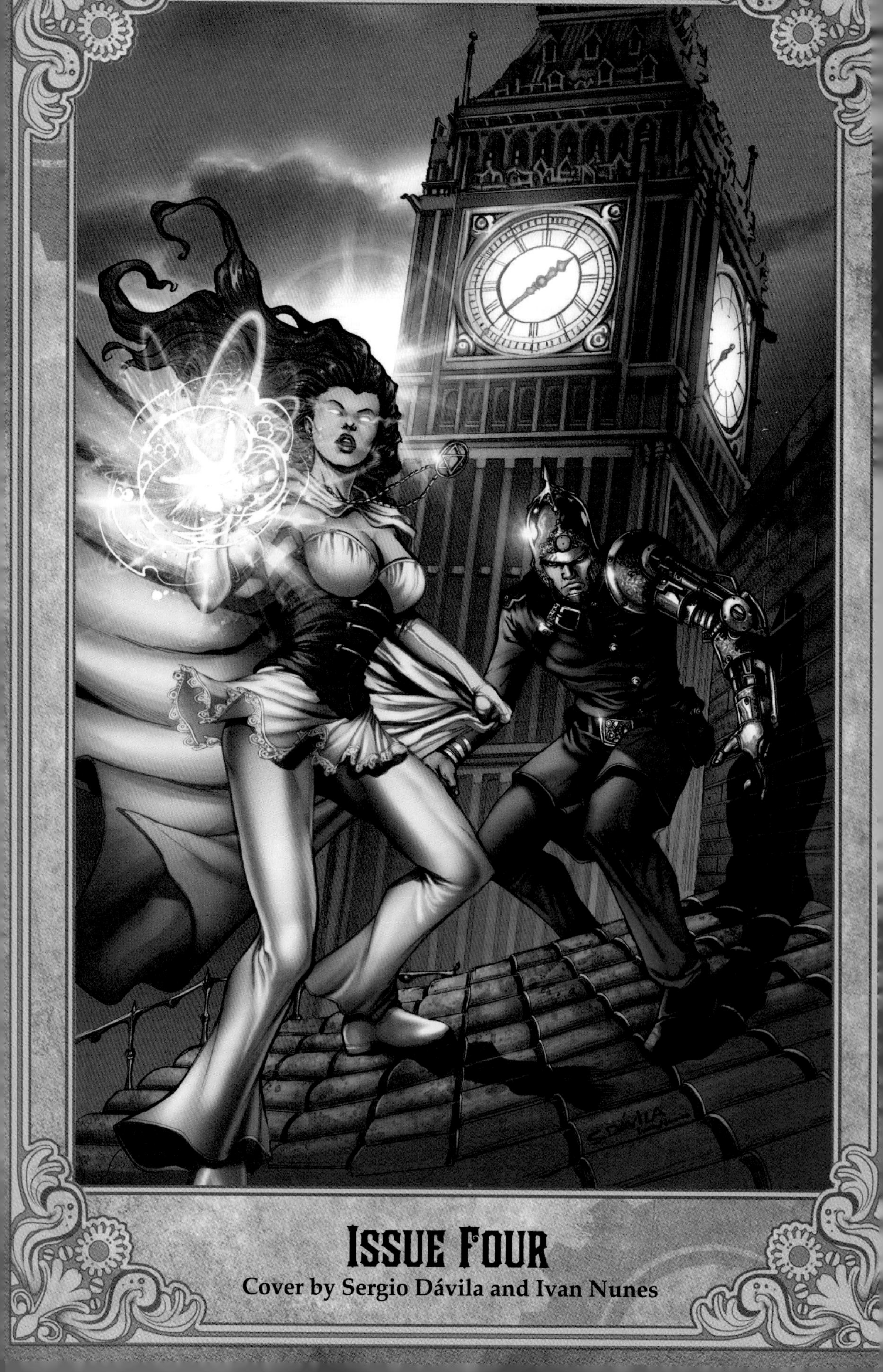

Issue Four

Cover by Sergio Dávila and Ivan Nunes

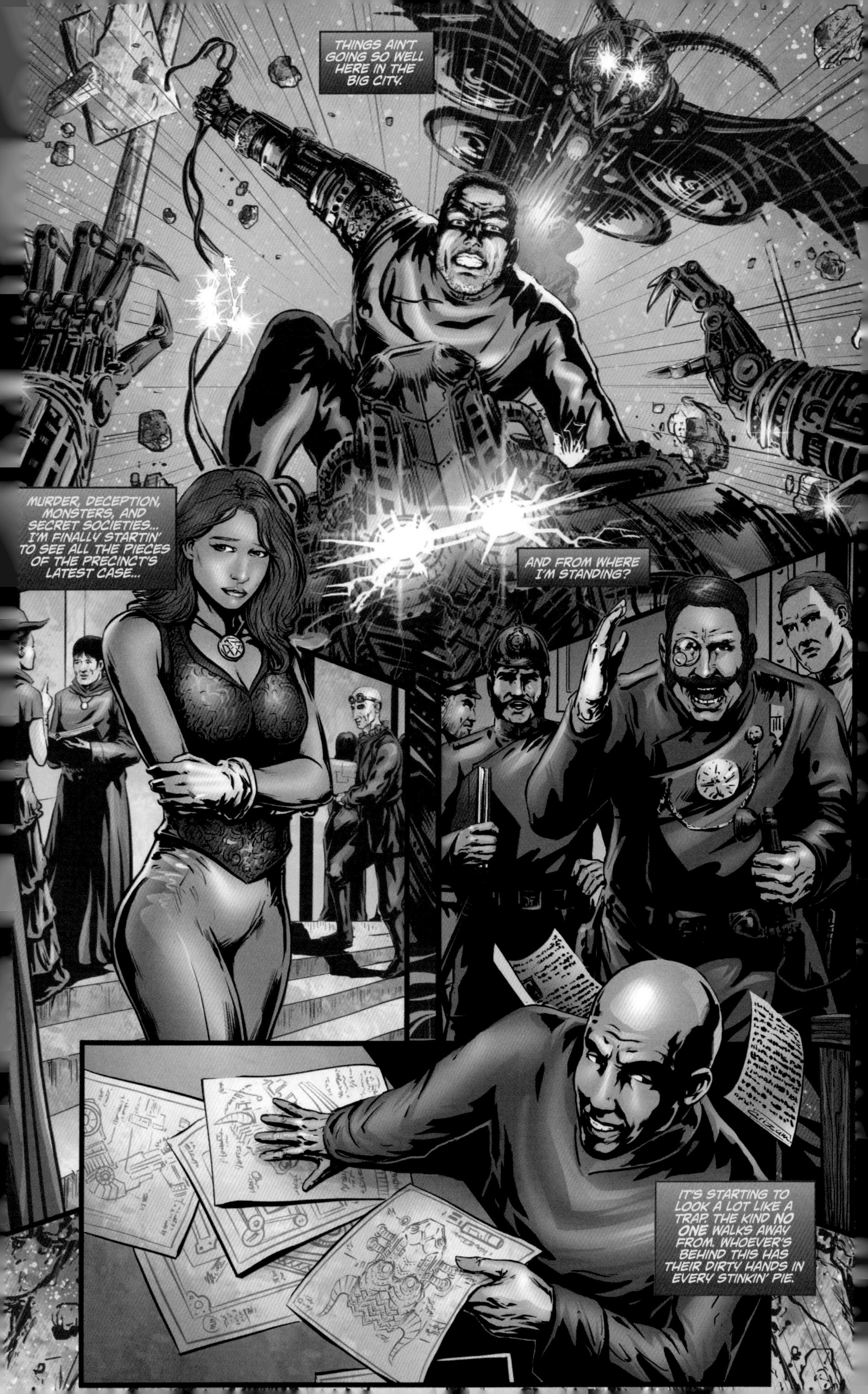
THINGS AIN'T GOING SO WELL HERE IN THE BIG CITY.
MURDER, DECEPTION, MONSTERS, AND SECRET SOCIETIES... I'M FINALLY STARTIN' TO SEE ALL THE PIECES OF THE PRECINCT'S LATEST CASE...
AND FROM WHERE I'M STANDING?
IT'S STARTING TO LOOK A LOT LIKE A TRAP. THE KIND NO ONE WALKS AWAY FROM. WHOEVER'S BEHIND THIS HAS THEIR DIRTY HANDS IN EVERY STINKIN' PIE.

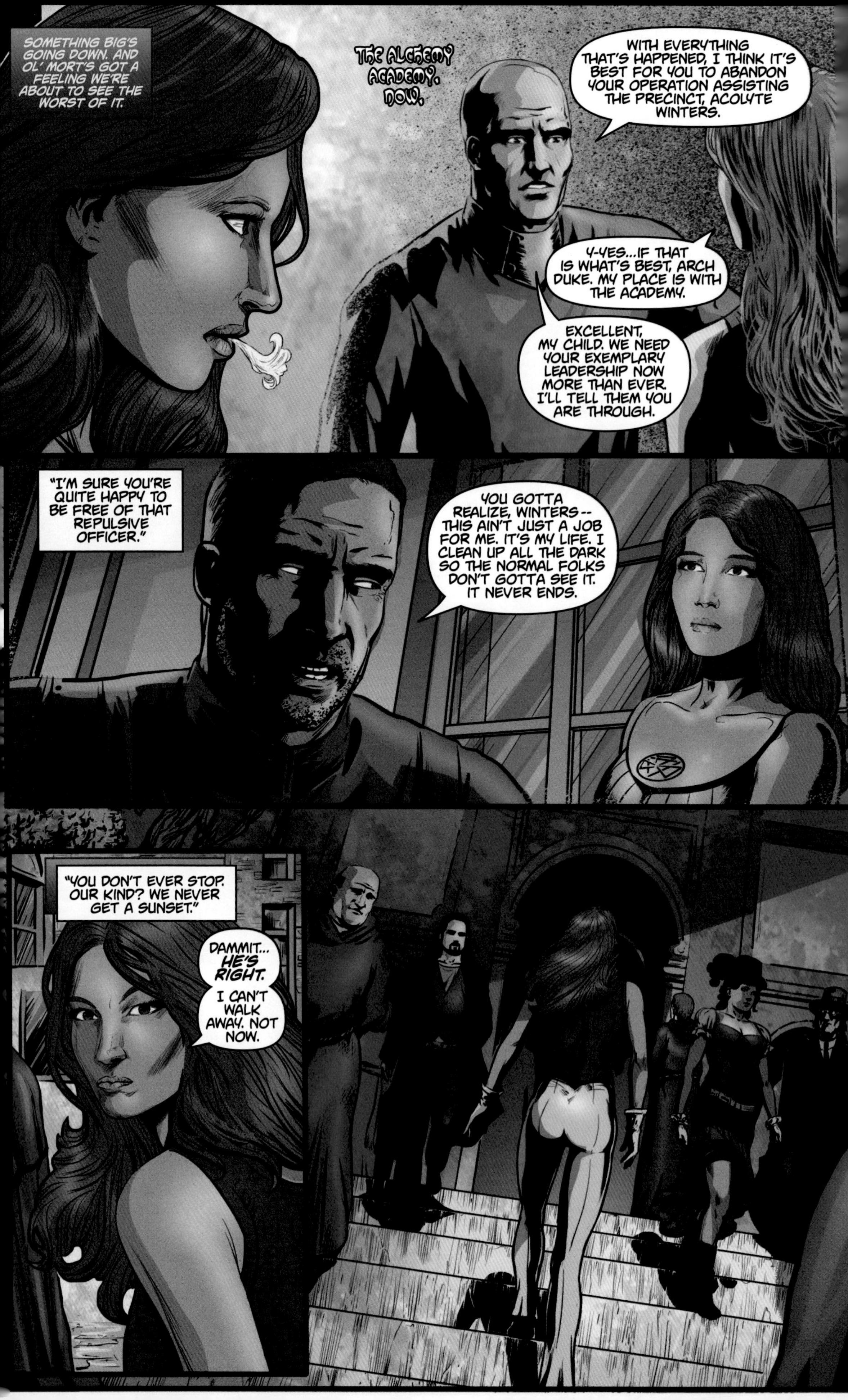
SOMETHING BIG'S GOING DOWN. AND OL' MORT'S GOT A FEELING WE'RE ABOUT TO SEE THE WORST OF IT.
THE ALCHEMY ACADEMY. NOW.
WITH EVERYTHING THAT'S HAPPENED, I THINK IT'S BEST FOR YOU TO ABANDON YOUR OPERATION ASSISTING THE PRECINCT, ACOLYTE WINTERS.
Y-YES...IF THAT IS WHAT'S BEST, ARCH DUKE. MY PLACE IS WITH THE ACADEMY.
EXCELLENT, MY CHILD. WE NEED YOUR EXEMPLARY LEADERSHIP NOW MORE THAN EVER. I'LL TELL THEM YOU ARE THROUGH.
"I'M SURE YOU'RE QUITE HAPPY TO BE FREE OF THAT REPULSIVE OFFICER."
YOU GOTTA REALIZE, WINTERS-- THIS AIN'T JUST A JOB FOR ME. IT'S MY LIFE. I CLEAN UP ALL THE DARK SO THE NORMAL FOLKS DON'T GOTTA SEE IT. IT NEVER ENDS.
"YOU DON'T EVER STOP. OUR KIND? WE NEVER GET A SUNSET."
DAMMIT... HE'S RIGHT.
I CAN'T WALK AWAY. NOT NOW.

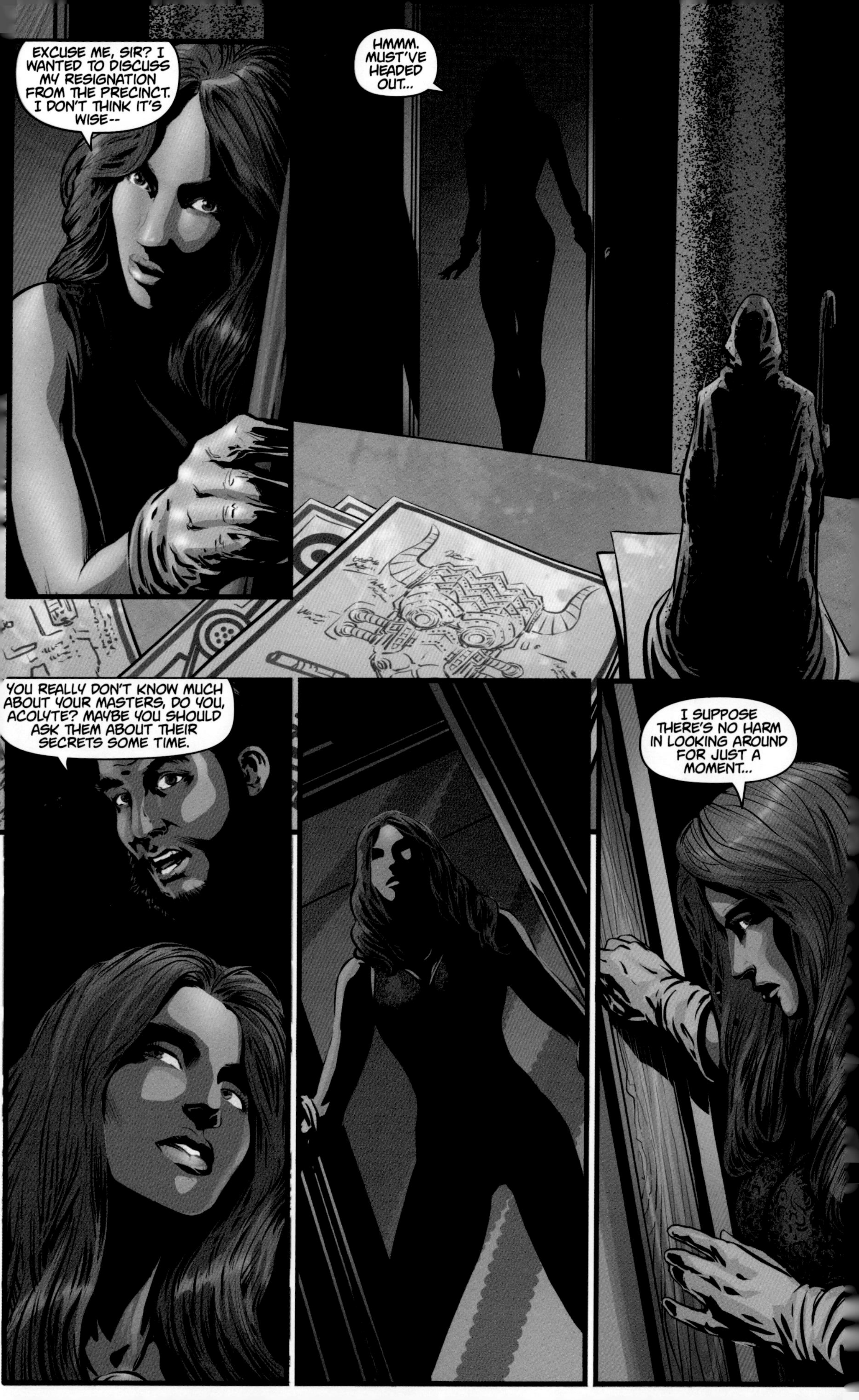
EXCUSE ME, SIR? I WANTED TO DISCUSS MY RESIGNATION FROM THE PRECINCT. I DON'T THINK IT'S WISE--
HMMM. MUST'VE HEADED OUT...
YOU REALLY DON'T KNOW MUCH ABOUT YOUR MASTERS, DO YOU, ACOLYTE? MAYBE YOU SHOULD ASK THEM ABOUT THEIR SECRETS SOME TIME.
I SUPPOSE THERE'S NO HARM IN LOOKING AROUND FOR JUST A MOMENT...

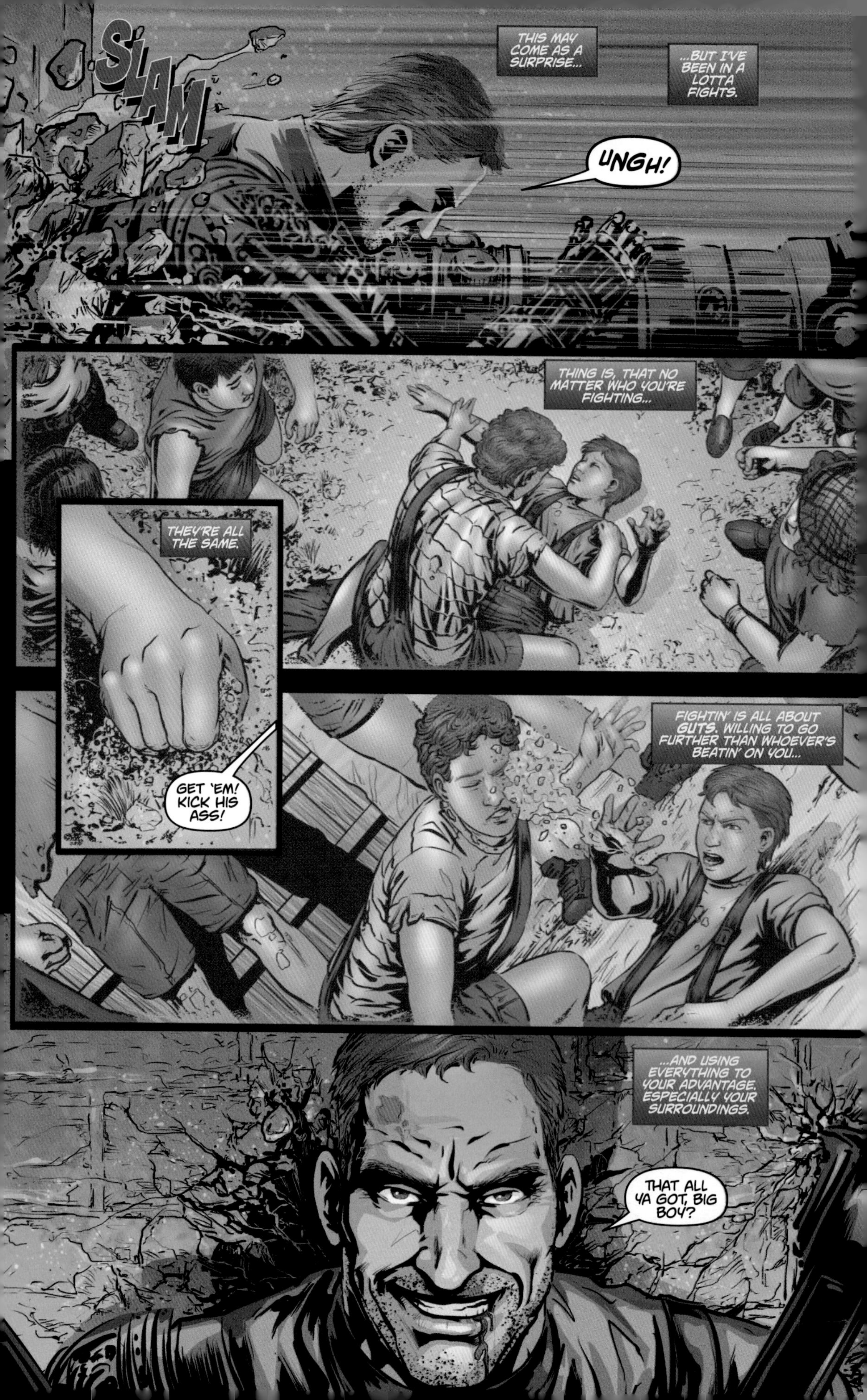
SLAM
THIS MAY COME AS A SURPRISE...
...BUT I'VE BEEN IN A LOTTA FIGHTS.
UNGH!
THING IS, THAT NO MATTER WHO YOU'RE FIGHTING...
THEY'RE ALL THE SAME.
GET 'EM! KICK HIS ASS!
FIGHTIN' IS ALL ABOUT GUTS. WILLING TO GO FURTHER THAN WHOEVER'S BEATIN' ON YOU...
...AND USING EVERYTHING TO YOUR ADVANTAGE. ESPECIALLY YOUR SURROUNDINGS.
THAT ALL YA GOT, BIG BOY?

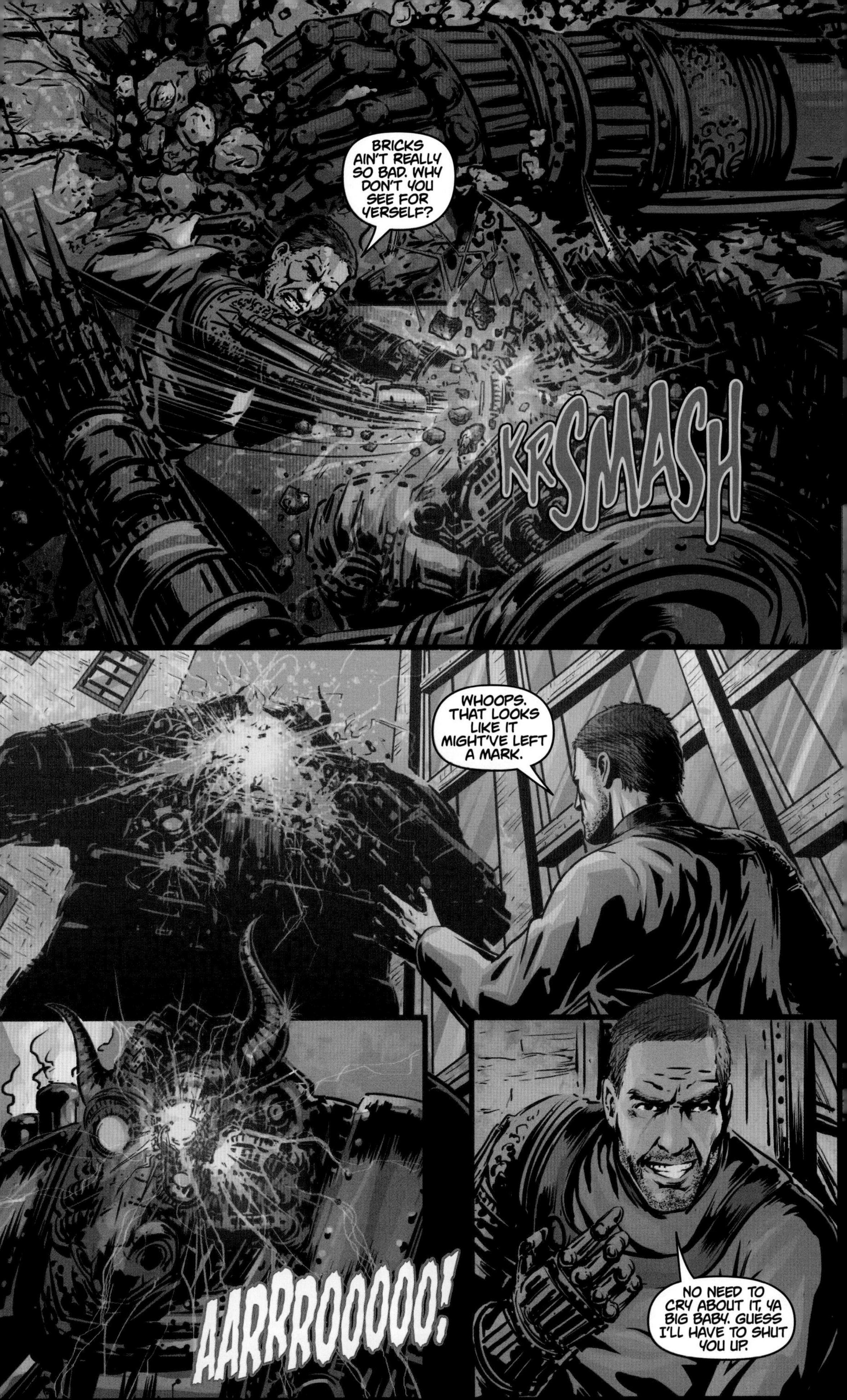
BRICKS AIN'T REALLY SO BAD. WHY DON'T YOU SEE FOR YERSELF?
KRSMASH
WHOOPS. THAT LOOKS LIKE IT MIGHT'VE LEFT A MARK.
AARRROOOOO!
NO NEED TO CRY ABOUT IT, YA BIG BABY. GUESS I'LL HAVE TO SHUT YOU UP.

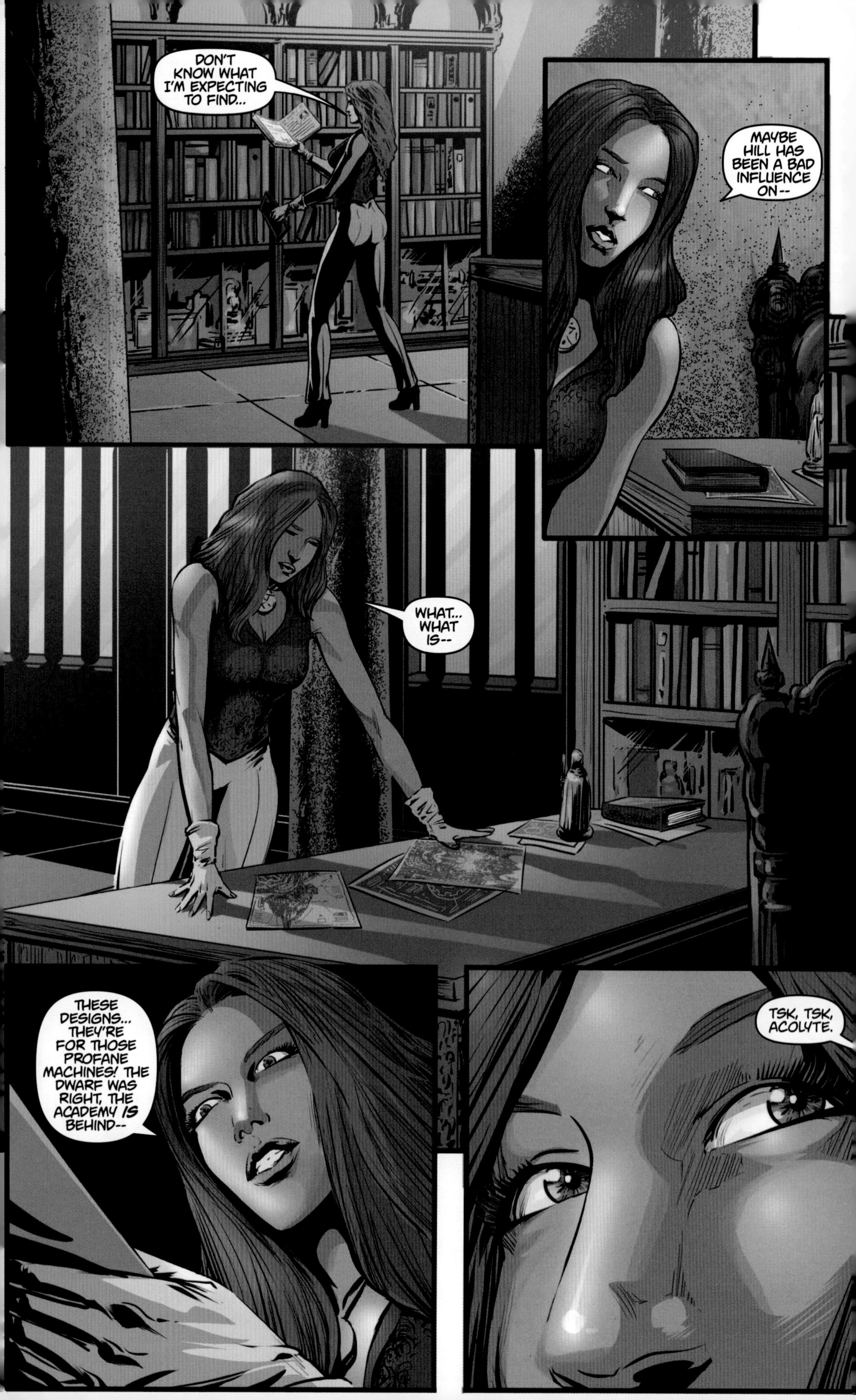
DON'T KNOW WHAT I'M EXPECTING TO FIND...
MAYBE HILL HAS BEEN A BAD INFLUENCE ON--
WHAT... WHAT IS--
THESE DESIGNS... THEY'RE FOR THOSE PROFANE MACHINES! THE DWARF WAS RIGHT, THE ACADEMY *IS* BEHIND--
TSK, TSK, ACOLYTE.

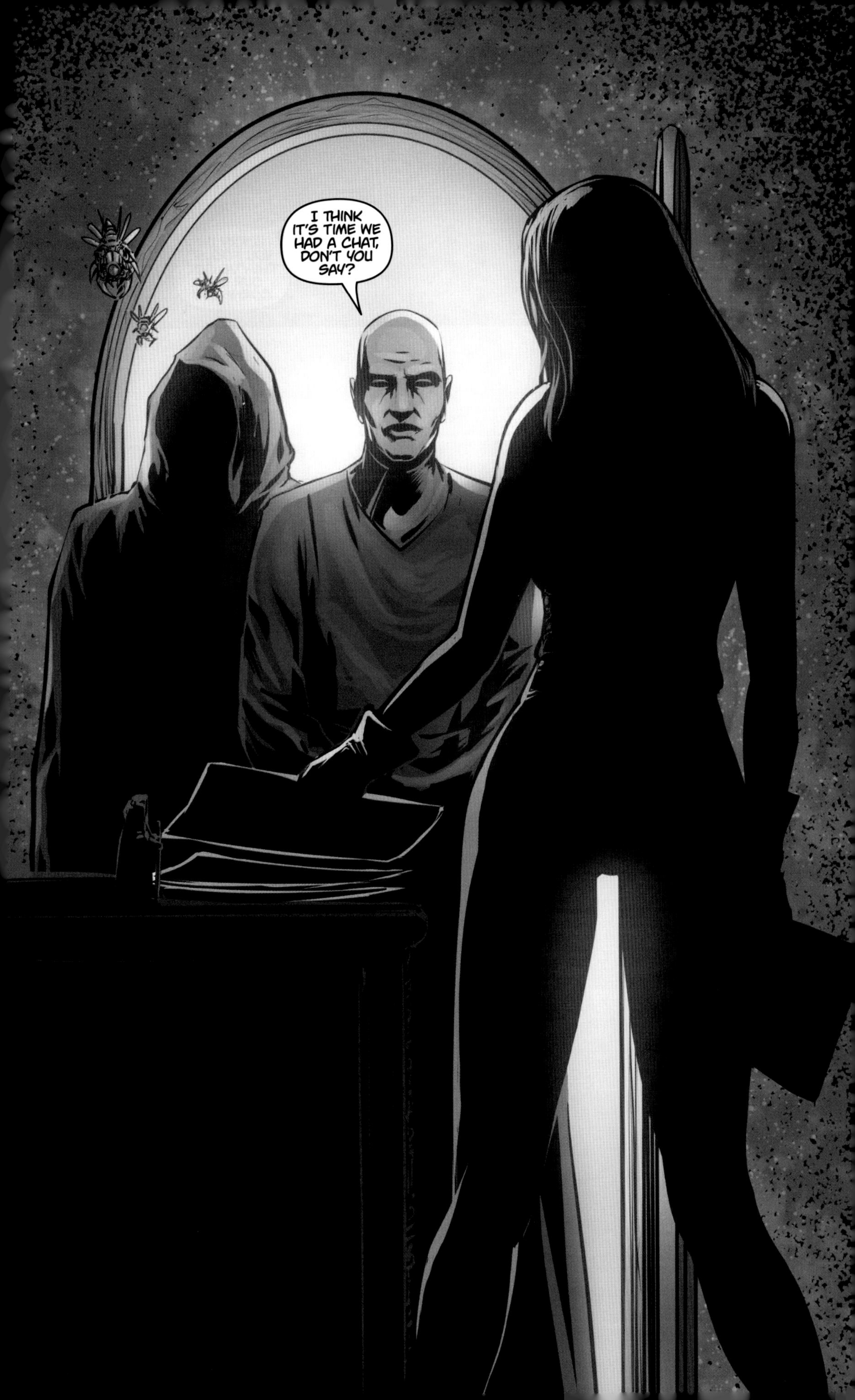
I THINK IT'S TIME WE HAD A CHAT, DON'T YOU SAY?

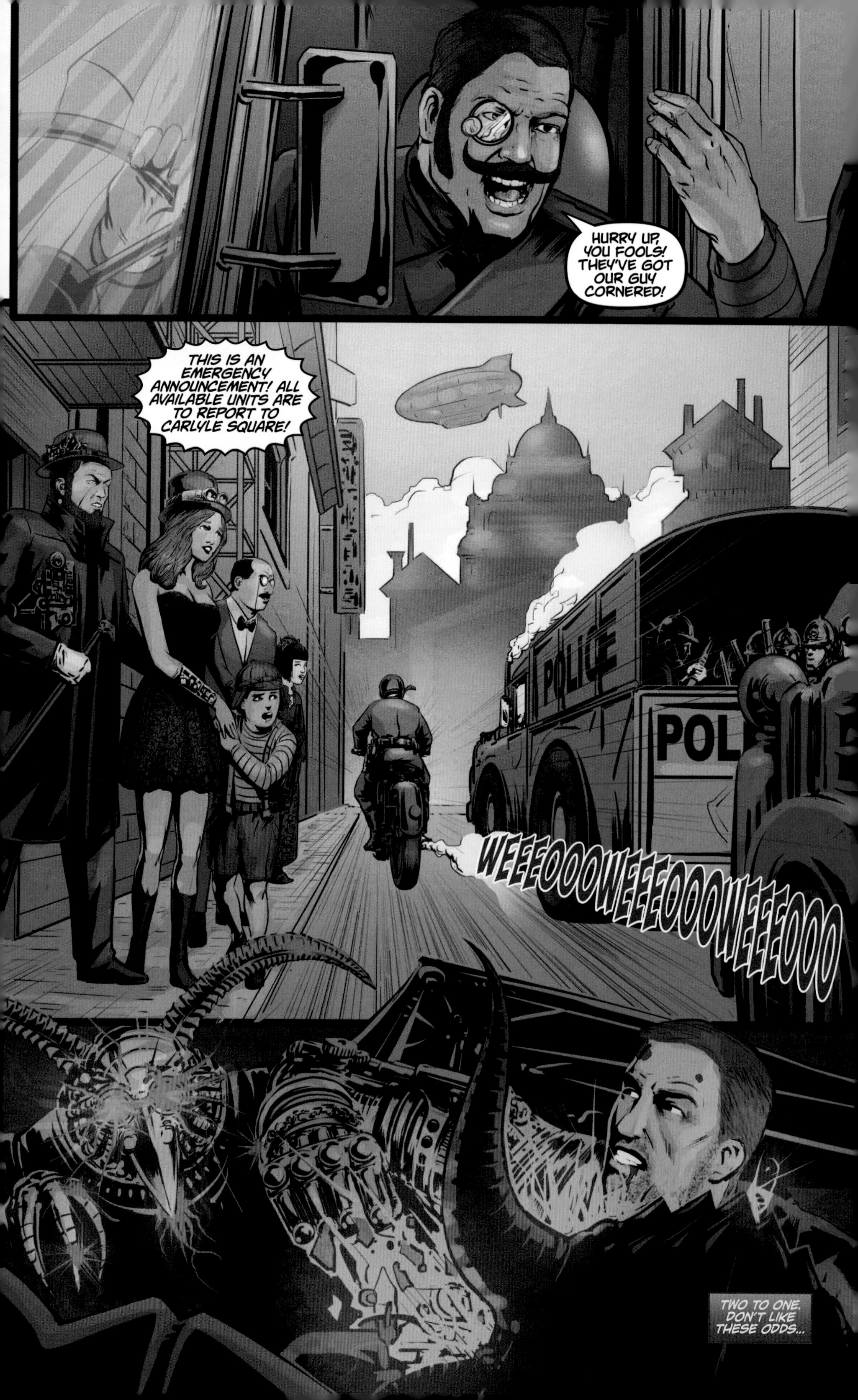
HURRY UP, YOU FOOLS! THEY'VE GOT OUR GUY CORNERED!
THIS IS AN EMERGENCY ANNOUNCEMENT! ALL AVAILABLE UNITS ARE TO REPORT TO CARLYLE SQUARE!
POLICE
POL
WEEEOOOWEEEOOOWEEEOOO
TWO TO ONE. DON'T LIKE THESE ODDS...

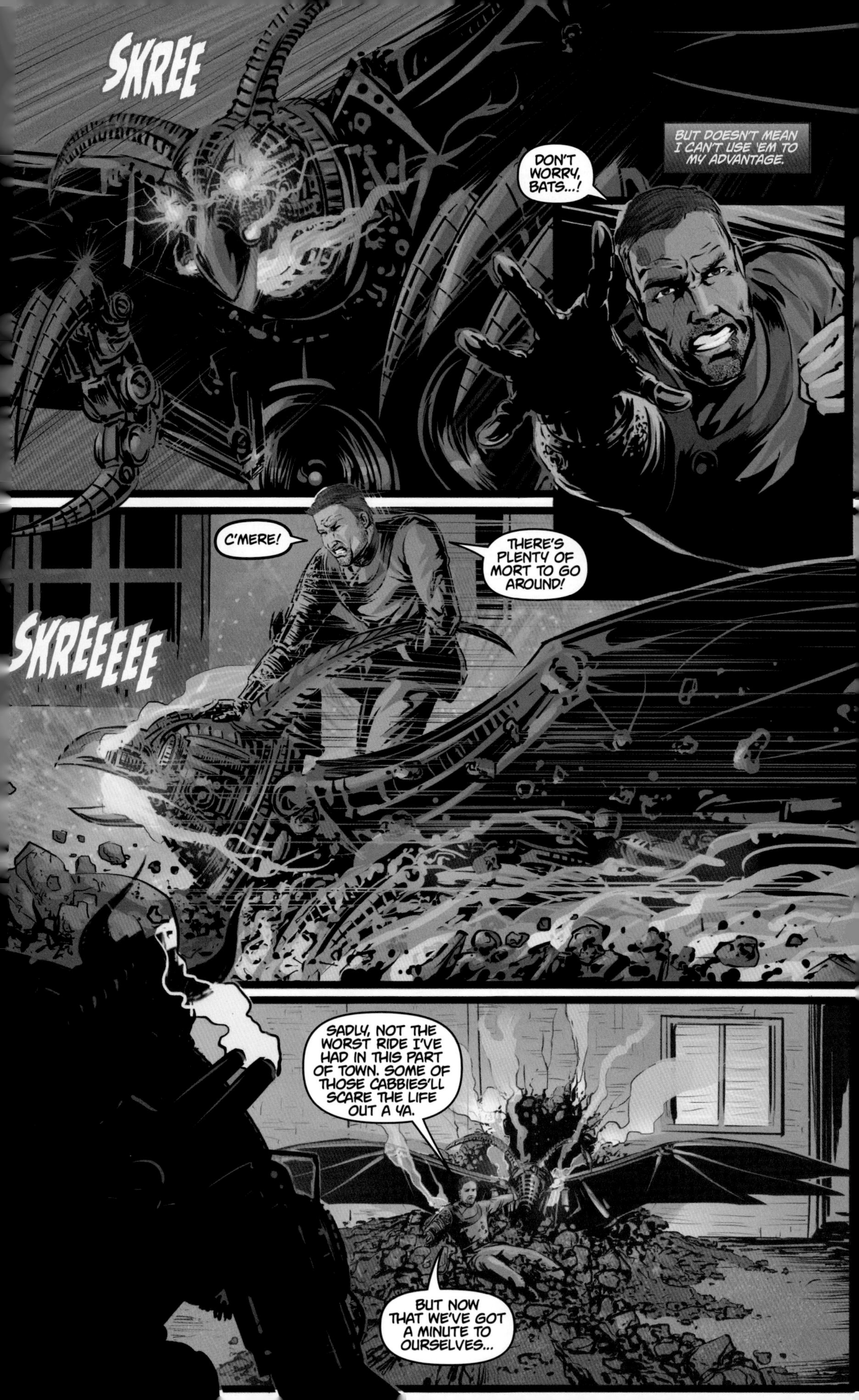
SKREE
BUT DOESN'T MEAN I CAN'T USE 'EM TO MY ADVANTAGE.
DON'T WORRY, BATS...!
C'MERE!
THERE'S PLENTY OF MORT TO GO AROUND!
SKREEEEE
SADLY, NOT THE WORST RIDE I'VE HAD IN THIS PART OF TOWN. SOME OF THOSE CABBIES'LL SCARE THE LIFE OUT A YA.
BUT NOW THAT WE'VE GOT A MINUTE TO OURSELVES...

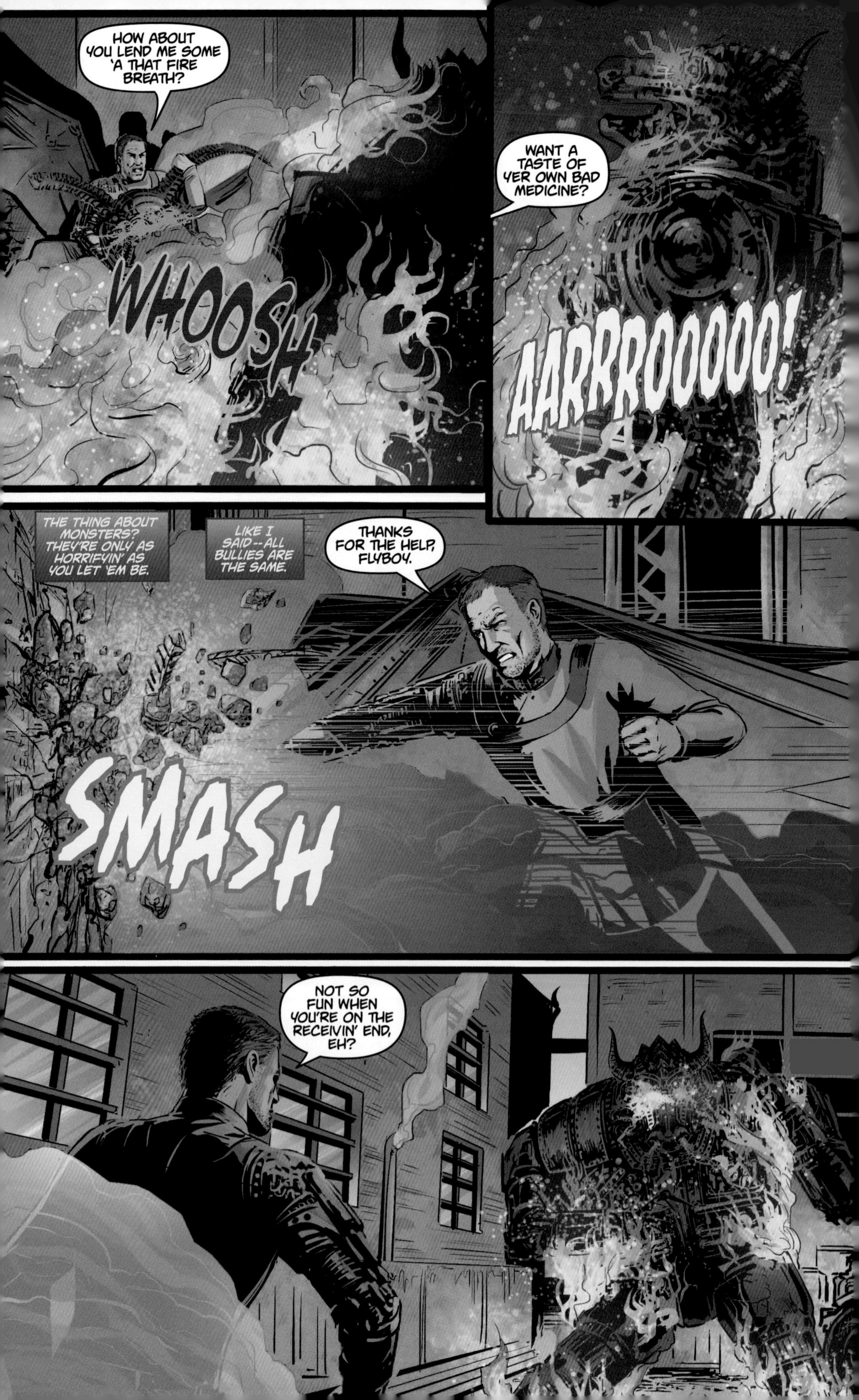
HOW ABOUT YOU LEND ME SOME 'A THAT FIRE BREATH?
WHOOSH
WANT A TASTE OF YER OWN BAD MEDICINE?
AARRROOOOO!
THE THING ABOUT MONSTERS? THEY'RE ONLY AS HORRIFYIN' AS YOU LET 'EM BE.
LIKE I SAID--ALL BULLIES ARE THE SAME.
THANKS FOR THE HELP, FLYBOY.
SMASH
NOT SO FUN WHEN YOU'RE ON THE RECEIVIN' END, EH?

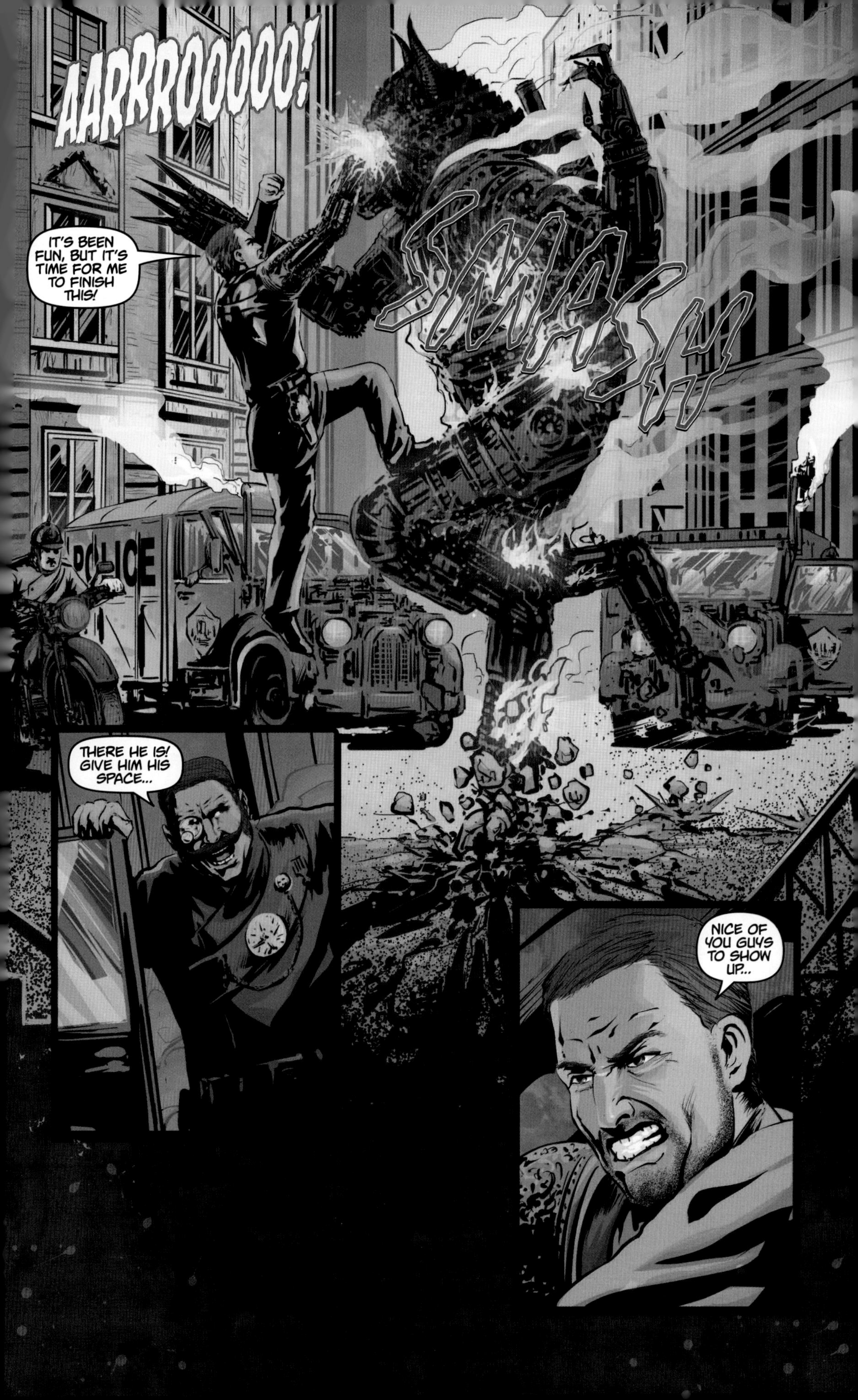
AARRROOOOO!
IT'S BEEN FUN, BUT IT'S TIME FOR ME TO FINISH THIS!
SMASH
POLICE
THERE HE IS! GIVE HIM HIS SPACE...
NICE OF YOU GUYS TO SHOW UP...

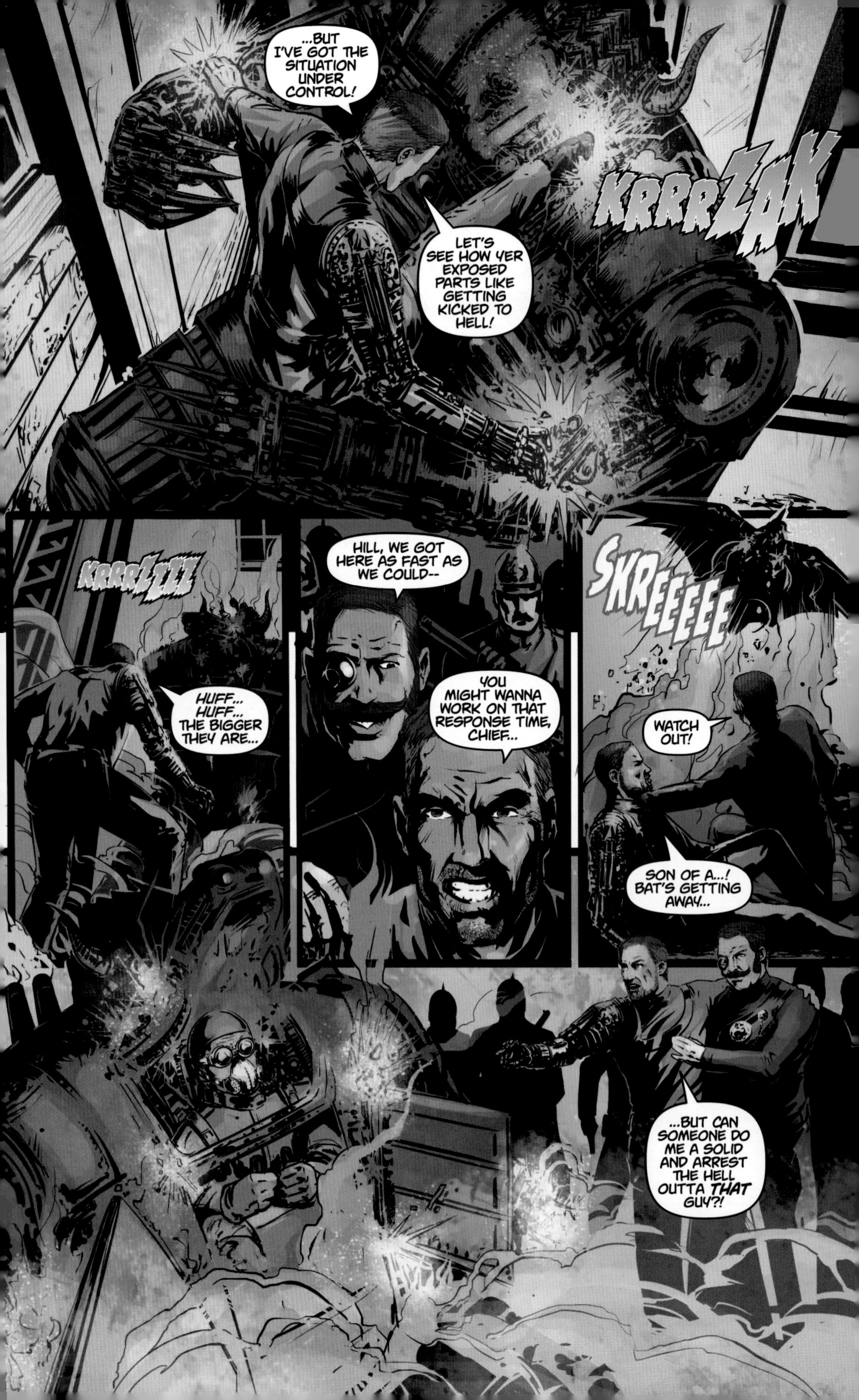
...BUT I'VE GOT THE SITUATION UNDER CONTROL!
KRRRZAK
LET'S SEE HOW YER EXPOSED PARTS LIKE GETTING KICKED TO HELL!
KRRRZZZZ
HUFF... HUFF... THE BIGGER THEY ARE...
HILL, WE GOT HERE AS FAST AS WE COULD--
YOU MIGHT WANNA WORK ON THAT RESPONSE TIME, CHIEF...
SKREEEEEE
WATCH OUT!
SON OF A...! BAT'S GETTING AWAY...
...BUT CAN SOMEONE DO ME A SOLID AND ARREST THE HELL OUTTA *THAT* GUY?!

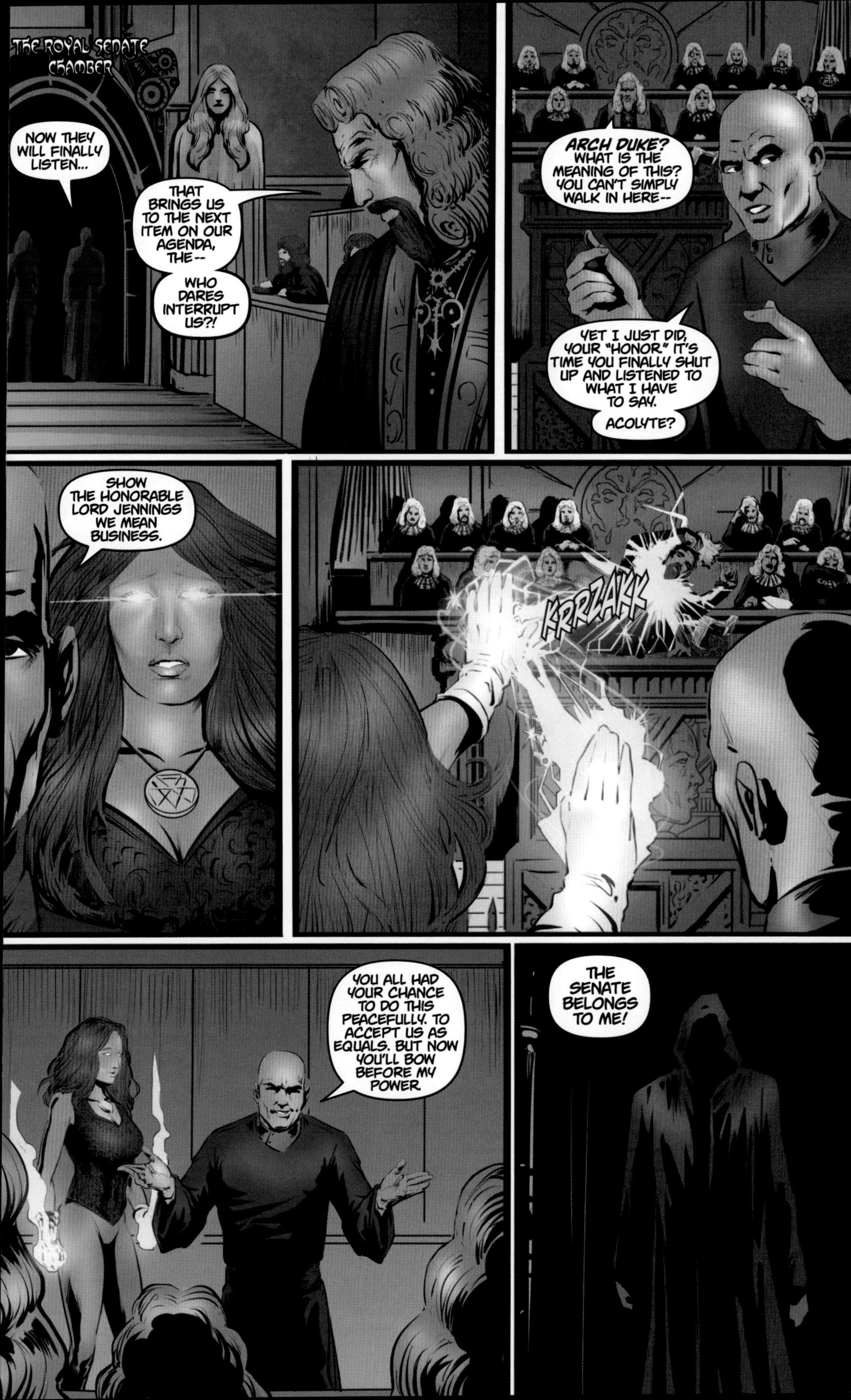
THE ROYAL SENATE CHAMBER
NOW THEY WILL FINALLY LISTEN...
THAT BRINGS US TO THE NEXT ITEM ON OUR AGENDA, THE--
WHO DARES INTERRUPT US?!
ARCH DUKE? WHAT IS THE MEANING OF THIS? YOU CAN'T SIMPLY WALK IN HERE--
YET I JUST DID, YOUR "HONOR." IT'S TIME YOU FINALLY SHUT UP AND LISTENED TO WHAT I HAVE TO SAY.
ACOLYTE?
SHOW THE HONORABLE LORD JENNINGS WE MEAN BUSINESS.
KRRZAKK
YOU ALL HAD YOUR CHANCE TO DO THIS PEACEFULLY. TO ACCEPT US AS EQUALS. BUT NOW YOU'LL BOW BEFORE MY POWER.
THE SENATE BELONGS TO ME!

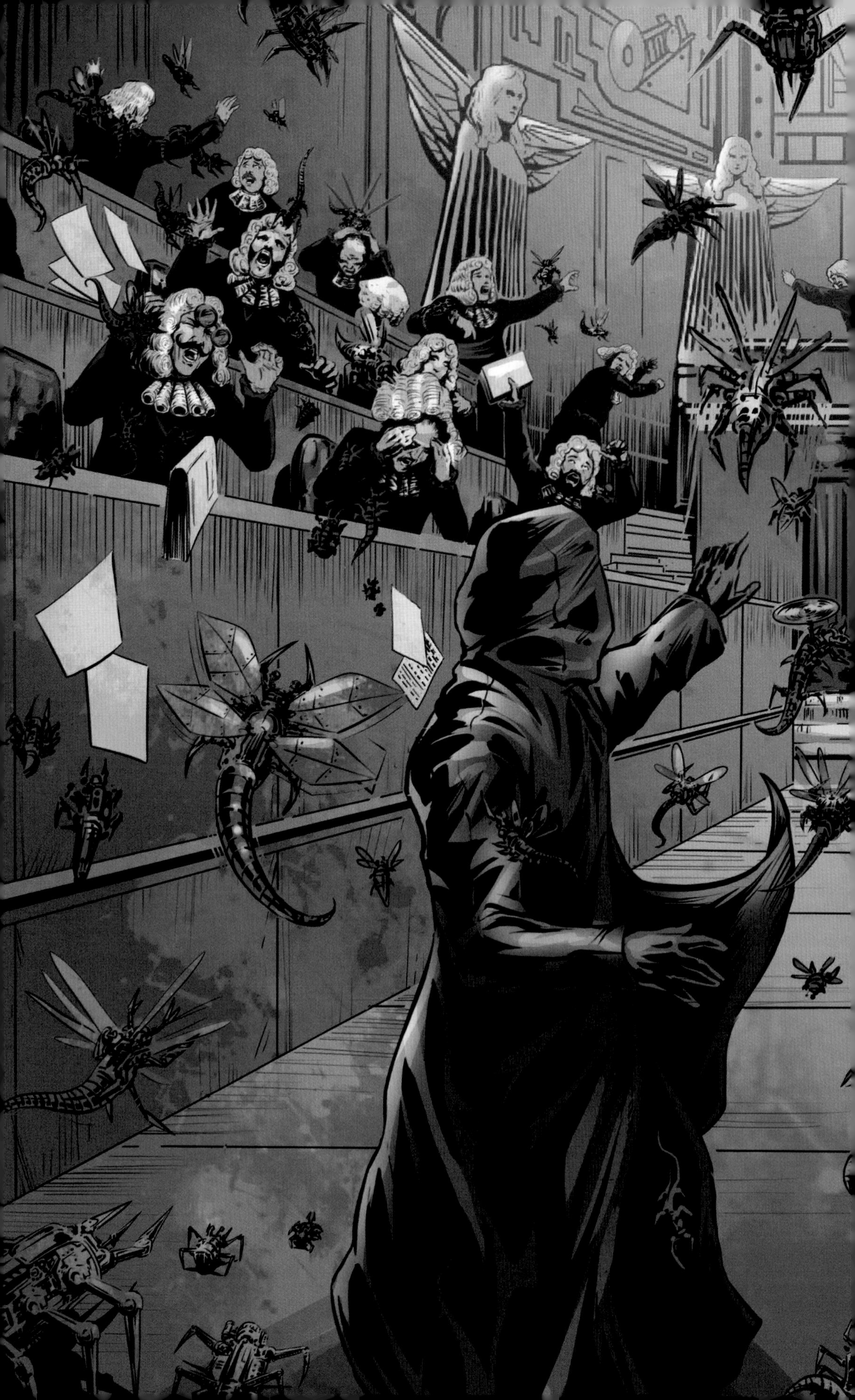

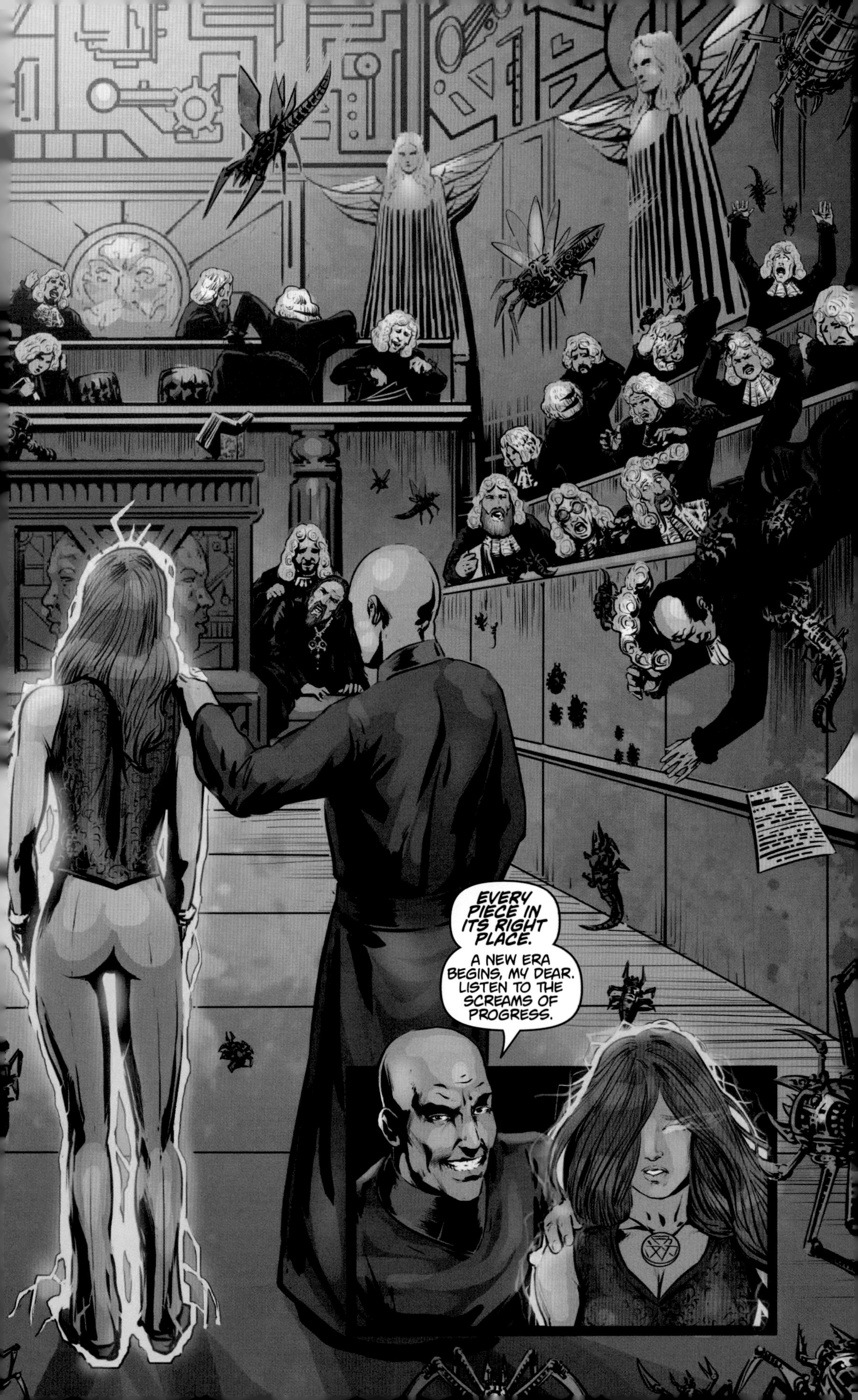
EVERY PIECE IN ITS RIGHT PLACE.
A NEW ERA BEGINS, MY DEAR. LISTEN TO THE SCREAMS OF PROGRESS.

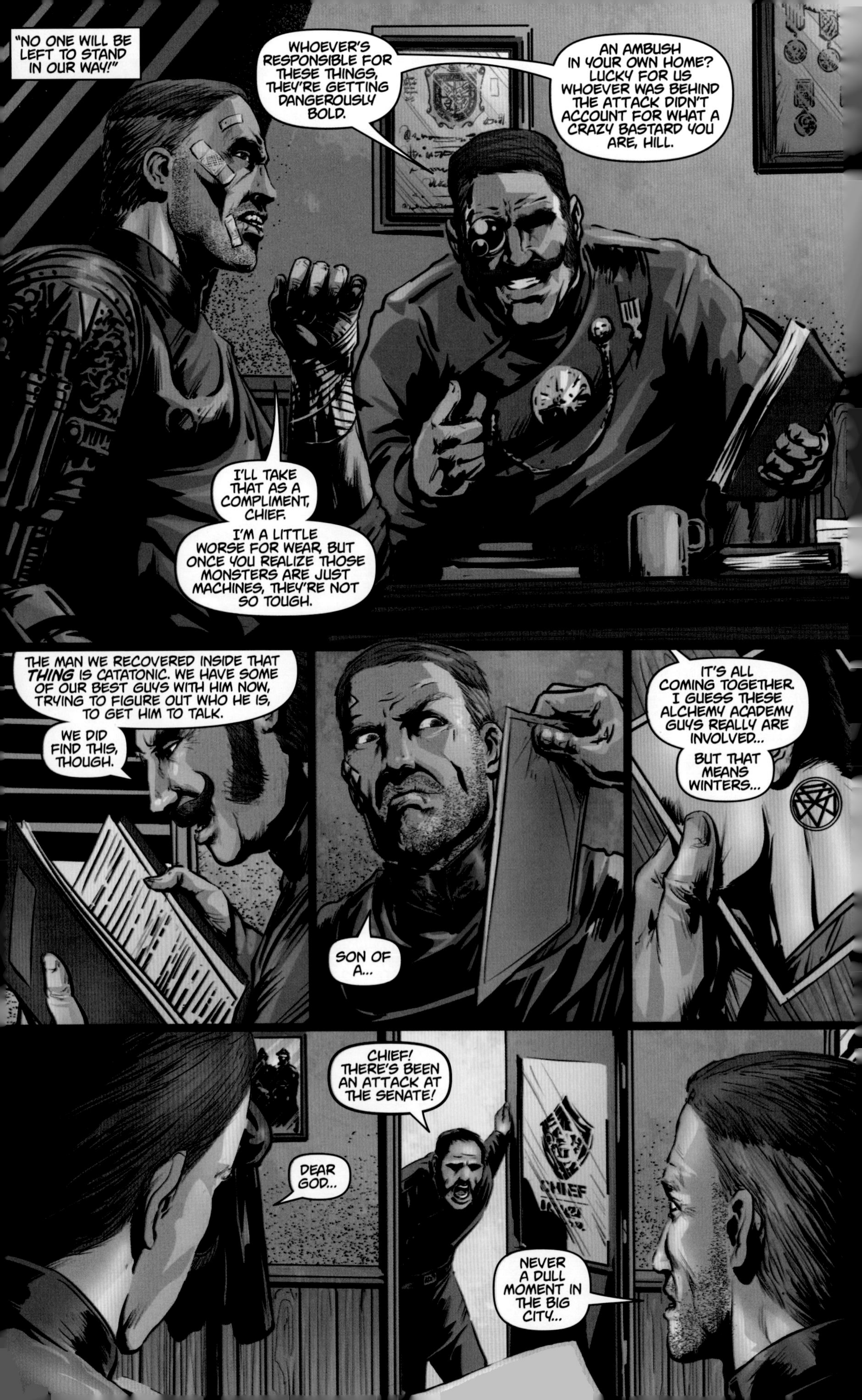
"NO ONE WILL BE LEFT TO STAND IN OUR WAY!"
WHOEVER'S RESPONSIBLE FOR THESE THINGS, THEY'RE GETTING DANGEROUSLY BOLD.
AN AMBUSH IN YOUR OWN HOME? LUCKY FOR US WHOEVER WAS BEHIND THE ATTACK DIDN'T ACCOUNT FOR WHAT A CRAZY BASTARD YOU ARE, HILL.
I'LL TAKE THAT AS A COMPLIMENT, CHIEF.
I'M A LITTLE WORSE FOR WEAR, BUT ONCE YOU REALIZE THOSE MONSTERS ARE JUST MACHINES, THEY'RE NOT SO TOUGH.
THE MAN WE RECOVERED INSIDE THAT *THING* IS CATATONIC. WE HAVE SOME OF OUR BEST GUYS WITH HIM NOW, TRYING TO FIGURE OUT WHO HE IS, TO GET HIM TO TALK.
WE DID FIND THIS, THOUGH.
SON OF A...
IT'S ALL COMING TOGETHER. I GUESS THESE ALCHEMY ACADEMY GUYS REALLY ARE INVOLVED...
BUT THAT MEANS WINTERS...
CHIEF! THERE'S BEEN AN ATTACK AT THE SENATE!
DEAR GOD...
CHIEF
NEVER A DULL MOMENT IN THE BIG CITY...

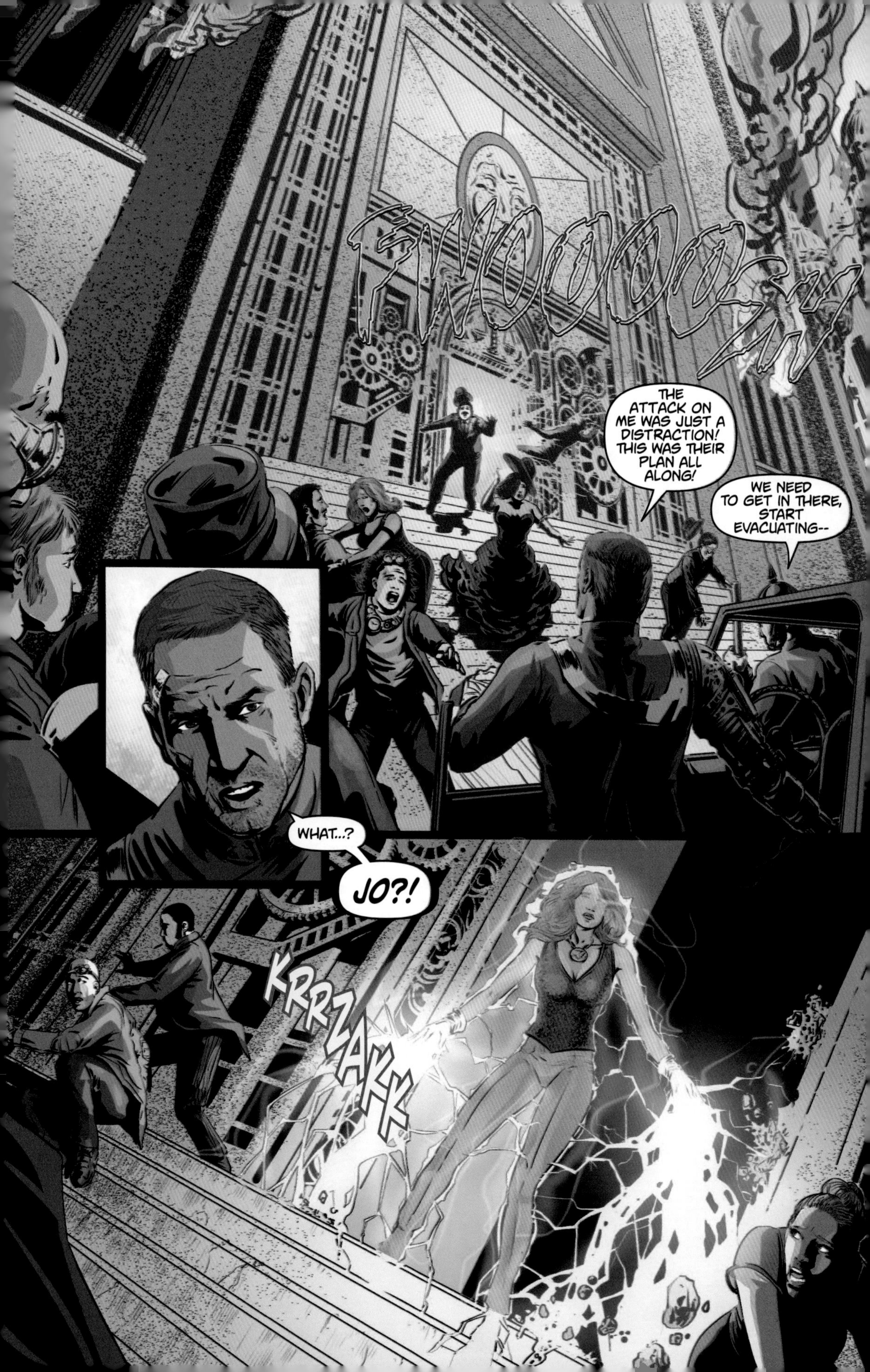
FWOOOOSHH
THE ATTACK ON ME WAS JUST A DISTRACTION! THIS WAS THEIR PLAN ALL ALONG!
WE NEED TO GET IN THERE, START EVACUATING--
WHAT...?
JO?!
KRRZAKK

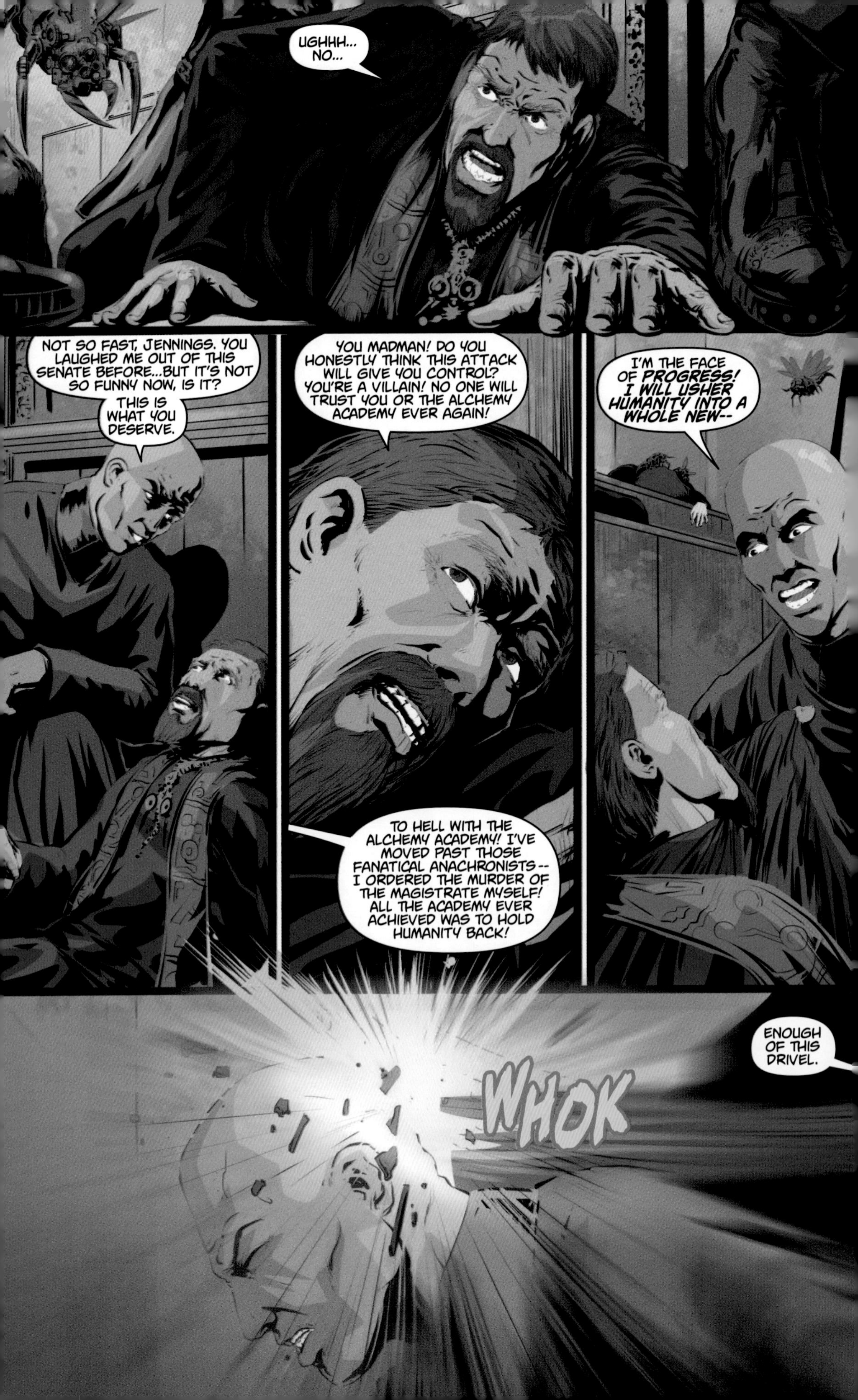
UGHHH... NO...
NOT SO FAST, JENNINGS. YOU LAUGHED ME OUT OF THIS SENATE BEFORE...BUT IT'S NOT SO FUNNY NOW, IS IT?
THIS IS WHAT YOU DESERVE.
YOU MADMAN! DO YOU HONESTLY THINK THIS ATTACK WILL GIVE YOU CONTROL? YOU'RE A VILLAIN! NO ONE WILL TRUST YOU OR THE ALCHEMY ACADEMY EVER AGAIN!
TO HELL WITH THE ALCHEMY ACADEMY! I'VE MOVED PAST THOSE FANATICAL ANACHRONISTS -- I ORDERED THE MURDER OF THE MAGISTRATE MYSELF! ALL THE ACADEMY EVER ACHIEVED WAS TO HOLD HUMANITY BACK!
I'M THE FACE OF PROGRESS! I WILL USHER HUMANITY INTO A WHOLE NEW--
ENOUGH OF THIS DRIVEL.
WHOK

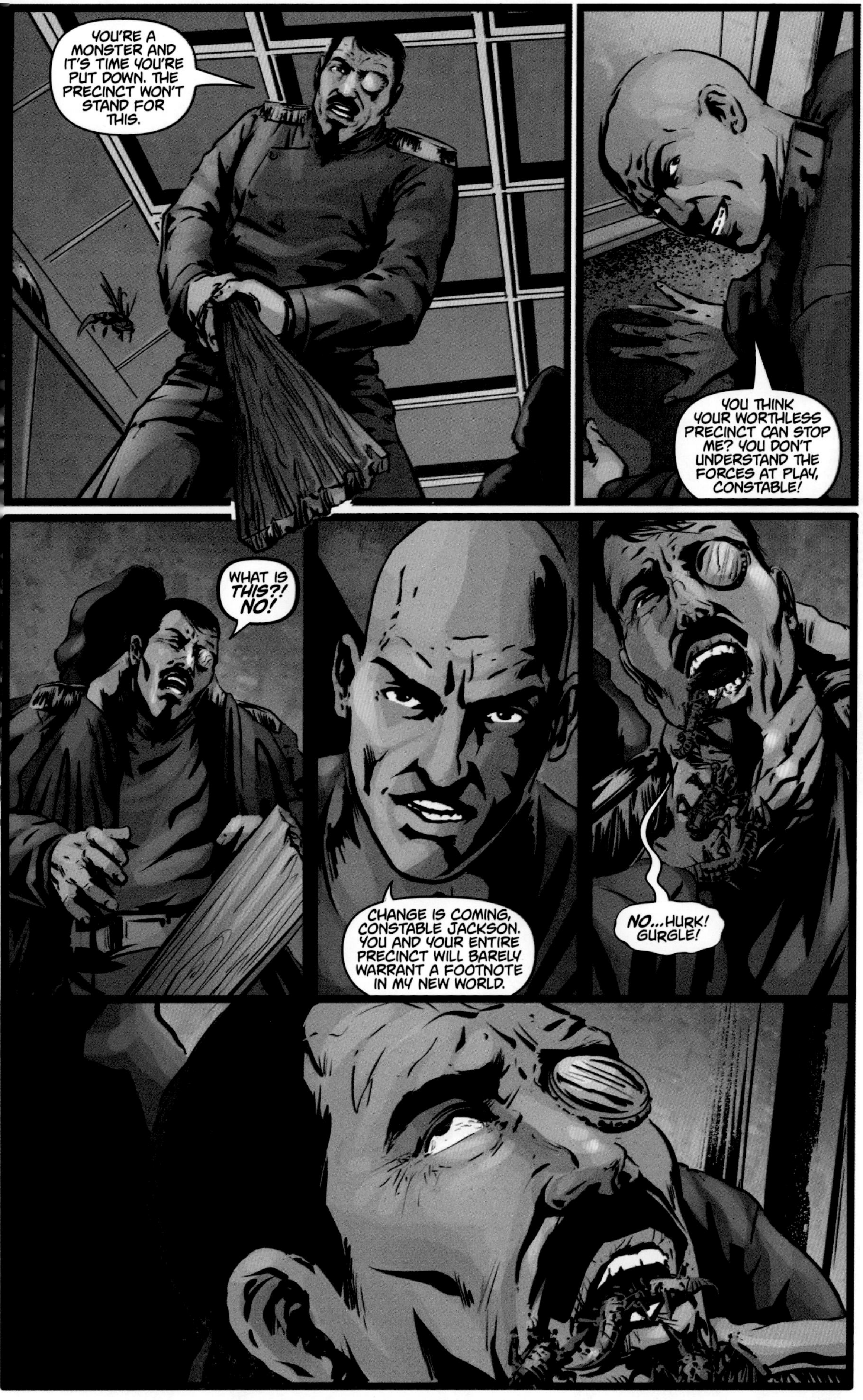
YOU'RE A MONSTER AND IT'S TIME YOU'RE PUT DOWN. THE PRECINCT WON'T STAND FOR THIS.
YOU THINK YOUR WORTHLESS PRECINCT CAN STOP ME? YOU DON'T UNDERSTAND THE FORCES AT PLAY, CONSTABLE!
WHAT IS THIS?! NO!
CHANGE IS COMING, CONSTABLE JACKSON. YOU AND YOUR ENTIRE PRECINCT WILL BARELY WARRANT A FOOTNOTE IN MY NEW WORLD.
NO... HURK! GURGLE!

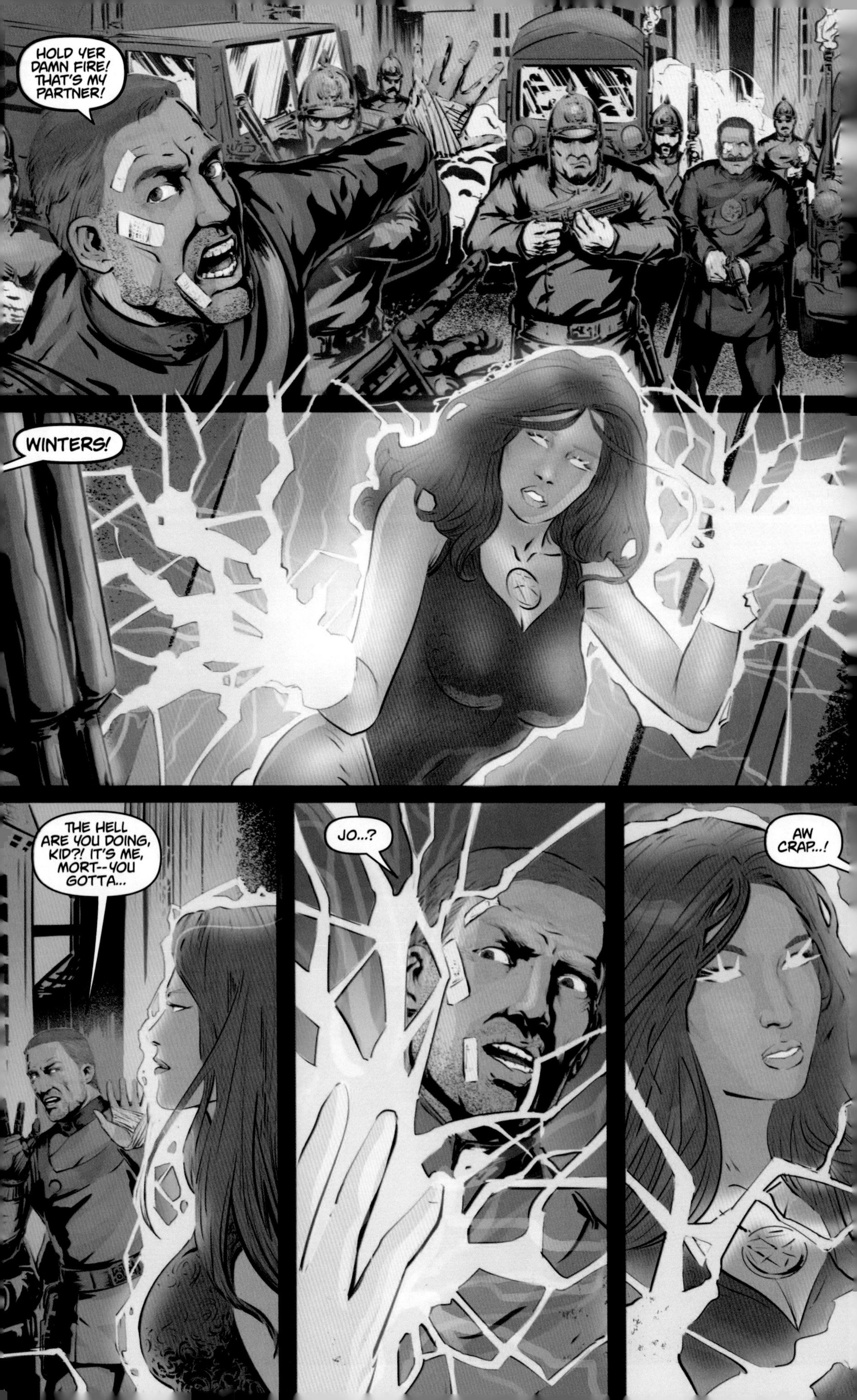
HOLD YER DAMN FIRE! THAT'S MY PARTNER!
WINTERS!
THE HELL ARE YOU DOING, KID?! IT'S ME, MORT--YOU GOTTA...
JO...?
AW CRAP...!

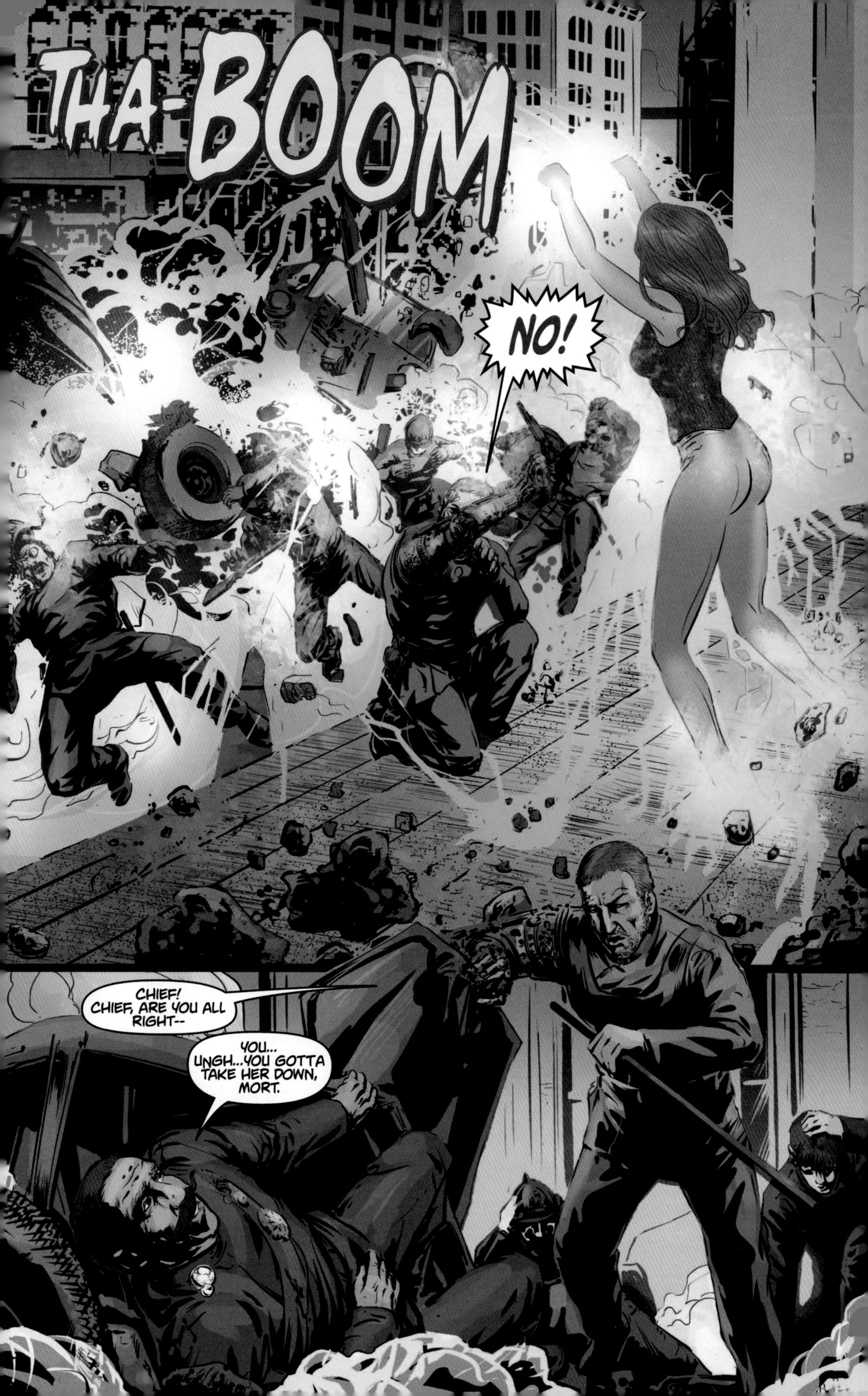
THA-BOOM
NO!
CHIEF! CHIEF, ARE YOU ALL RIGHT--
YOU... UNGH...YOU GOTTA TAKE HER DOWN, MORT.

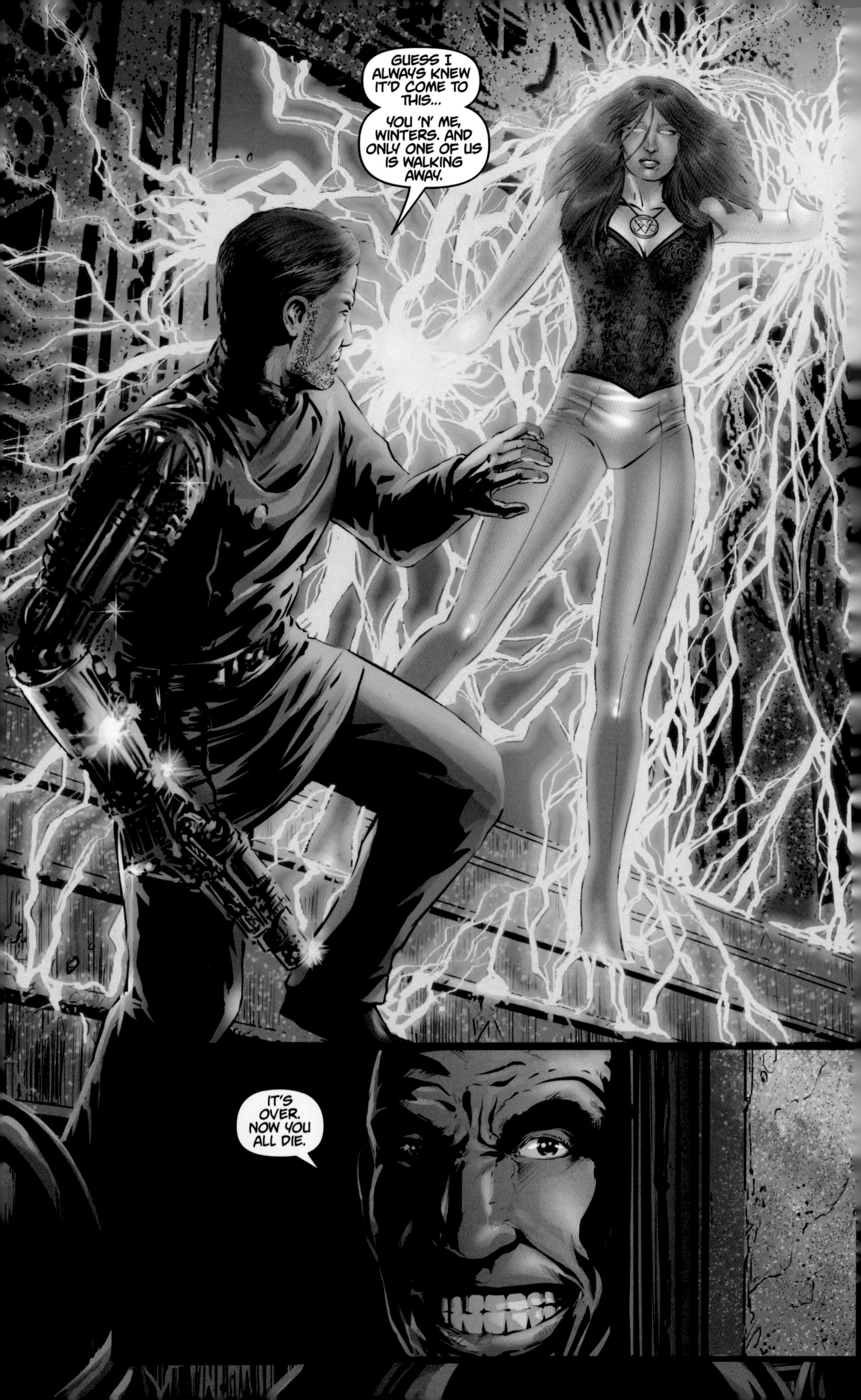
GUESS I ALWAYS KNEW IT'D COME TO THIS...
YOU 'N' ME, WINTERS. AND ONLY ONE OF US IS WALKING AWAY.
IT'S OVER. NOW YOU ALL DIE.

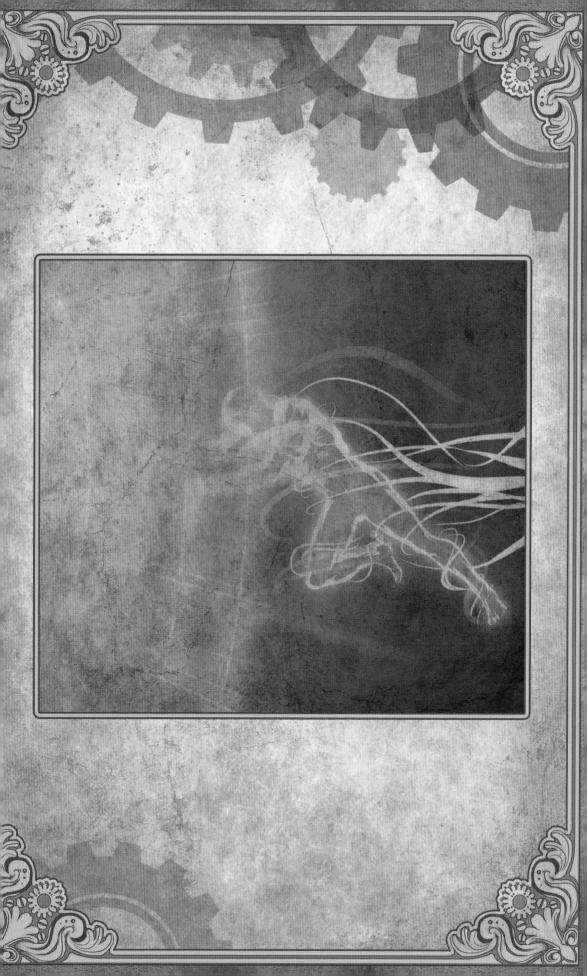

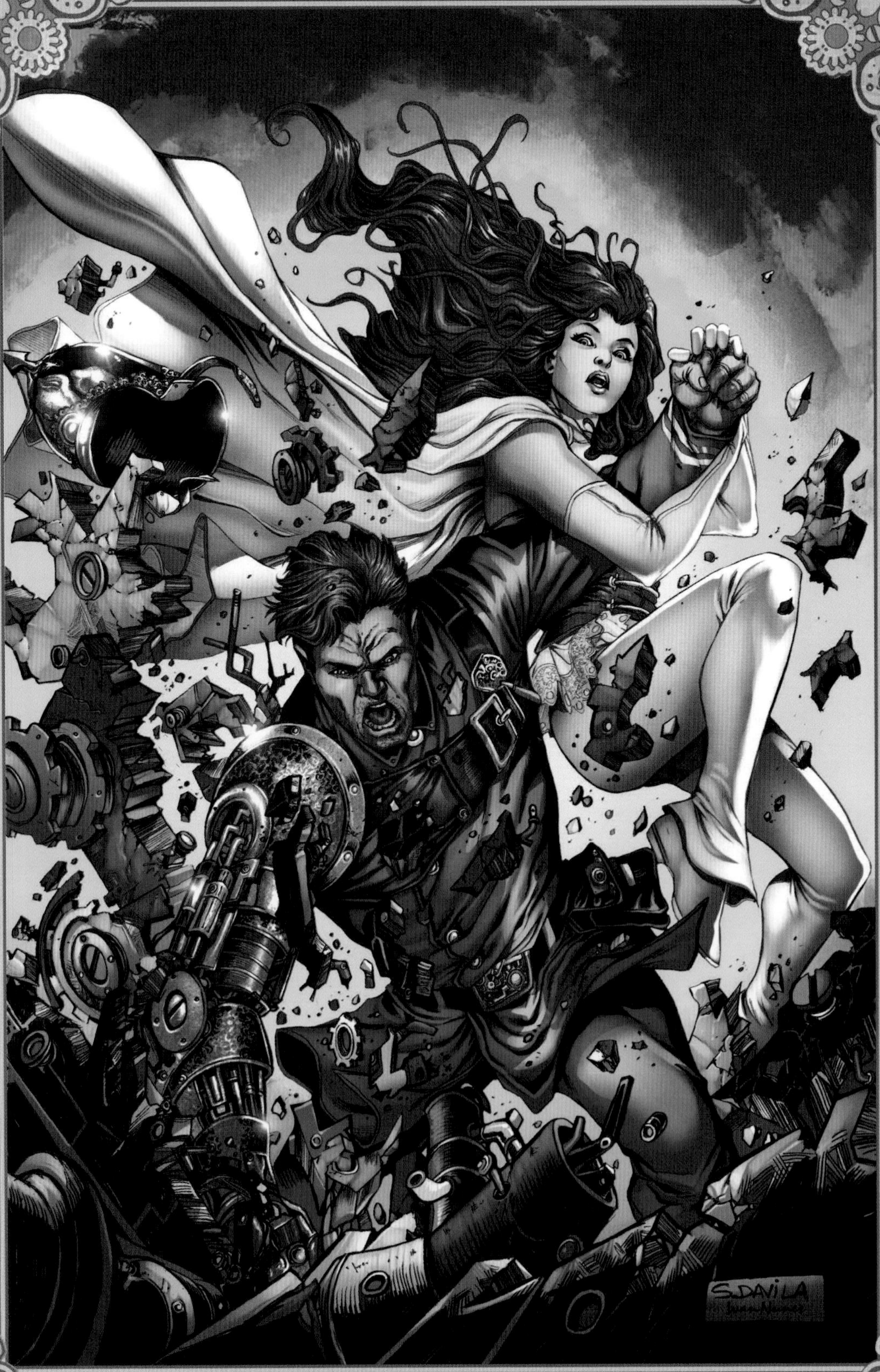
S.DAVILA

ISSUE FIVE

Cover by Sergio Dávila and Ivan Nunes

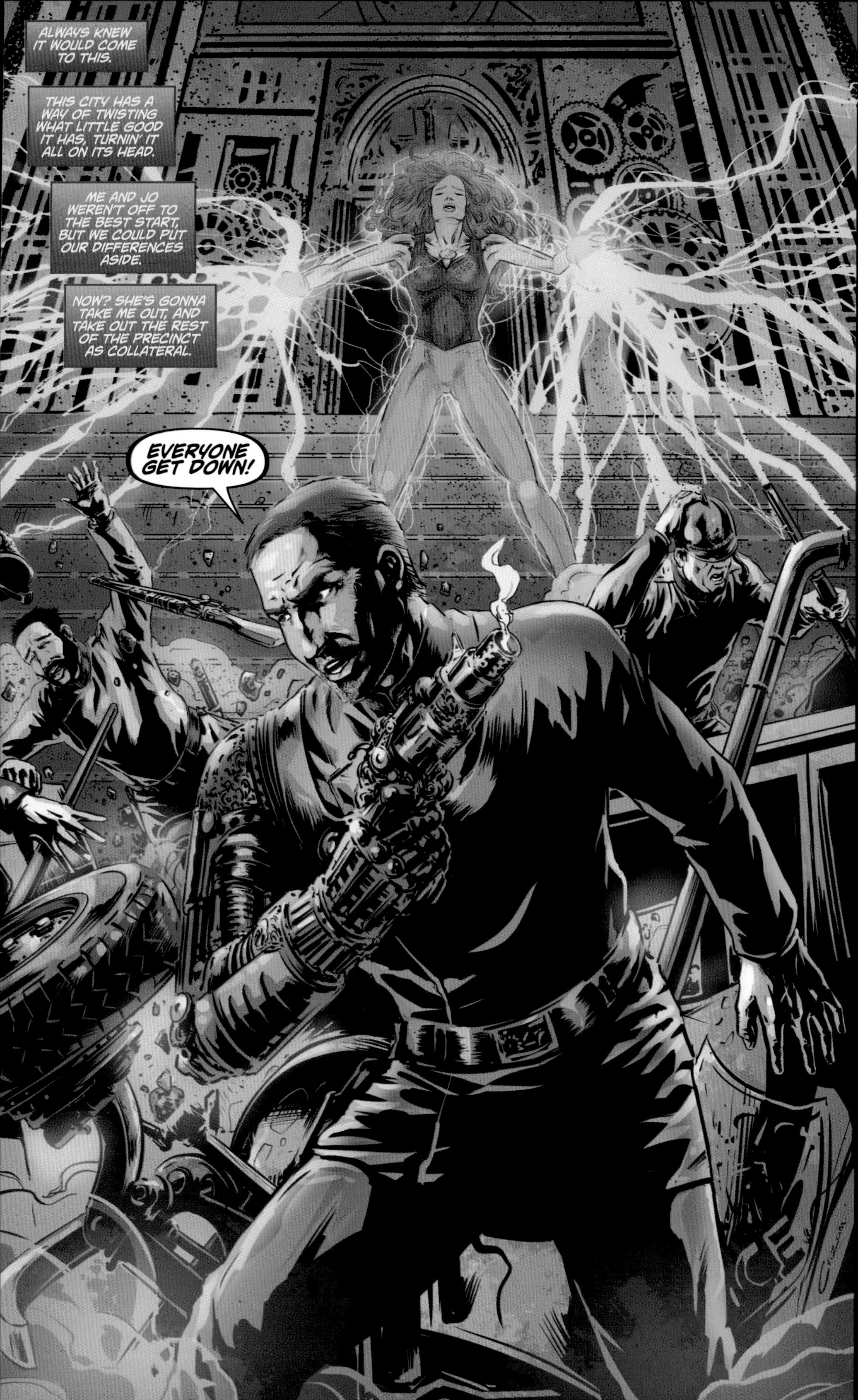
ALWAYS KNEW IT WOULD COME TO THIS.
THIS CITY HAS A WAY OF TWISTING WHAT LITTLE GOOD IT HAS, TURNIN' IT ALL ON ITS HEAD.
ME AND JO WEREN'T OFF TO THE BEST START, BUT WE COULD PUT OUR DIFFERENCES ASIDE.
NOW? SHE'S GONNA TAKE ME OUT, AND TAKE OUT THE REST OF THE PRECINCT AS COLLATERAL.
EVERYONE GET DOWN!

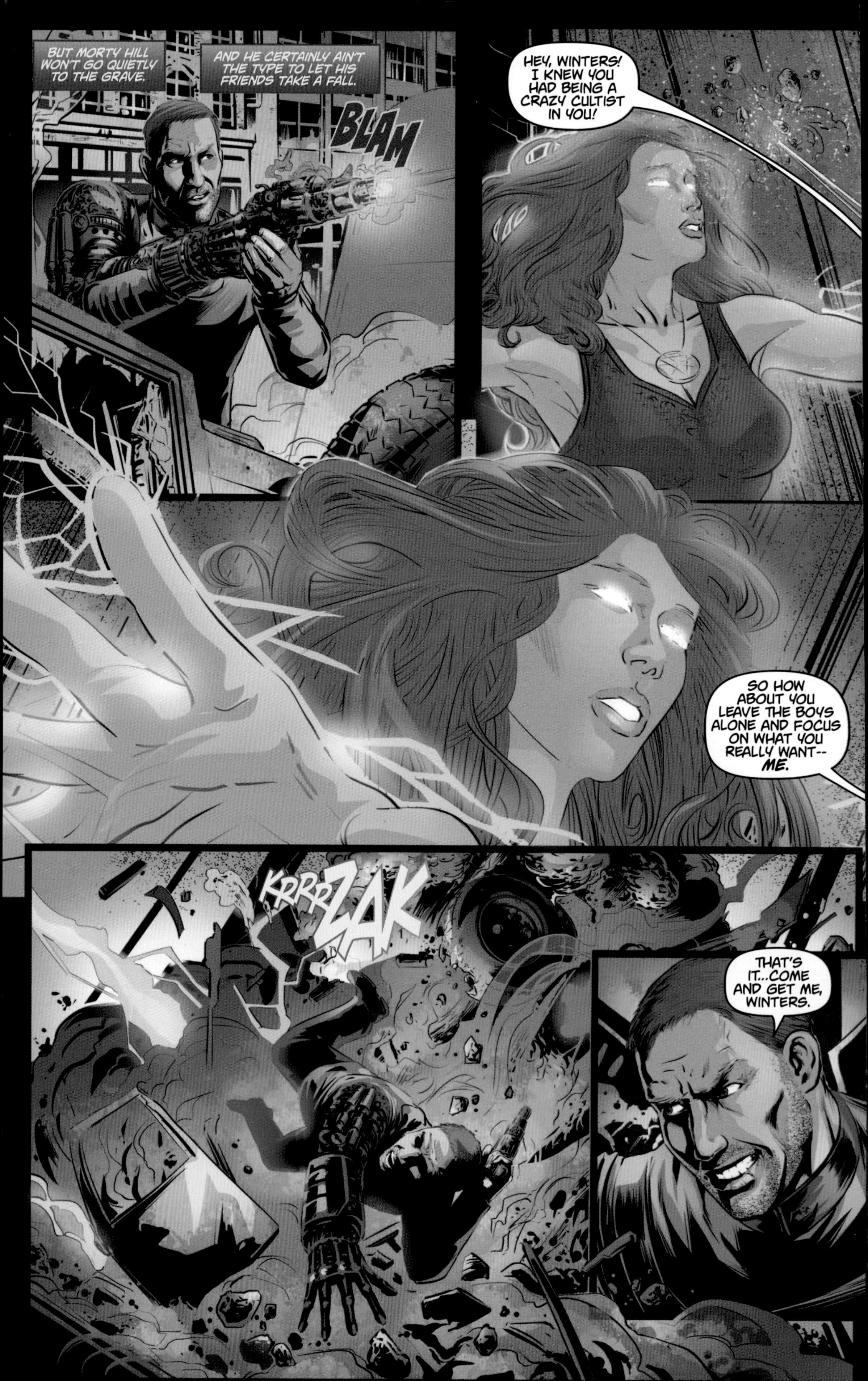
BUT MORTY HILL WON'T GO QUIETLY TO THE GRAVE.
AND HE CERTAINLY AIN'T THE TYPE TO LET HIS FRIENDS TAKE A FALL.
BLAM
HEY, WINTERS! I KNEW YOU HAD BEING A CRAZY CULTIST IN YOU!
SO HOW ABOUT YOU LEAVE THE BOYS ALONE AND FOCUS ON WHAT YOU REALLY WANT-- ME.
KRRRZAK
THAT'S IT...COME AND GET ME, WINTERS.

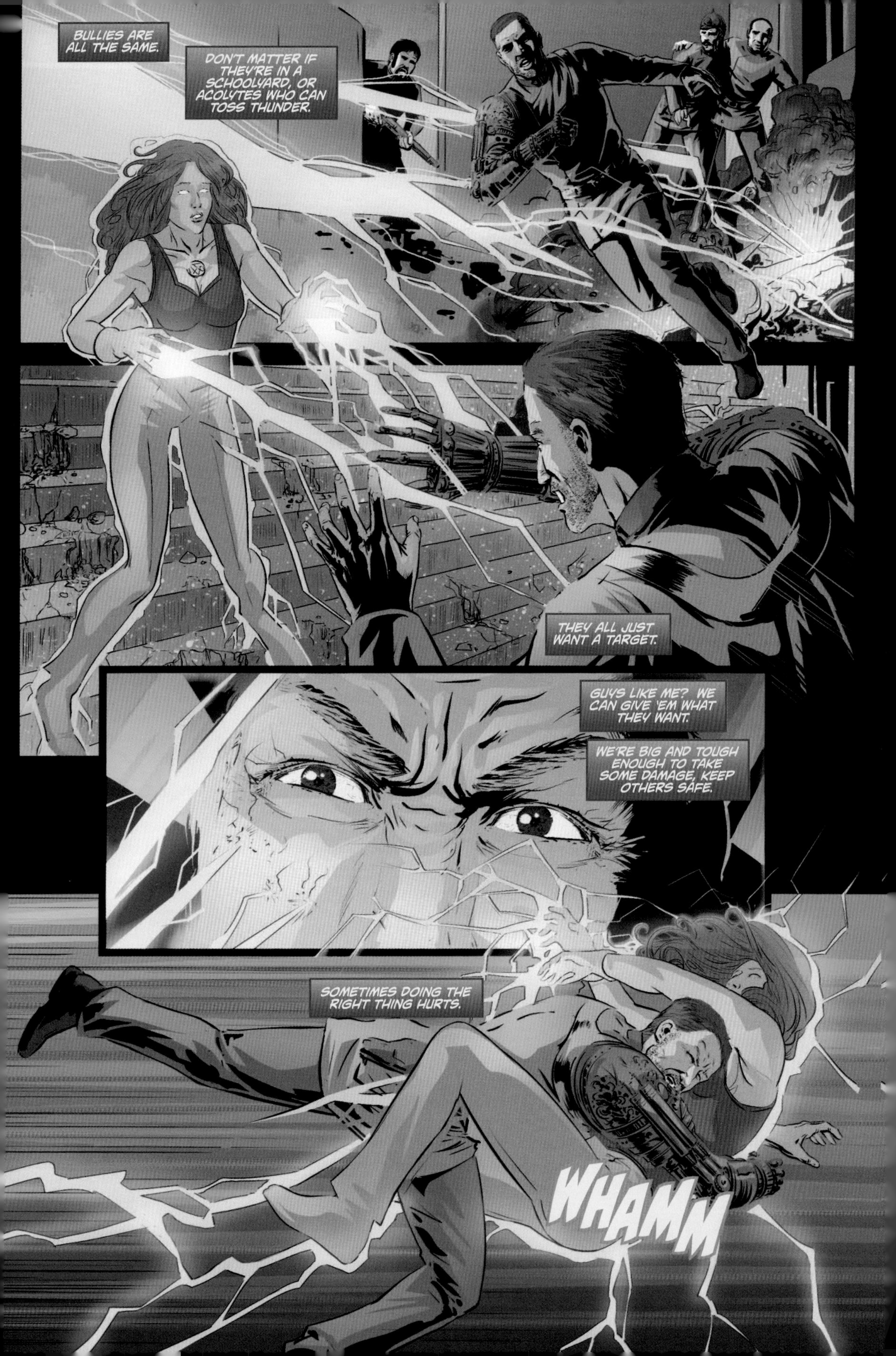
BULLIES ARE ALL THE SAME.
DON'T MATTER IF THEY'RE IN A SCHOOLYARD, OR ACOLYTES WHO CAN TOSS THUNDER.
THEY ALL JUST WANT A TARGET.
GUYS LIKE ME? WE CAN GIVE 'EM WHAT THEY WANT.
WE'RE BIG AND TOUGH ENOUGH TO TAKE SOME DAMAGE, KEEP OTHERS SAFE.
SOMETIMES DOING THE RIGHT THING HURTS.
WHAMM

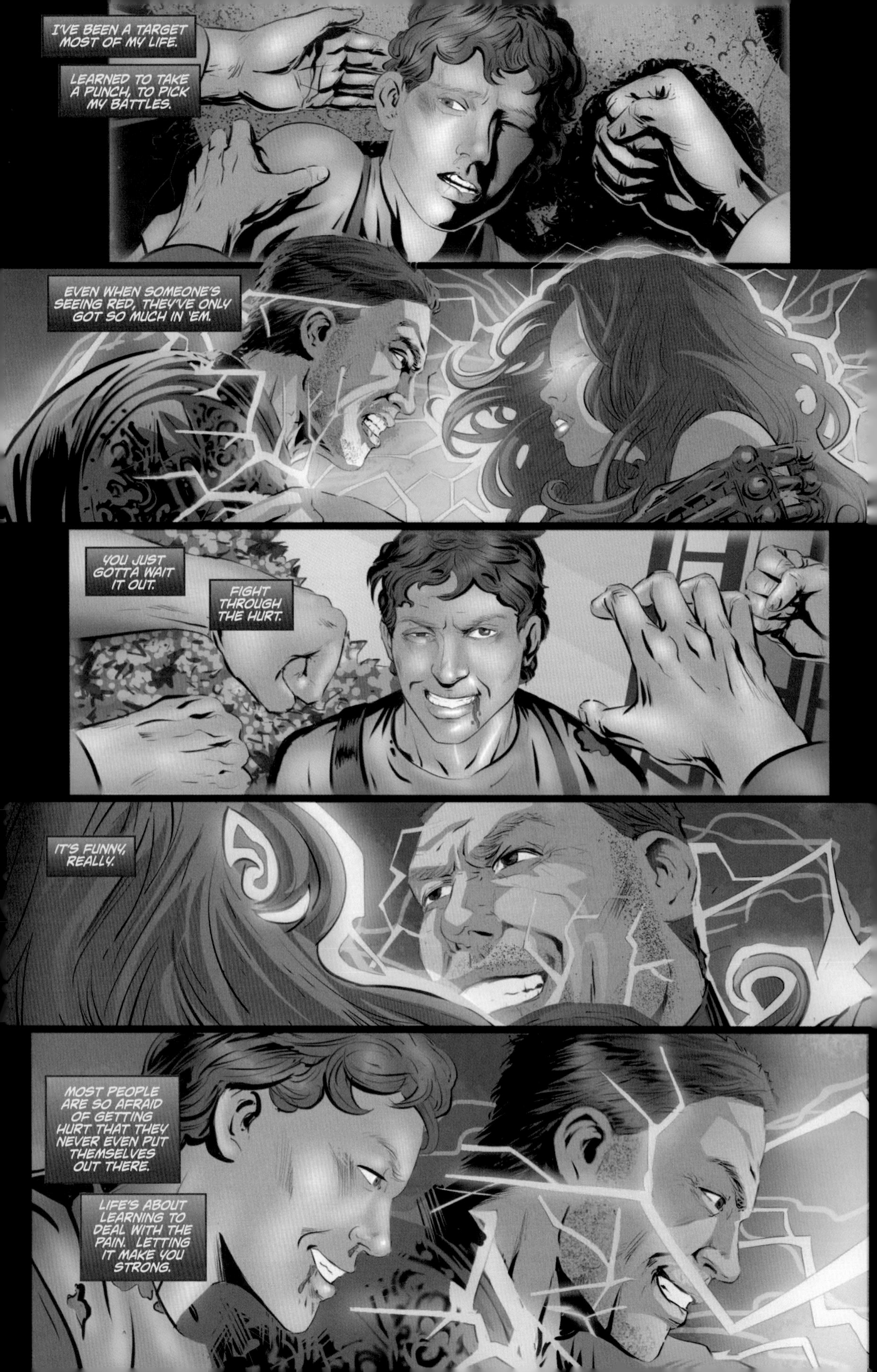
I'VE BEEN A TARGET MOST OF MY LIFE.
LEARNED TO TAKE A PUNCH, TO PICK MY BATTLES.
EVEN WHEN SOMEONE'S SEEING RED, THEY'VE ONLY GOT SO MUCH IN 'EM.
YOU JUST GOTTA WAIT IT OUT.
FIGHT THROUGH THE HURT.
IT'S FUNNY, REALLY.
MOST PEOPLE ARE SO AFRAID OF GETTING HURT THAT THEY NEVER EVEN PUT THEMSELVES OUT THERE.
LIFE'S ABOUT LEARNING TO DEAL WITH THE PAIN. LETTING IT MAKE YOU STRONG.

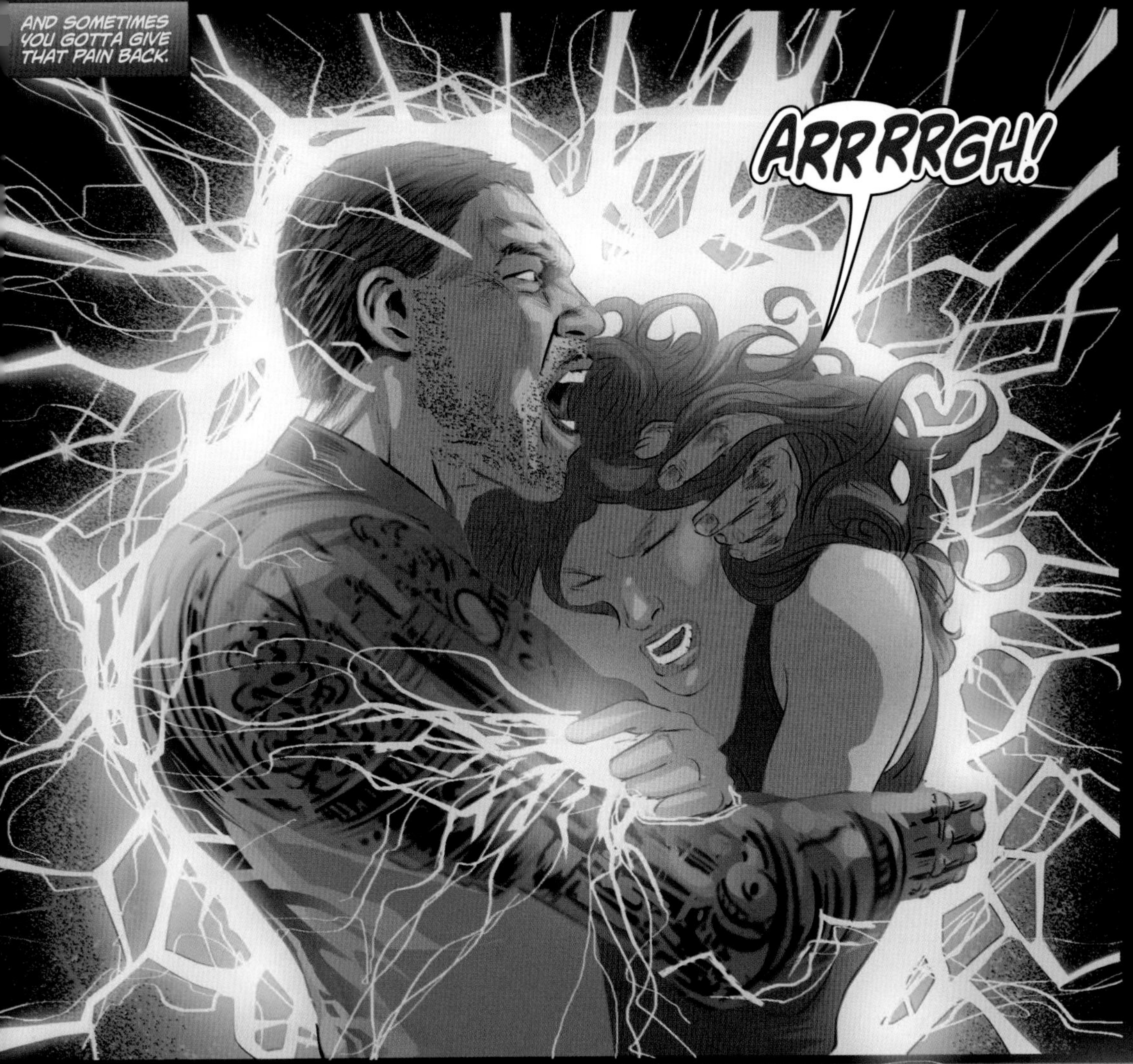
AND SOMETIMES YOU GOTTA GIVE THAT PAIN BACK.
ARRRRGH!

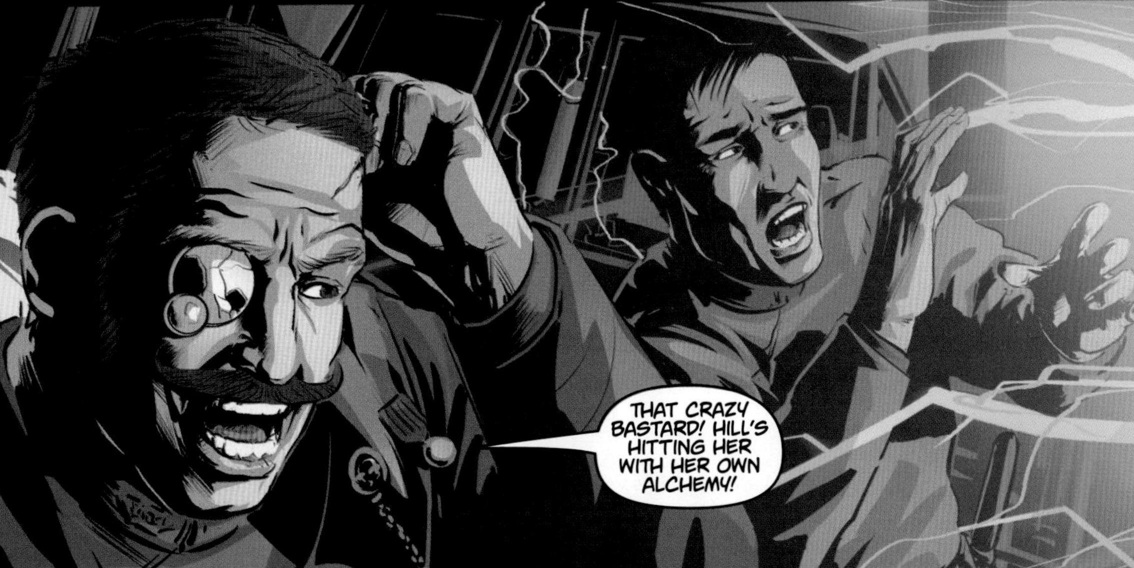
THAT CRAZY BASTARD! HILL'S HITTING HER WITH HER OWN ALCHEMY!

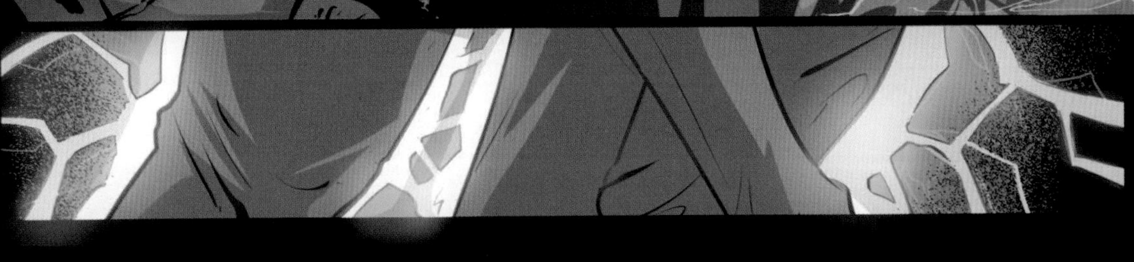

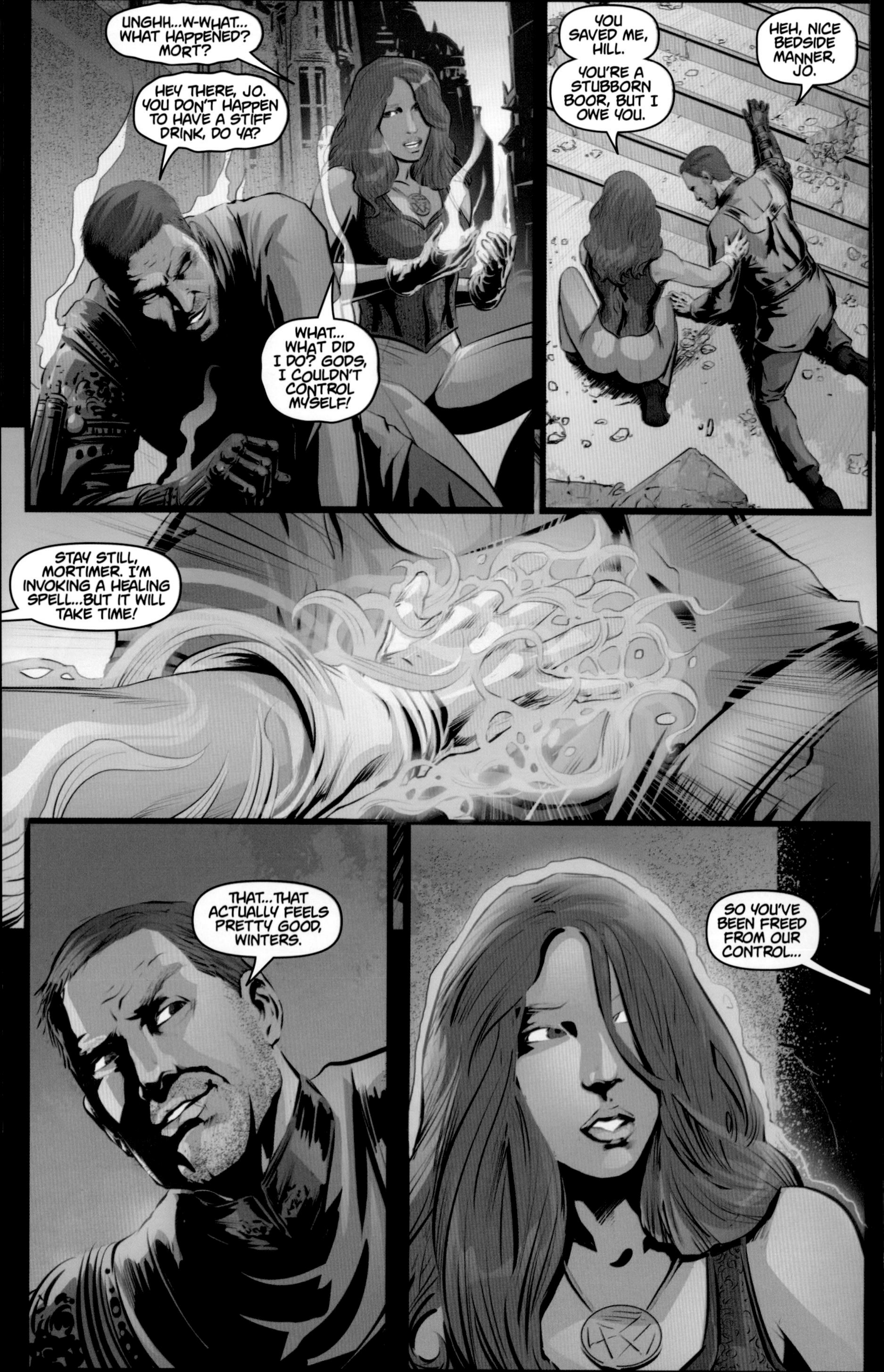
UNGHH...W-WHAT... WHAT HAPPENED? MORT?
HEY THERE, JO. YOU DON'T HAPPEN TO HAVE A STIFF DRINK, DO YA?
WHAT... WHAT DID I DO? GODS, I COULDN'T CONTROL MYSELF!
YOU SAVED ME, HILL.
YOU'RE A STUBBORN BOOR, BUT I OWE YOU.
HEH, NICE BEDSIDE MANNER, JO.
STAY STILL, MORTIMER. I'M INVOKING A HEALING SPELL...BUT IT WILL TAKE TIME!
THAT...THAT ACTUALLY FEELS PRETTY GOOD, WINTERS.
SO YOU'VE BEEN FREED FROM OUR CONTROL...

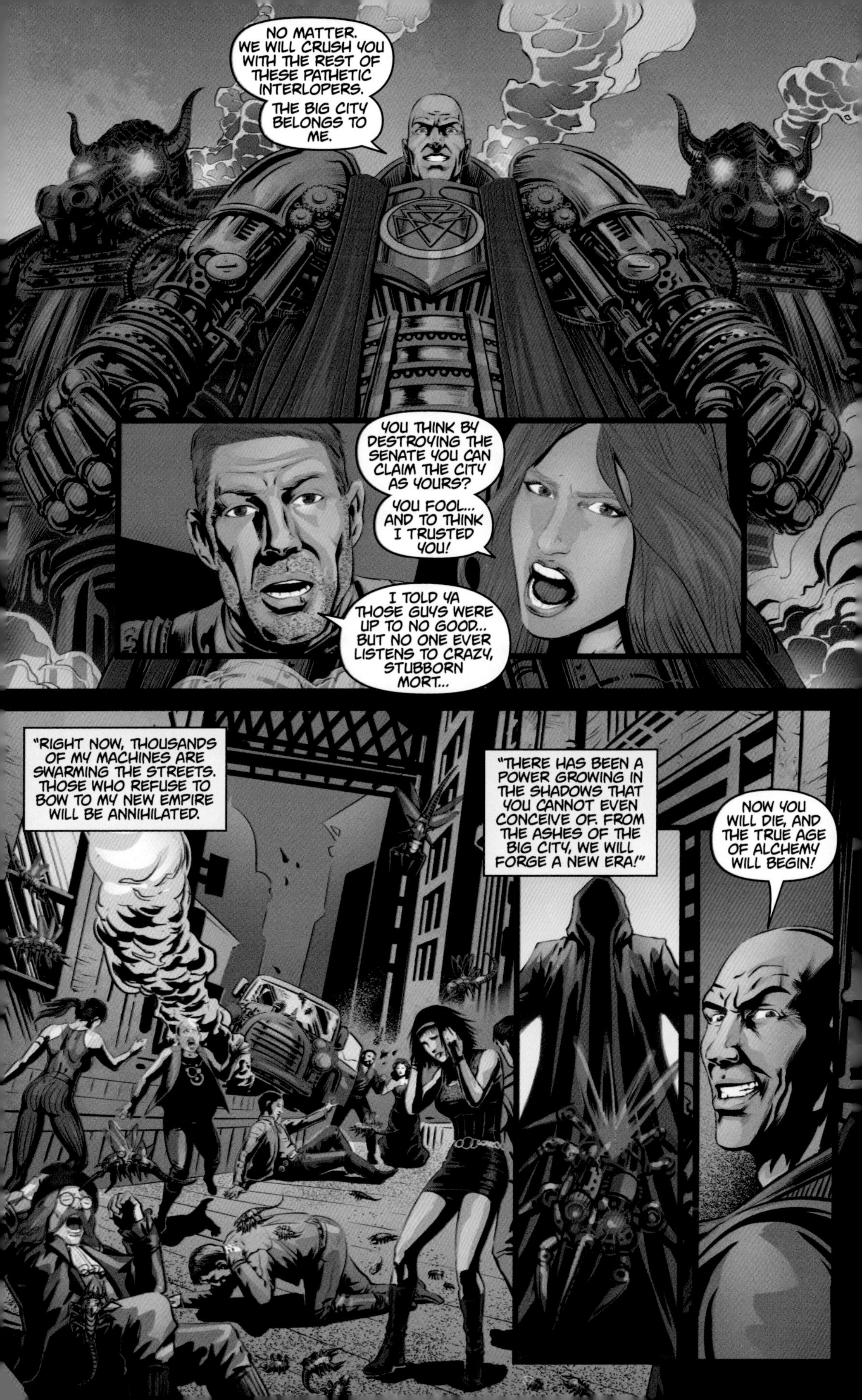
NO MATTER. WE WILL CRUSH YOU WITH THE REST OF THESE PATHETIC INTERLOPERS.
THE BIG CITY BELONGS TO ME.
YOU THINK BY DESTROYING THE SENATE YOU CAN CLAIM THE CITY AS YOURS?
YOU FOOL... AND TO THINK I TRUSTED YOU!
I TOLD YA THOSE GUYS WERE UP TO NO GOOD... BUT NO ONE EVER LISTENS TO CRAZY, STUBBORN MORT...
"RIGHT NOW, THOUSANDS OF MY MACHINES ARE SWARMING THE STREETS. THOSE WHO REFUSE TO BOW TO MY NEW EMPIRE WILL BE ANNIHILATED.
"THERE HAS BEEN A POWER GROWING IN THE SHADOWS THAT YOU CANNOT EVEN CONCEIVE OF. FROM THE ASHES OF THE BIG CITY, WE WILL FORGE A NEW ERA!"
NOW YOU WILL DIE, AND THE TRUE AGE OF ALCHEMY WILL BEGIN!

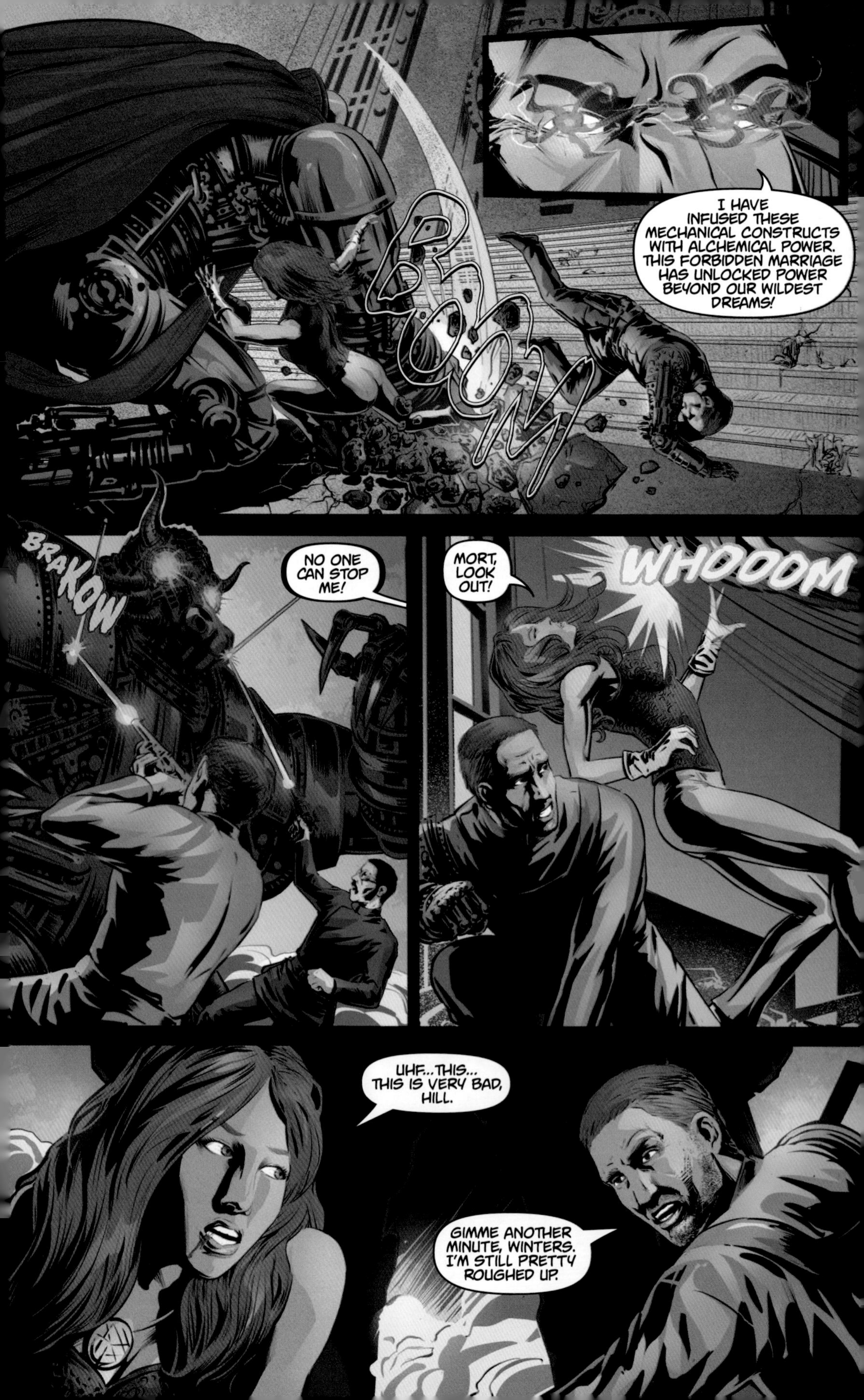

BOOOM
I HAVE INFUSED THESE MECHANICAL CONSTRUCTS WITH ALCHEMICAL POWER. THIS FORBIDDEN MARRIAGE HAS UNLOCKED POWER BEYOND OUR WILDEST DREAMS!
BRAKOW
NO ONE CAN STOP ME!
MORT, LOOK OUT!
WHOOOM
UHF... THIS... THIS IS VERY BAD, HILL.
GIMME ANOTHER MINUTE, WINTERS. I'M STILL PRETTY ROUGHED UP.

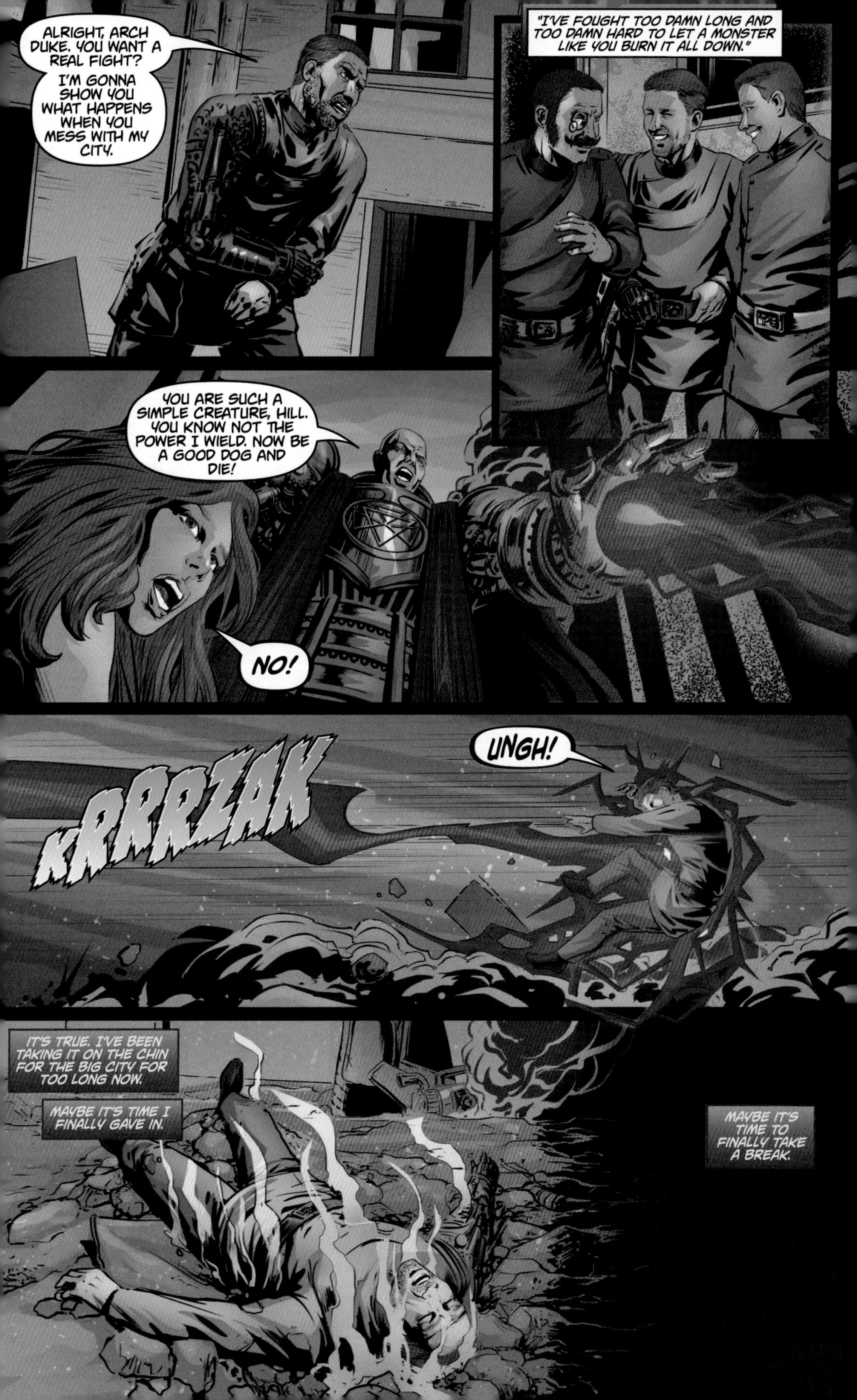
ALRIGHT, ARCH DUKE. YOU WANT A REAL FIGHT?
I'M GONNA SHOW YOU WHAT HAPPENS WHEN YOU MESS WITH MY CITY.
"I'VE FOUGHT TOO DAMN LONG AND TOO DAMN HARD TO LET A MONSTER LIKE YOU BURN IT ALL DOWN."
YOU ARE SUCH A SIMPLE CREATURE, HILL. YOU KNOW NOT THE POWER I WIELD. NOW BE A GOOD DOG AND DIE!
NO!
KRRRZAK
UNGH!
IT'S TRUE. I'VE BEEN TAKING IT ON THE CHIN FOR THE BIG CITY FOR TOO LONG NOW.
MAYBE IT'S TIME I FINALLY GAVE IN.
MAYBE IT'S TIME TO FINALLY TAKE A BREAK.

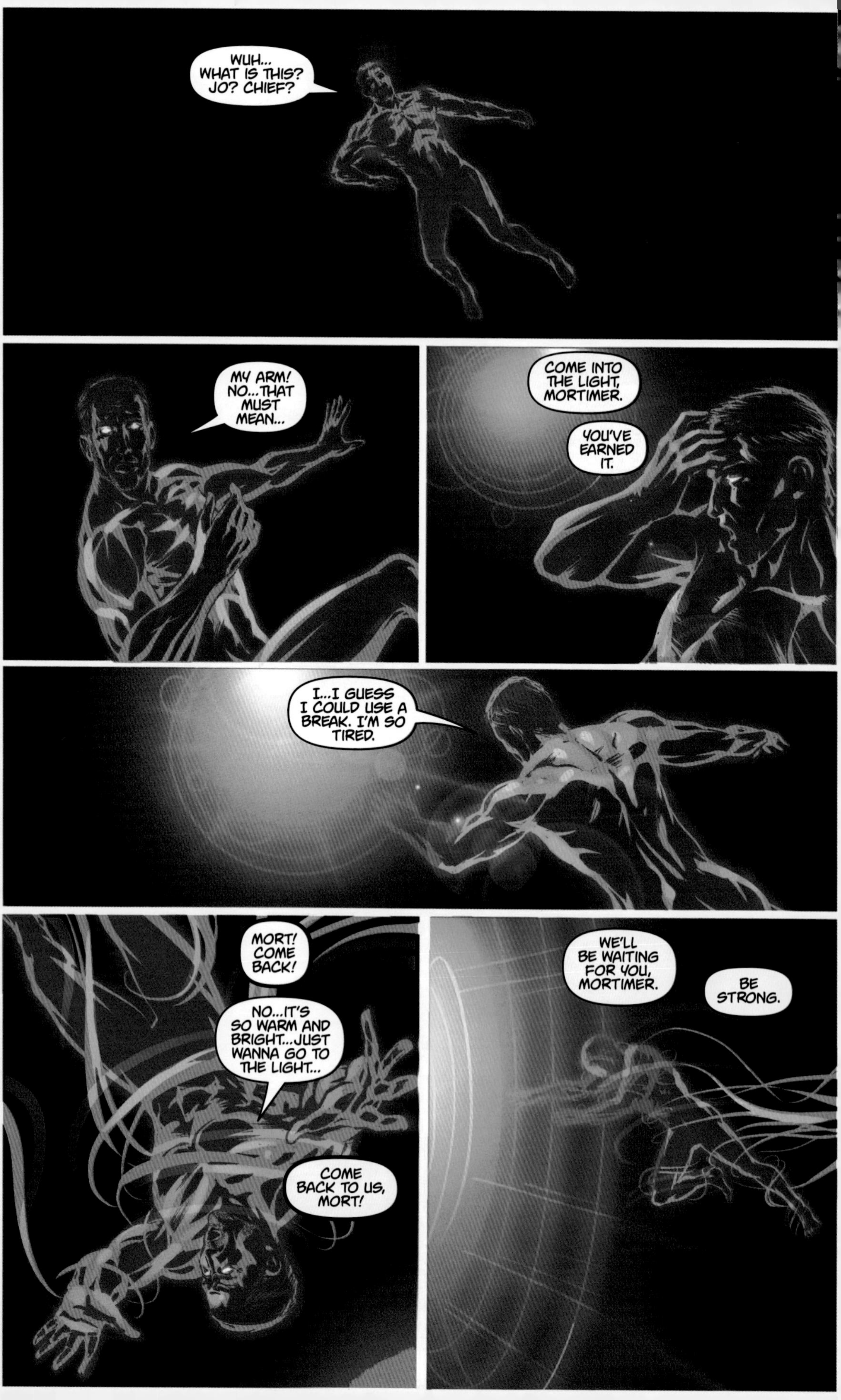
WUH... WHAT IS THIS? JO? CHIEF?
MY ARM! NO...THAT MUST MEAN...
COME INTO THE LIGHT, MORTIMER.
YOU'VE EARNED IT.
I...I GUESS I COULD USE A BREAK. I'M SO TIRED.
MORT! COME BACK!
NO...IT'S SO WARM AND BRIGHT...JUST WANNA GO TO THE LIGHT...
COME BACK TO US, MORT!
WE'LL BE WAITING FOR YOU, MORTIMER.
BE STRONG.

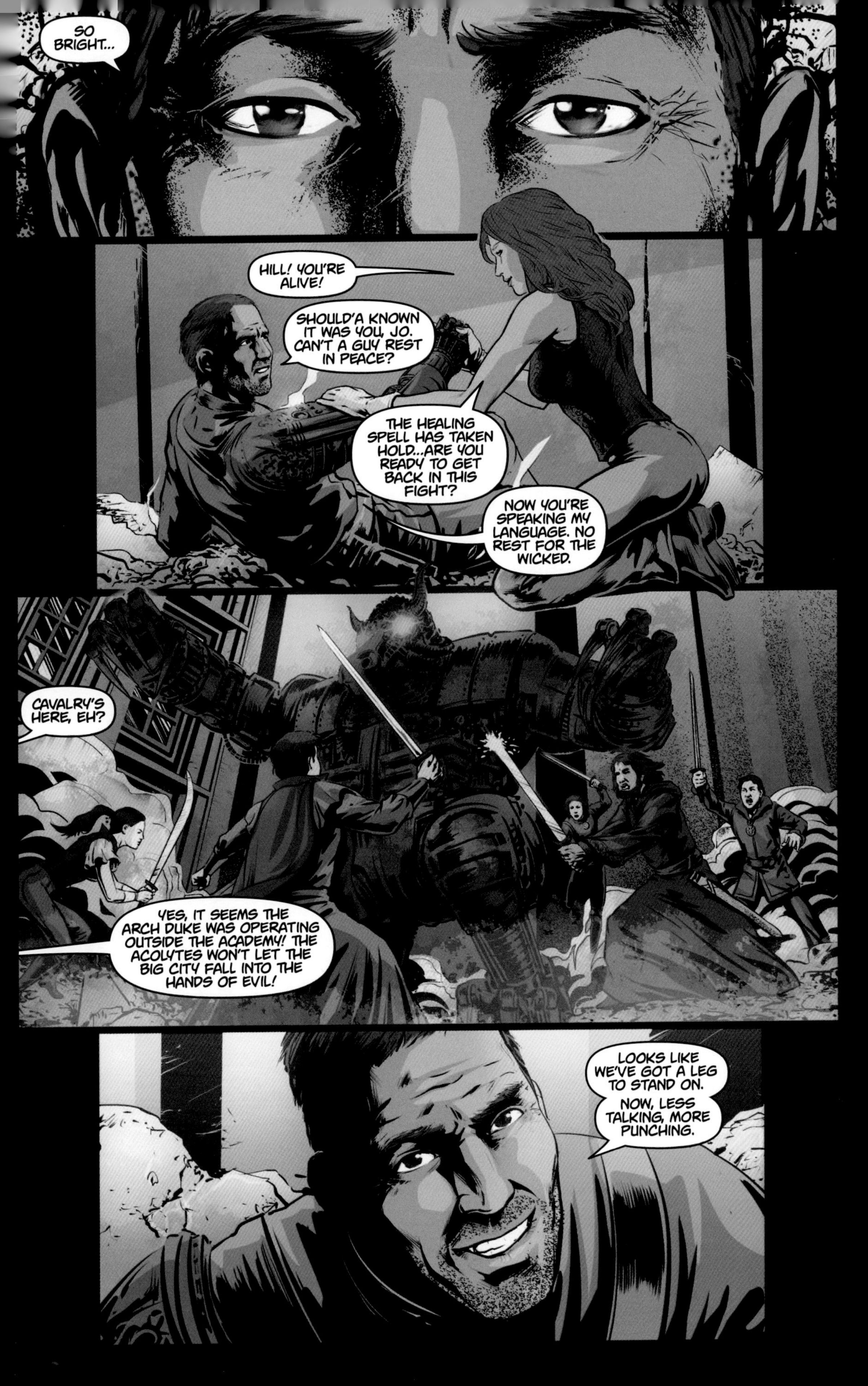
SO BRIGHT...
HILL! YOU'RE ALIVE!
SHOULD'A KNOWN IT WAS YOU, JO. CAN'T A GUY REST IN PEACE?
THE HEALING SPELL HAS TAKEN HOLD...ARE YOU READY TO GET BACK IN THIS FIGHT?
NOW YOU'RE SPEAKING MY LANGUAGE. NO REST FOR THE WICKED.
CAVALRY'S HERE, EH?
YES, IT SEEMS THE ARCH DUKE WAS OPERATING OUTSIDE THE ACADEMY! THE ACOLYTES WON'T LET THE BIG CITY FALL INTO THE HANDS OF EVIL!
LOOKS LIKE WE'VE GOT A LEG TO STAND ON.
NOW, LESS TALKING, MORE PUNCHING.

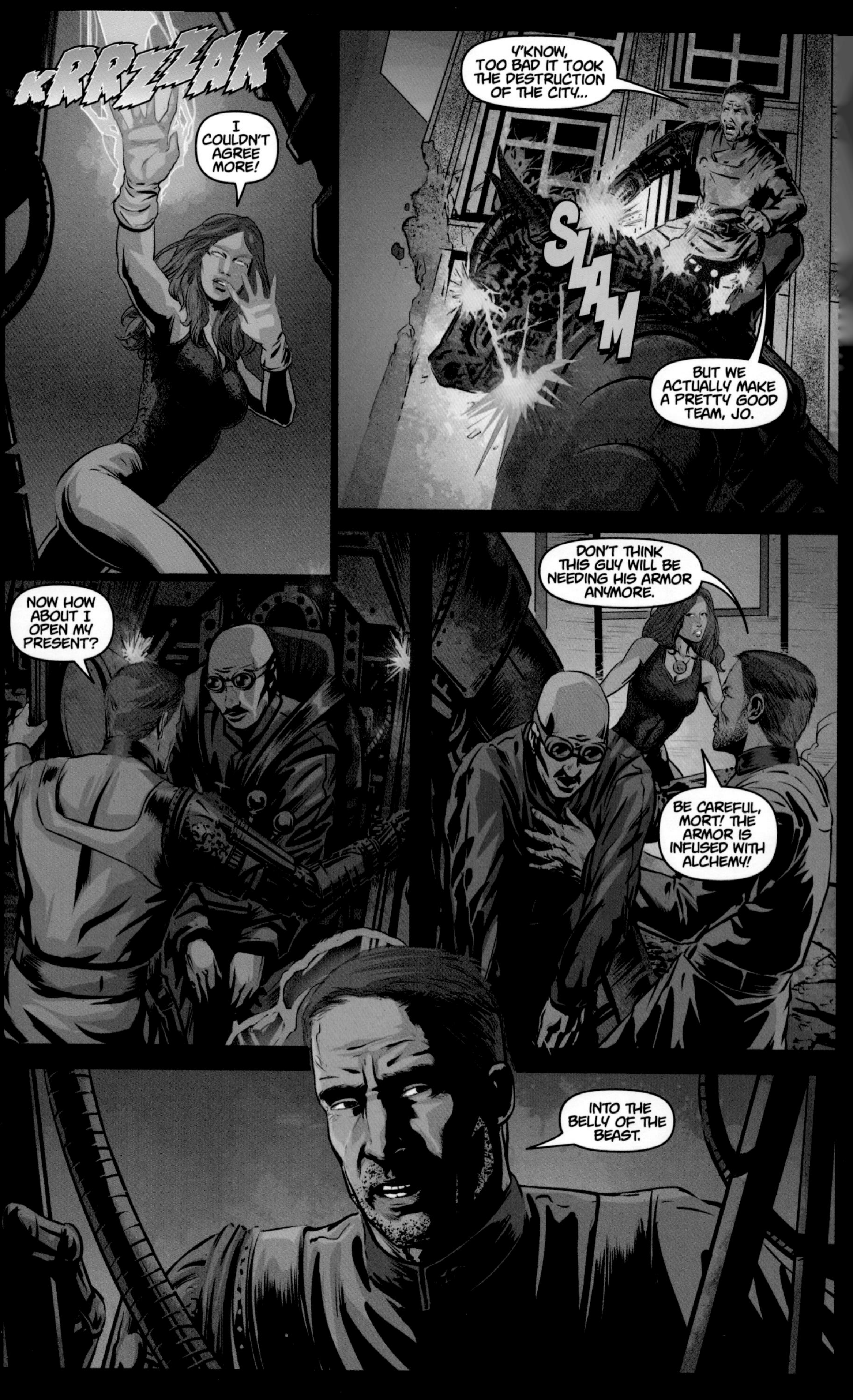
KRRZZAK
I COULDN'T AGREE MORE!
Y'KNOW, TOO BAD IT TOOK THE DESTRUCTION OF THE CITY...
SLAM
BUT WE ACTUALLY MAKE A PRETTY GOOD TEAM, JO.
NOW HOW ABOUT I OPEN MY PRESENT?
DON'T THINK THIS GUY WILL BE NEEDING HIS ARMOR ANYMORE.
BE CAREFUL, MORT! THE ARMOR IS INFUSED WITH ALCHEMY!
INTO THE BELLY OF THE BEAST.

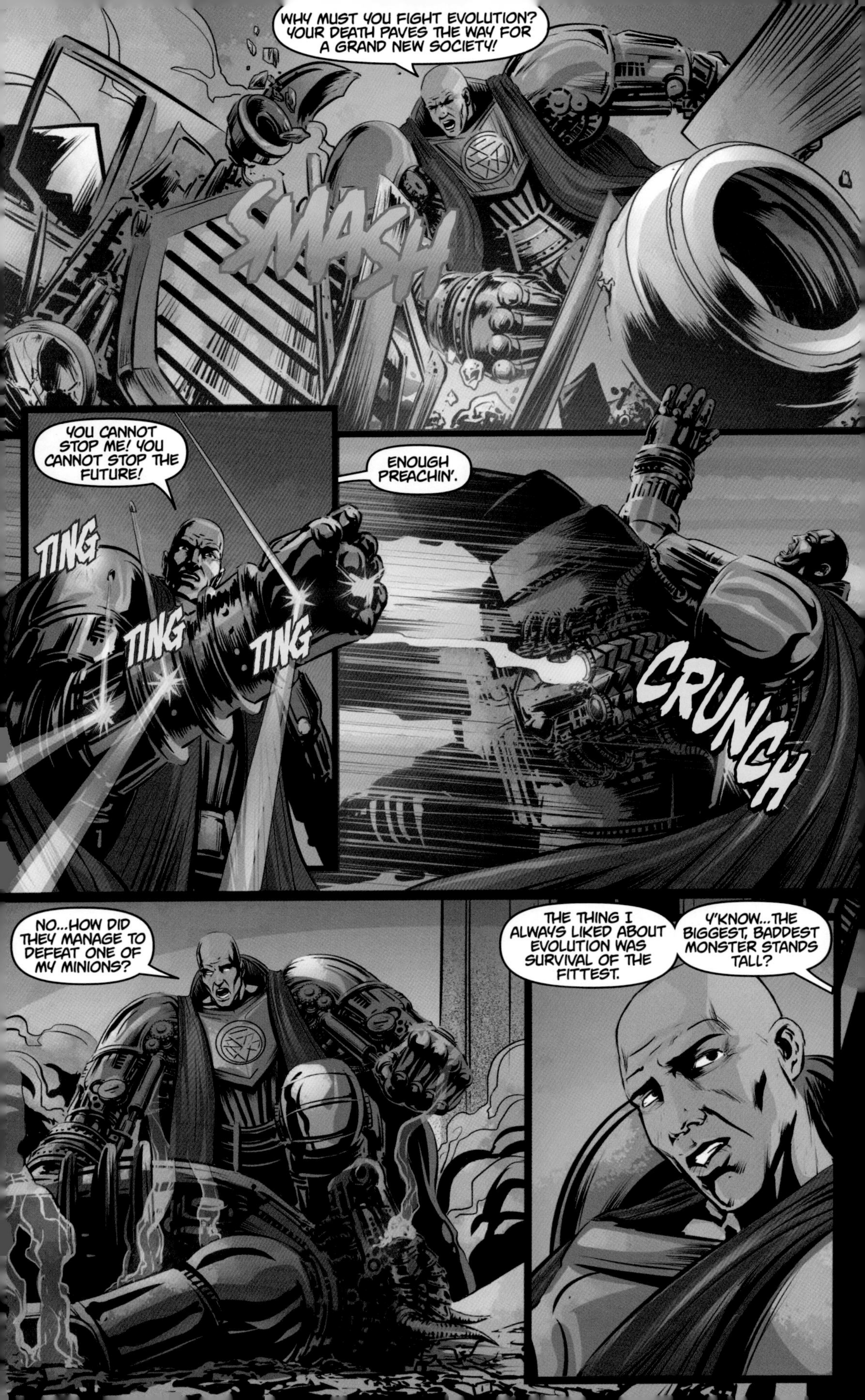
WHY MUST YOU FIGHT EVOLUTION? YOUR DEATH PAVES THE WAY FOR A GRAND NEW SOCIETY!
SMASH
YOU CANNOT STOP ME! YOU CANNOT STOP THE FUTURE!
TING
TING
TING
ENOUGH PREACHIN'.
CRUNCH
NO...HOW DID THEY MANAGE TO DEFEAT ONE OF MY MINIONS?
THE THING I ALWAYS LIKED ABOUT EVOLUTION WAS SURVIVAL OF THE FITTEST.
Y'KNOW...THE BIGGEST, BADDEST MONSTER STANDS TALL?

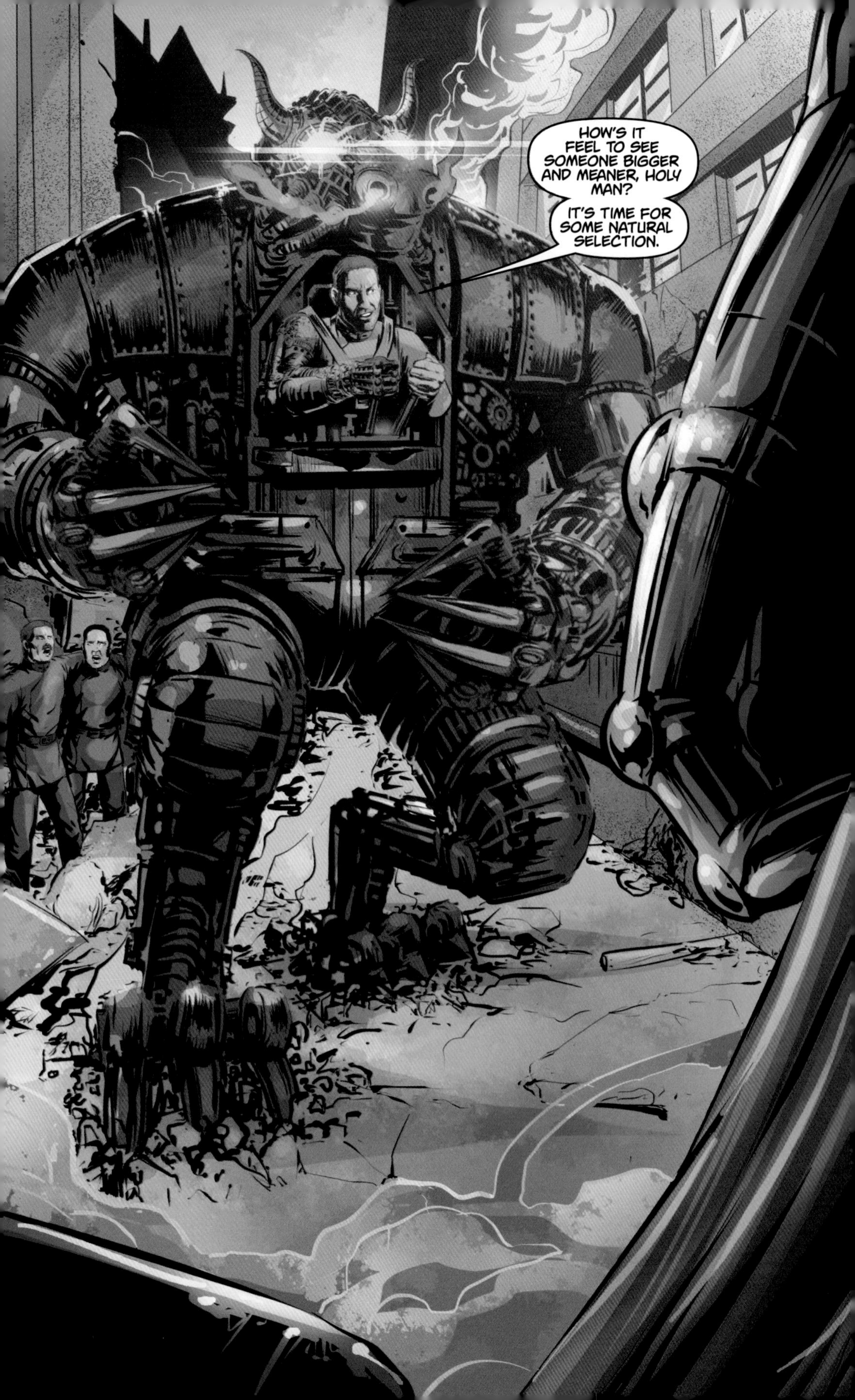
HOW'S IT FEEL TO SEE SOMEONE BIGGER AND MEANER, HOLY MAN?
IT'S TIME FOR SOME NATURAL SELECTION.

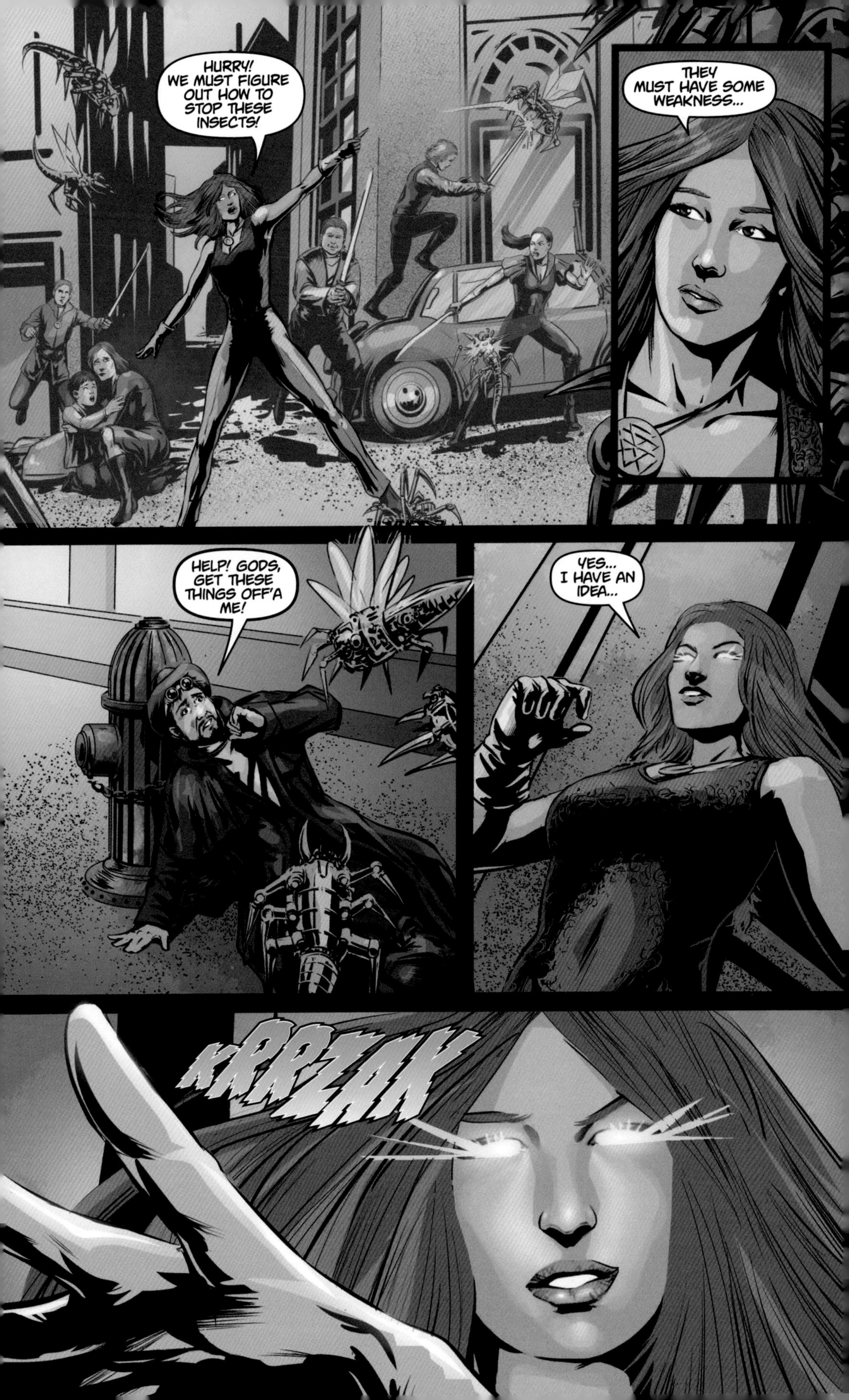
HURRY! WE MUST FIGURE OUT HOW TO STOP THESE INSECTS!
THEY MUST HAVE SOME WEAKNESS...
HELP! GODS, GET THESE THINGS OFF'A ME!
YES... I HAVE AN IDEA...
KRRZAK

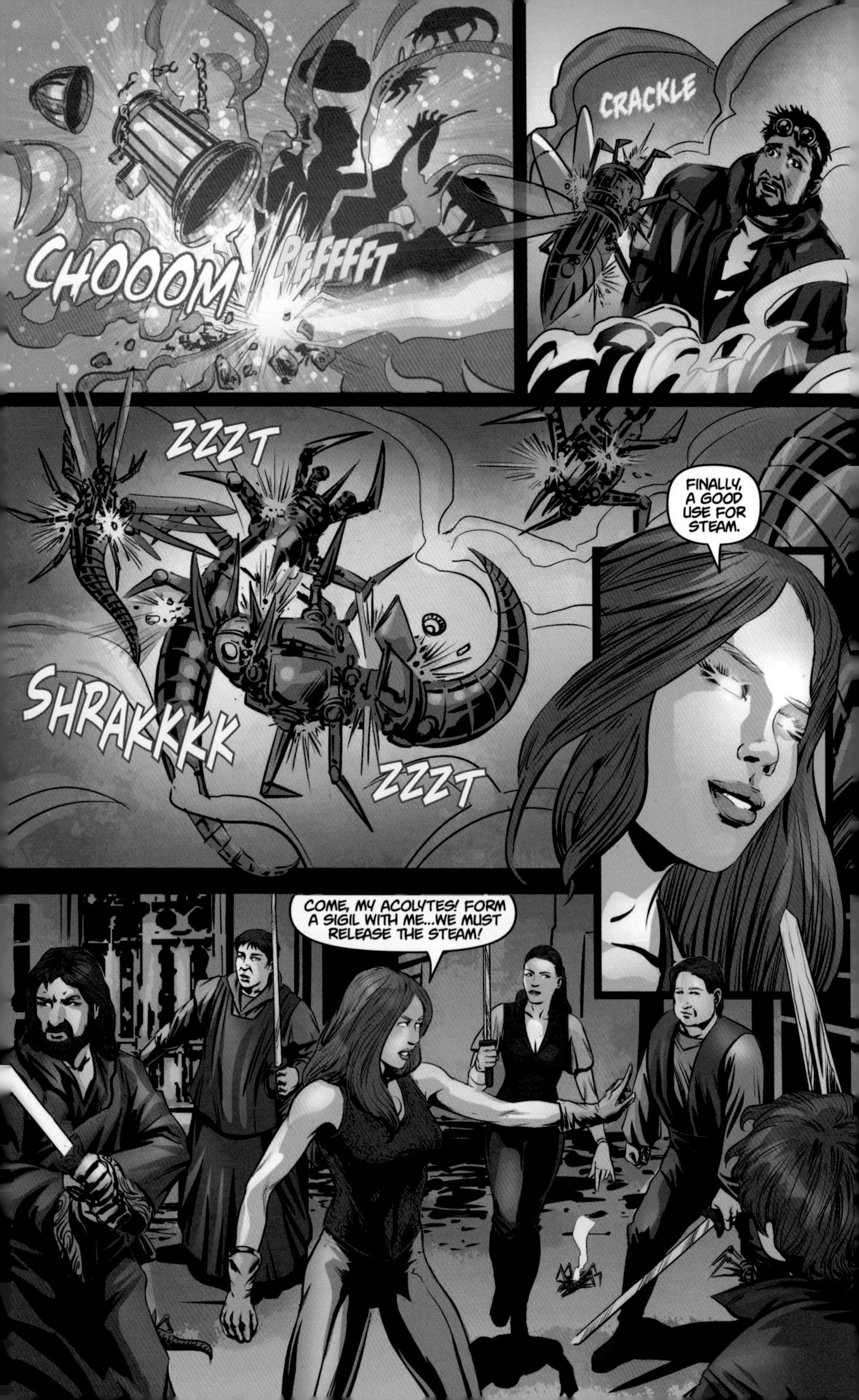
CHOOOM
PFFFFFT
CRACKLE
ZZZT
SHRAKKKK
ZZZT
FINALLY, A GOOD USE FOR STEAM.
COME, MY ACOLYTES! FORM A SIGIL WITH ME...WE MUST RELEASE THE STEAM!

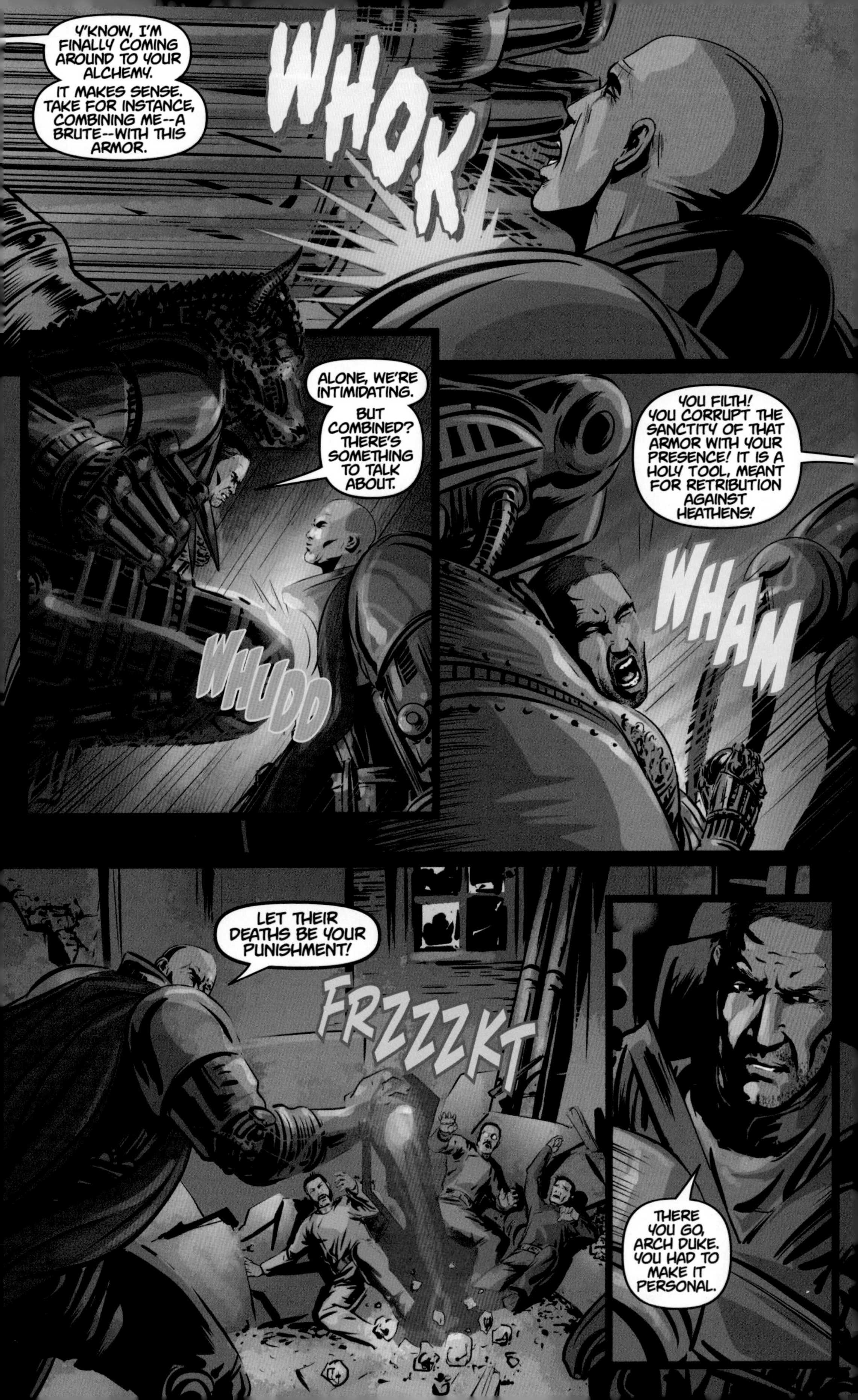
Y'KNOW, I'M FINALLY COMING AROUND TO YOUR ALCHEMY.
IT MAKES SENSE. TAKE FOR INSTANCE, COMBINING ME--A BRUTE--WITH THIS ARMOR.
WHOK
ALONE, WE'RE INTIMIDATING.
BUT COMBINED? THERE'S SOMETHING TO TALK ABOUT.
WHUDD
YOU FILTH! YOU CORRUPT THE SANCTITY OF THAT ARMOR WITH YOUR PRESENCE! IT IS A HOLY TOOL, MEANT FOR RETRIBUTION AGAINST HEATHENS!
WHAM
LET THEIR DEATHS BE YOUR PUNISHMENT!
FRZZZKT
THERE YOU GO, ARCH DUKE. YOU HAD TO MAKE IT PERSONAL.

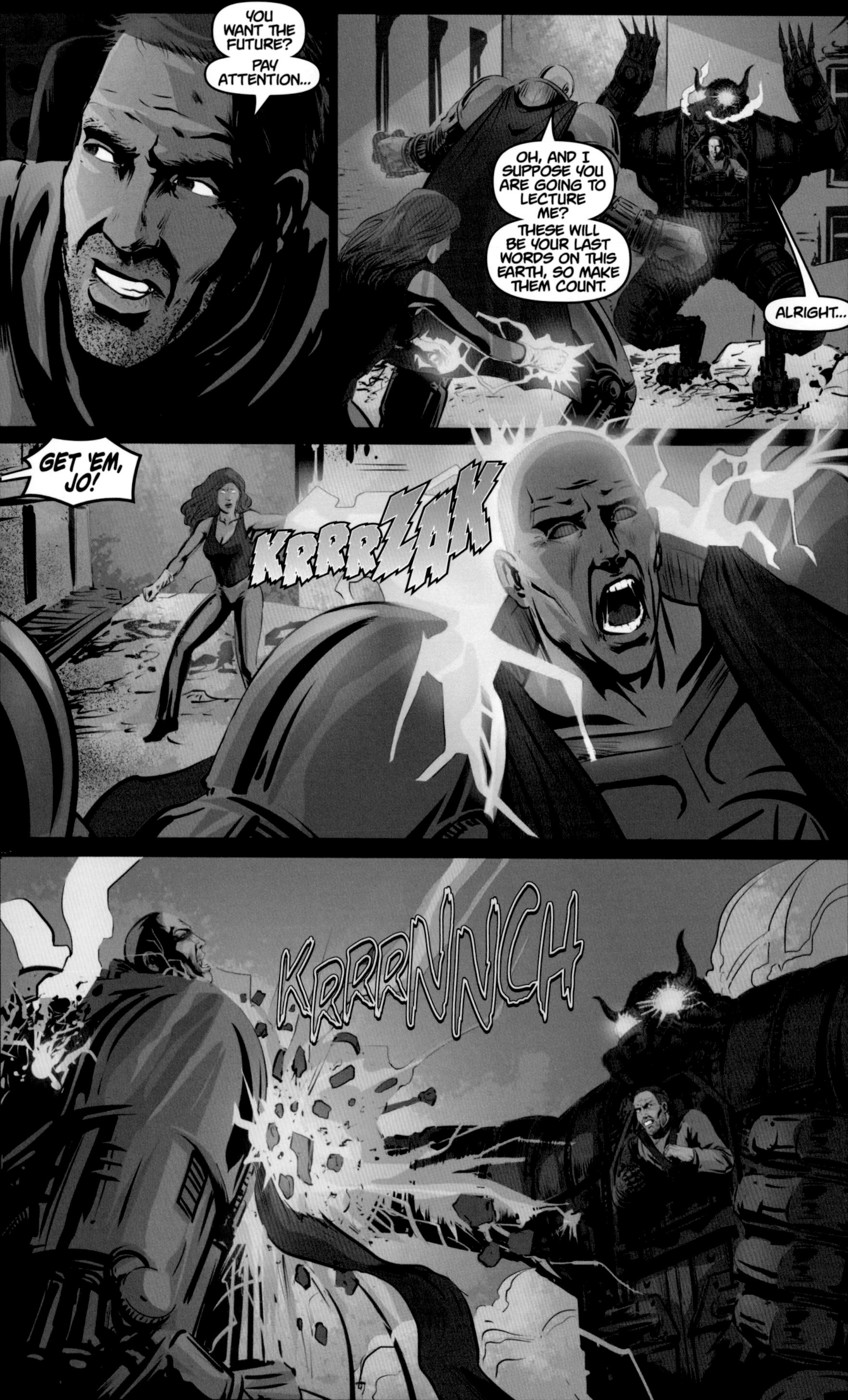
YOU WANT THE FUTURE? PAY ATTENTION...
OH, AND I SUPPOSE YOU ARE GOING TO LECTURE ME? THESE WILL BE YOUR LAST WORDS ON THIS EARTH, SO MAKE THEM COUNT.
ALRIGHT...
GET 'EM, JO!
KRRRZAK
KRRRNNCH

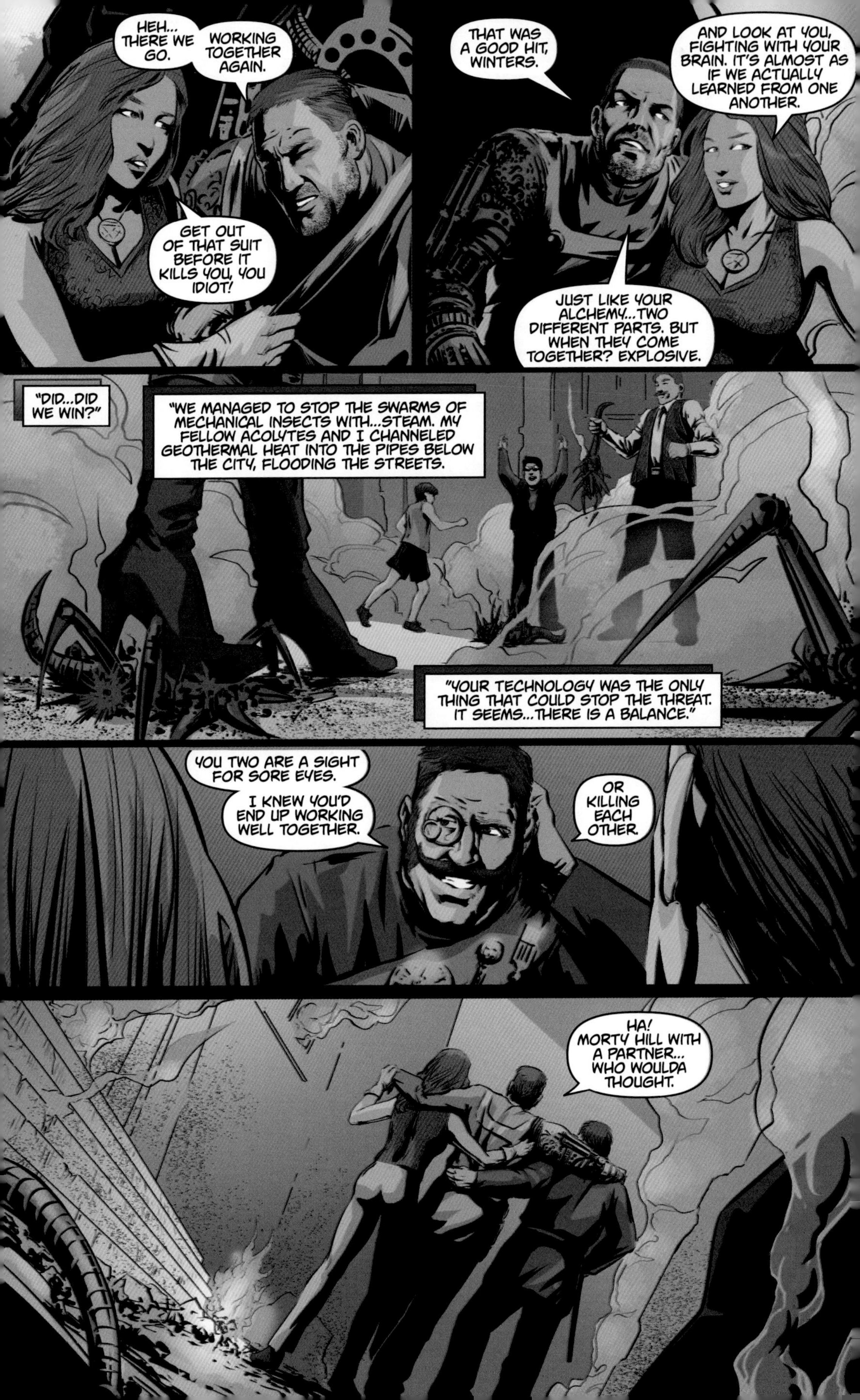
HEH... THERE WE GO.
WORKING TOGETHER AGAIN.
GET OUT OF THAT SUIT BEFORE IT KILLS YOU, YOU IDIOT!
THAT WAS A GOOD HIT, WINTERS.
AND LOOK AT YOU, FIGHTING WITH YOUR BRAIN. IT'S ALMOST AS IF WE ACTUALLY LEARNED FROM ONE ANOTHER.
JUST LIKE YOUR ALCHEMY...TWO DIFFERENT PARTS. BUT WHEN THEY COME TOGETHER? EXPLOSIVE.
"DID...DID WE WIN?"
"WE MANAGED TO STOP THE SWARMS OF MECHANICAL INSECTS WITH...STEAM. MY FELLOW ACOLYTES AND I CHANNELED GEOTHERMAL HEAT INTO THE PIPES BELOW THE CITY, FLOODING THE STREETS.
"YOUR TECHNOLOGY WAS THE ONLY THING THAT COULD STOP THE THREAT. IT SEEMS...THERE IS A BALANCE."
YOU TWO ARE A SIGHT FOR SORE EYES.
I KNEW YOU'D END UP WORKING WELL TOGETHER.
OR KILLING EACH OTHER.
HA! MORTY HILL WITH A PARTNER... WHO WOULDA THOUGHT.

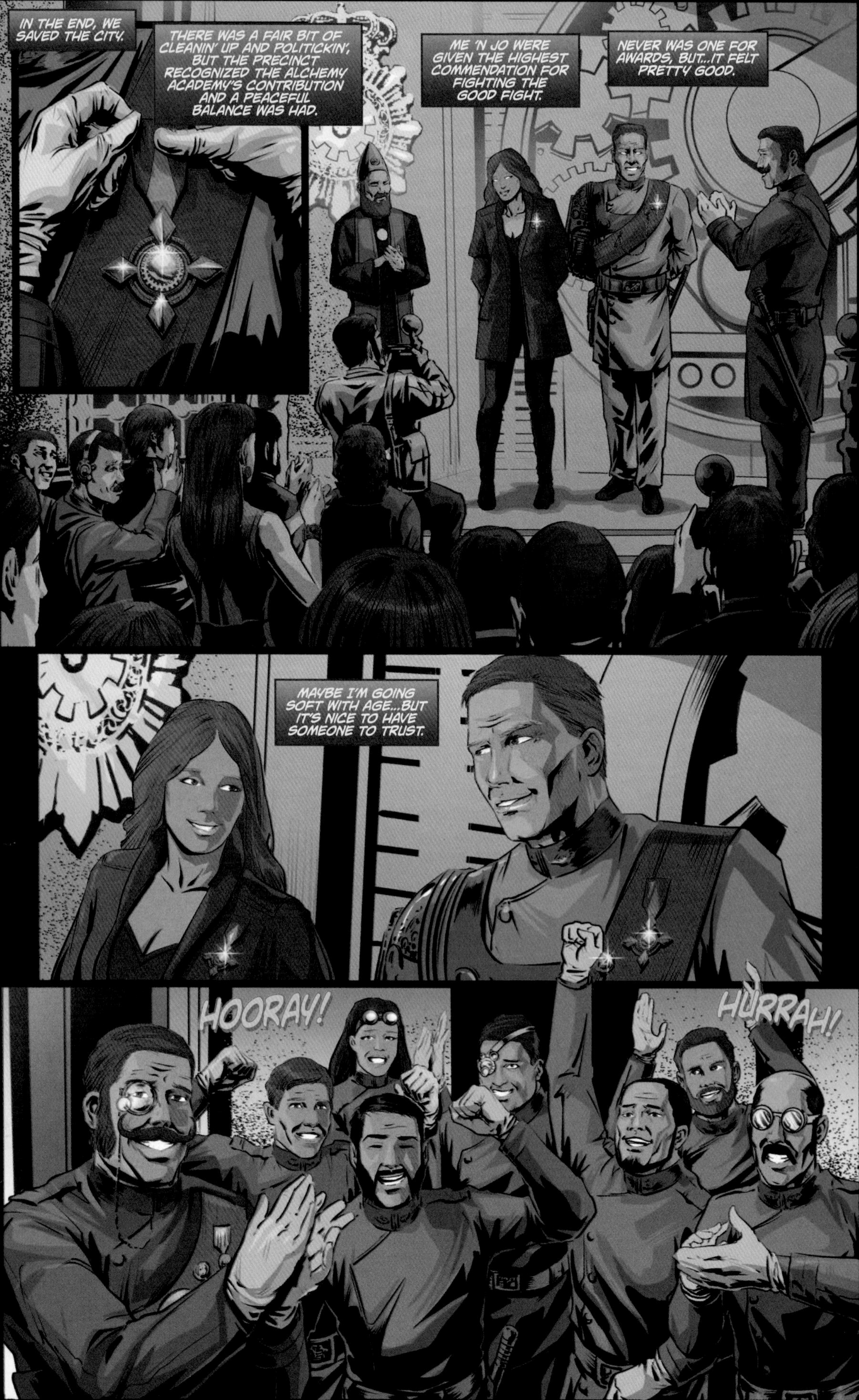
IN THE END, WE SAVED THE CITY.
THERE WAS A FAIR BIT OF CLEANIN' UP AND POLITICKIN', BUT THE PRECINCT RECOGNIZED THE ALCHEMY ACADEMY'S CONTRIBUTION AND A PEACEFUL BALANCE WAS HAD.
ME 'N JO WERE GIVEN THE HIGHEST COMMENDATION FOR FIGHTING THE GOOD FIGHT.
NEVER WAS ONE FOR AWARDS, BUT...IT FELT PRETTY GOOD.
MAYBE I'M GOING SOFT WITH AGE...BUT IT'S NICE TO HAVE SOMEONE TO TRUST.
HOORAY!
HURRAH!

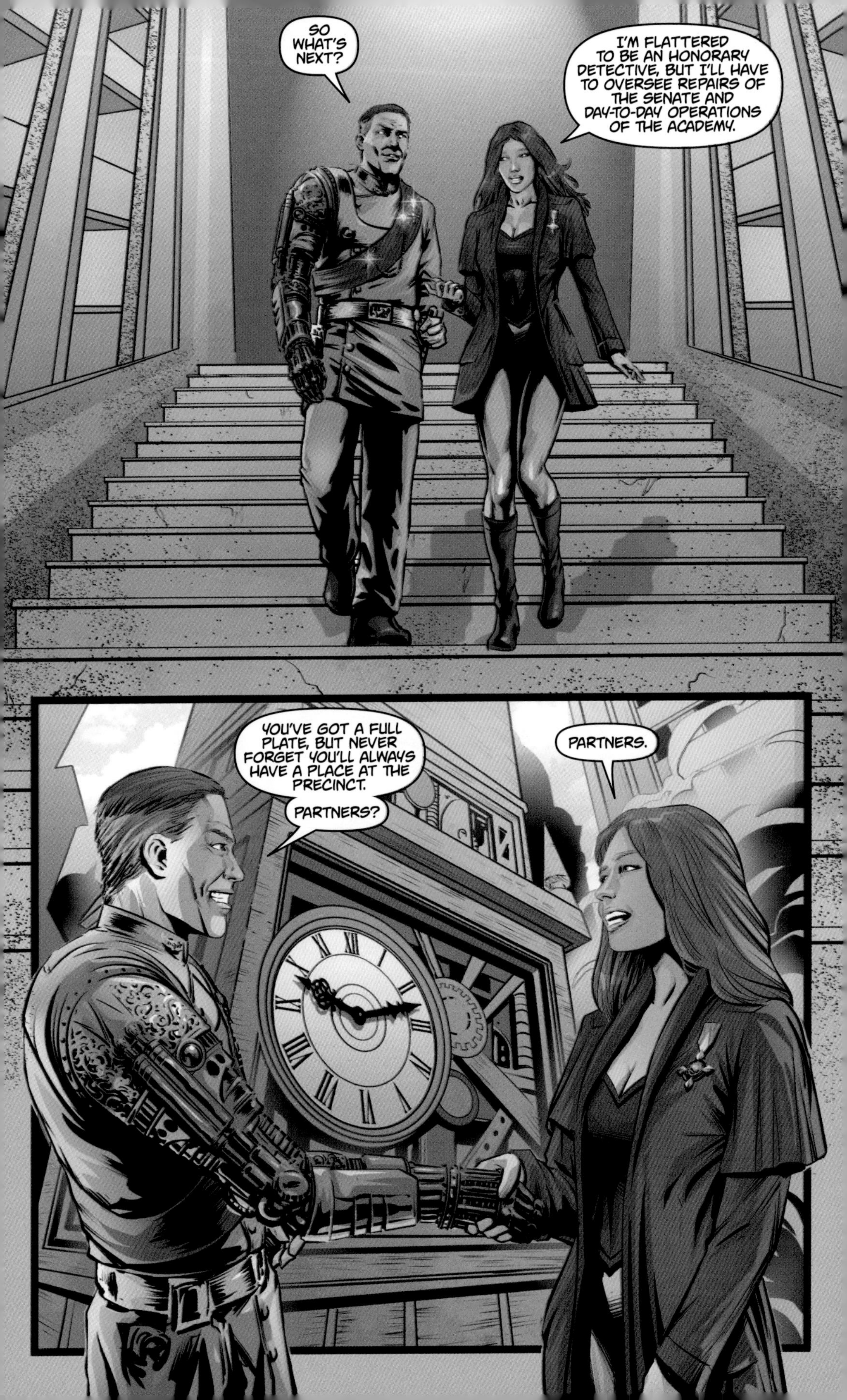
SO WHAT'S NEXT?
I'M FLATTERED TO BE AN HONORARY DETECTIVE, BUT I'LL HAVE TO OVERSEE REPAIRS OF THE SENATE AND DAY-TO-DAY OPERATIONS OF THE ACADEMY.
YOU'VE GOT A FULL PLATE, BUT NEVER FORGET YOU'LL ALWAYS HAVE A PLACE AT THE PRECINCT.
PARTNERS?
PARTNERS.

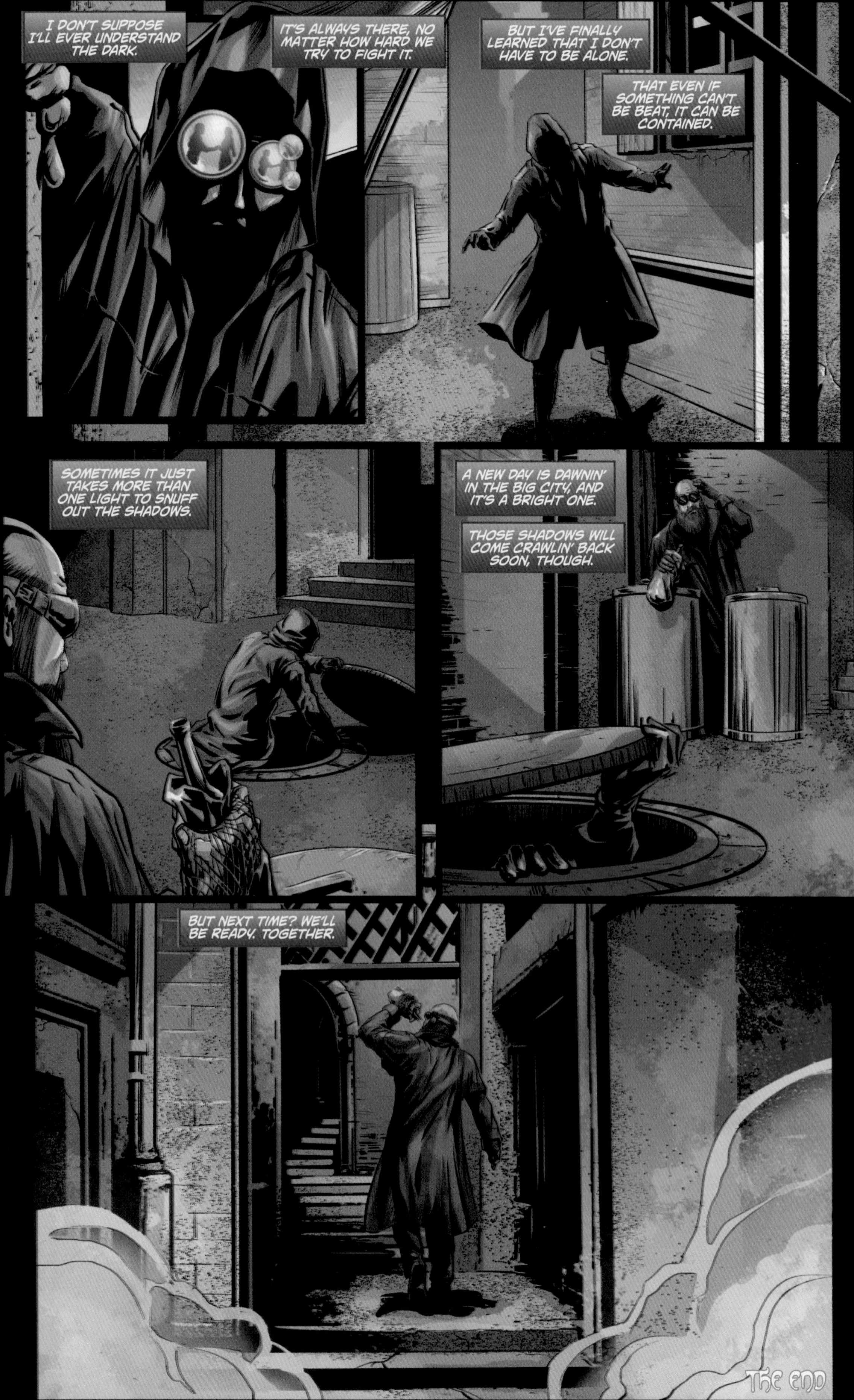
I DON'T SUPPOSE I'LL EVER UNDERSTAND THE DARK.
IT'S ALWAYS THERE, NO MATTER HOW HARD WE TRY TO FIGHT IT.
BUT I'VE FINALLY LEARNED THAT I DON'T HAVE TO BE ALONE.
THAT EVEN IF SOMETHING CAN'T BE BEAT, IT CAN BE CONTAINED.
SOMETIMES IT JUST TAKES MORE THAN ONE LIGHT TO SNUFF OUT THE SHADOWS.
A NEW DAY IS DAWNIN' IN THE BIG CITY, AND IT'S A BRIGHT ONE.
THOSE SHADOWS WILL COME CRAWLIN' BACK SOON, THOUGH.
BUT NEXT TIME? WE'LL BE READY. TOGETHER.
THE END

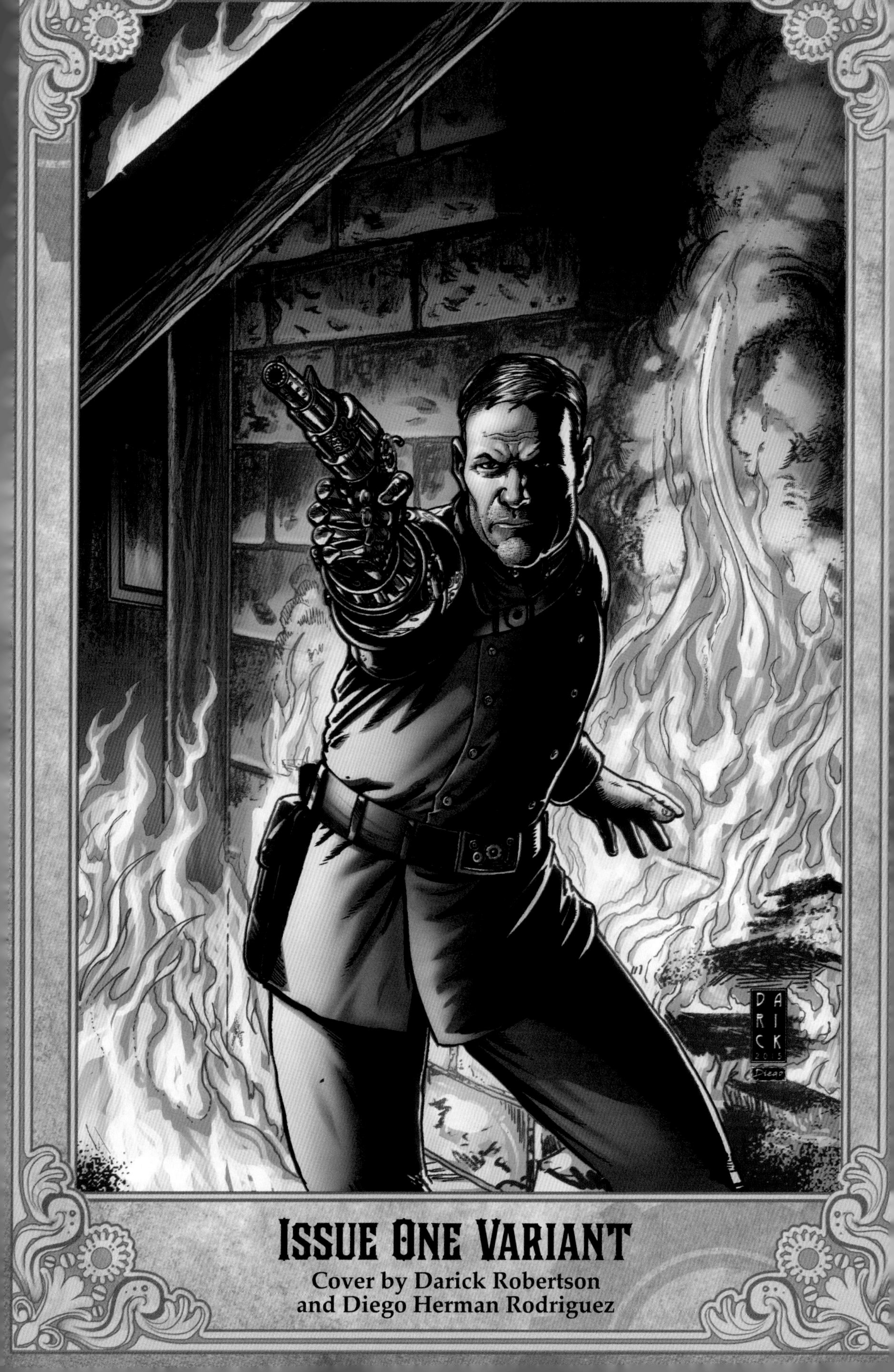

Issue One Variant

Cover by Darick Robertson
and Diego Herman Rodriguez

THE EISNER-AWARD-WINNING WRITER OF FABLES
PRESENTS YOUR FAVORITE DYNAMITE CHARACTERS
AS YOU'VE NEVER SEEN THEM BEFORE!

"HIGHEST POSSIBLE RECOMMENDATION"
- SCI-FI PULSE (LEGENDERRY: A STEAMPUNK ADVENTURE)

"THE ACTION IS CINEMATIC AND LARGER THAN LIFE WITH
BIG EXPLOSIONS AND CRASHES THAT ARE OVER-THE-TOP."
- GEEKS WITH WIVES (LEGENDERRY: GREEN HORNET)

"WRITER *MARC ANDREYKO* AND ARTIST *ANEKE* DELIVER A TRULY
FASCINATING TALE, WITH THE CROSS IN GENRE'S BEING FABULOUSLY HANDLED."
- UNLEASH THE FANBOY (LEGENDERRY: RED SONJA)

"WORTH CHECKING OUT. OVERALL GRADE: A."
- SCI-FI PULSE (LEGENDERRY: VAMPIRELLA)

"IT'S A FANTASTIC AND FUNNY MELDING OF TWO THINGS I REALLY LIKE,
AND AN EASY RECOMMENDATION TO ANYONE WHO LIKES THEIR
COMICS STRANGE AND SILLY."
- GEEKALITY (STEAMPUNK: BATTLESTAR GALACTICA 1880)

LEGENDERRY
A STEAMPUNK ADVENTURE

EXPLORE THE STEAMPUNK WORLD OF DYNAMITE

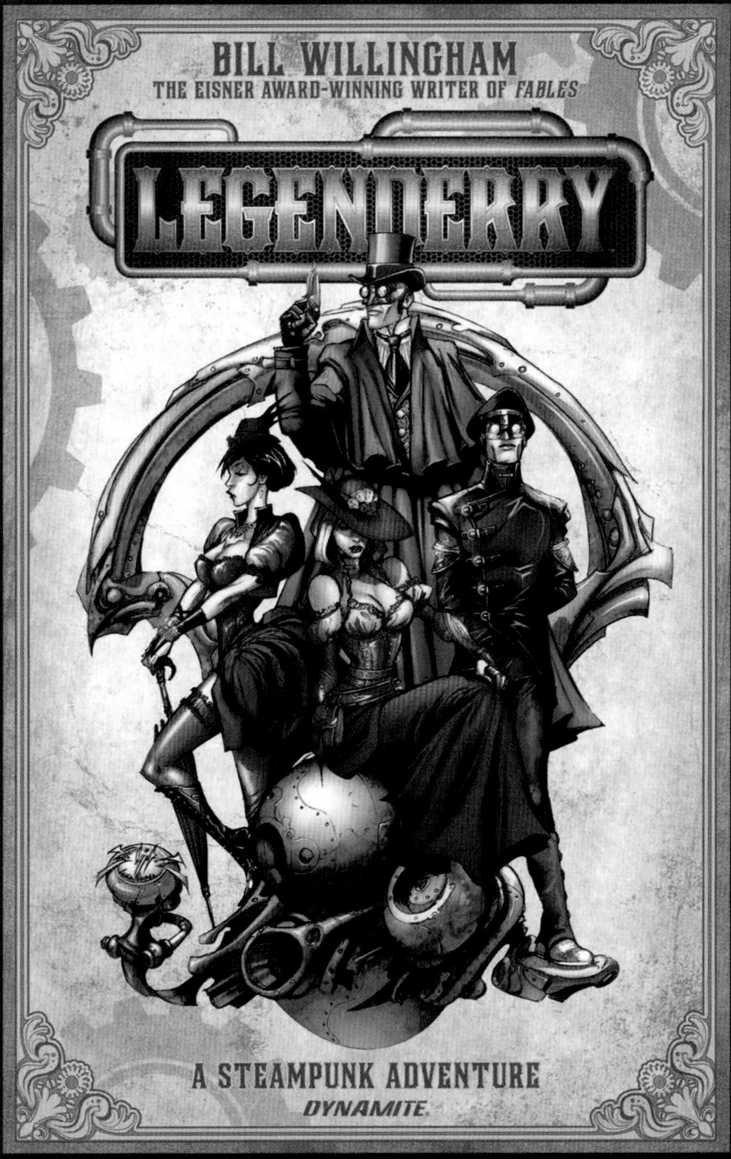
BILL WILLINGHAM
THE EISNER AWARD-WINNING WRITER OF FABLES
LEGENDERRY
A STEAMPUNK ADVENTURE
DYNAMITE

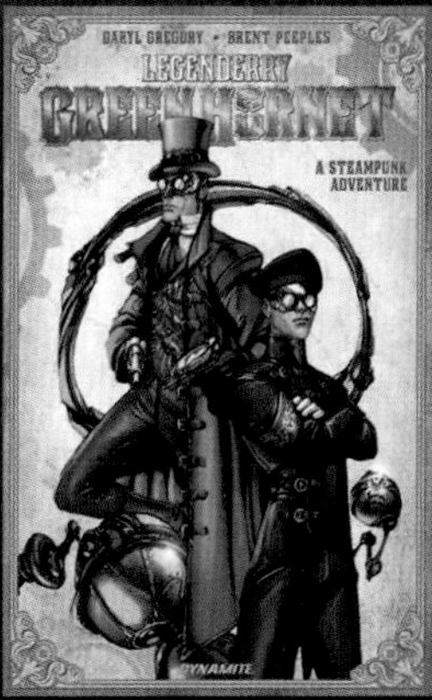
DARYL GREGORY • BRENT PEEPLES
LEGENDERRY
A STEAMPUNK ADVENTURE
DYNAMITE

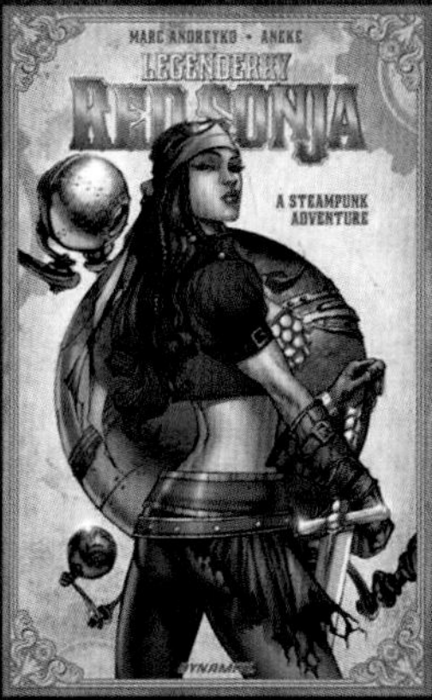
MARC ANDREYKO • ANEKE
LEGENDERRY
RED SONJA
A STEAMPUNK ADVENTURE

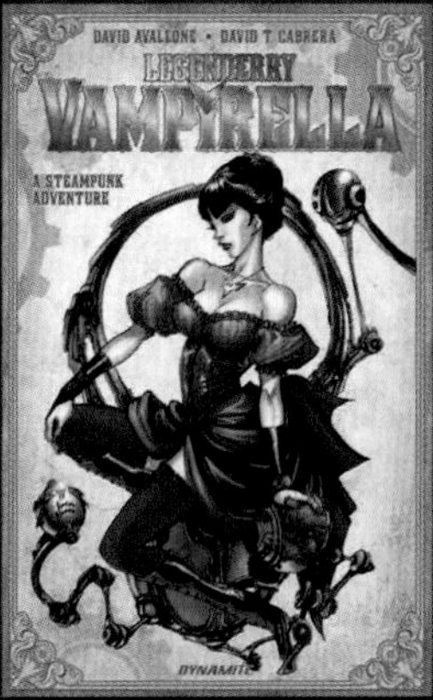
DAVID AVALLONE • DAVID T. CABRERA
LEGENDERRY
VAMPIRELLA
A STEAMPUNK ADVENTURE

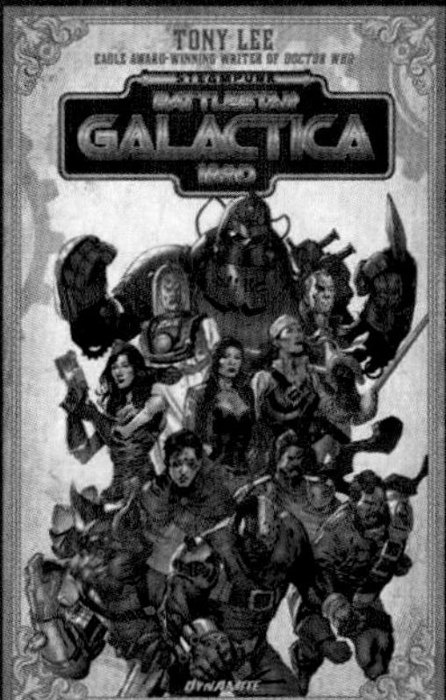
TONY LEE
GALACTICA

LEGENDERRY
WRITTEN BY BILL WILLINGHAM
ART BY SERGIO DAVILA, COVER BY JOE BENITEZ

LEGENDERRY GREEN HORNET
WRITTEN BY DAVE AVALLONE
ART BY DAVID T. CABRERA, COVER BY JOE BENITEZ AND IVAN NUNES

LEGENDERRY RED SONJA
WRITTEN BY MARC ANDREYKO
ART BY ANEKE AND JUAN RAMIREZ, COVER BY JOE BENITEZ AND IVAN NUNES

LEGENDERRY VAMPIRELLA
WRITTEN BY DARYL GREGORY
ART BY BRENT PEEPLES, COVER BY JOE BENITEZ AND IVAN NUNES

STEAMPUNK BATTLESTAR GALACTICA 1880
WRITTEN BY BILL WILLINGHAM
ART BY SERGIO DÁVILA, COVER BY JOE BENITEZ AND IVAN NUNES

PRECINCT

A STEAMPUNK ADVENTURE